SMUGGLING ~~DAYS~~

AND

SMUGGLING WAYS;

SMUGGLING DAYS

AND

SMUGGLING WAYS;

BY

LIEUT. THE HON. HENRY N. SHORE, R.N.,

with a new Introduction
by
Edward Carson

Republished EP Publishing Ltd., 1972
First published Cassell & Co., Ltd., London, 1892

Republished 1972 by EP Publishing Limited
East Ardsley, Wakefield
Yorkshire, England
by kind permission of the copyright holder

Copyright © 1972 in new Introduction by
EP Publishing Limited

ISBN 0 85409 931 X

Please address all enquiries to EP Publishing Ltd.
(address as above)

Reprinted in Great Britain by
Scolar Press Limited, Menston, Yorkshire

INTRODUCTION

by EDWARD CARSON

There have been many accounts of smuggling in the eighteenth and early nineteenth centuries, a period generally regarded as the 'heyday of smuggling', but most were based more on fiction than fact and relied to a large extent on the uncorroborated stories of those who claimed to have been smugglers. Commander Shore's account was, however, based mainly on official records, his own experience in the Coastguard and personal contact with those who had been actively engaged in smuggling and combating smuggling.

Henry Noel Shore, 5th Baron Teignmouth, was born in 1847, being descended from John Shore, 1st Baron Teignmouth (1751–1834), who had risen from a humble position with the East India Company to become Governor-General of India in 1792 and a member of the Supreme Council of Bengal, giving evidence in favour of Warren Hastings and later becoming the first president of the British and Foreign Bible Society.

In 1861 H. N. Shore entered the Royal Navy as a cadet, was commissioned as lieutenant in 1872 and, after some years' service in the Far East, was appointed as Inspecting Officer of the Coastguard at Greenock in 1881. He was transferred to Fowey in 1886 and was promoted to Commander but ill-health caused him to retire from the Service in 1891.

It was during his service with the Coastguard that he became interested in the history of smuggling and, as he himself tells us, 'succeeded, by dint of searching out old smugglers and coastguard pensioners, in rescuing a mass of curious information from the oblivion to which modern indifference and respectability would fain have consigned it'. He recorded the results of these studies in 'Smuggling Days and Smuggling Ways' which was published in 1891.

Commander Shore composed a number of other works including 'The Flight of the Lapwing in China, Japan and Formosa', an account based on his naval experiences in the Far East, 'Old Foye Days' and 'Three Pleasant Springs in Portugal'. He was no mean artist and had works exhibited at the Royal Institutes and the Royal Scottish and Royal Irish Academies.

His account of smuggling is factual and not at all romanticised but is none the less exciting for, incredible though some of the tales of the bloody deeds of the smuggling gangs might appear to the modern reader, there is ample documentary evidence to show that the gangs treated those who opposed them or informed on them with the greatest inhumanity. One of the most outrageous of these episodes, that dealing with the attack by the infamous Hawkhurst Gang on the Custom House at Poole and the subsequent dastardly murders committed by members of the gang, is described in detail.

Although the author relied to a large extent on official records, it is probable that he did not have access to the numerous Customs records recently centralized at the Customs headquarters in London making it now possible to look at the situation from the point of view of the revenue officials. The reader might gain the impression that the Customs Preventive Service was largely ineffective in the eighteenth century both on account of their inadequate force and lack of zeal and there is no doubt that the Tide Waiter or lonely Riding Officer normally regarded discretion as the better part of valour when confronted by anything up to a hundred determined and well-armed smugglers.

Nevertheless, the officers themselves constantly reported such cases to the Board of Customs, lamenting their own inadequacy and begging for military assistance. Some officials were exceedingly zealous and often quite successful in their attempts at outwitting the smugglers and sometimes to such an extent that they were subject to constant threats. Mr. Florence, Riding Officer at Wareham, for example, received a letter in August 1789 in which a smuggler threatened 'I will blow your brains out by night or day' while the Anglesey smugglers, incensed against Captain Gambold of the Customs cutter 'Pelham' in 1770 threatened that they would sink him wherever they met with him.

It is also clear from Customs records that for a large part of the eighteenth century naval vessels actively cooperated with the revenue cutters in their fight against the smugglers, many such instances being reported by Customs collectors. We find, for instance, the Portsmouth Collector informing the Board of Customs that 'the very great exertions by Captain Thornbrough, commander of H.M.S. frigate the 'Hebe' whose activity and zeal for the Revenue deserve the highest commendation, has proved of great advantage in diminishing the practice of smuggling'. On the other hand the Board of Customs found themselves obliged to remind the commanders of the revenue vessels that their primary duty was the protection of the revenue and not the capturing of enemy ships. Customs vessels bearing 'letters of marque' were in fact expected to assist the navy at times and during the Napoleonic wars their effectiveness as a revenue protection force was greatly impaired by the fact that so many of the vessels were serving with the Navy.

It is also now possible to reconstruct the early history of the Coastguard, with whose later history Commander Shore was so well acquainted. The author refers to the 'scientific period' in the history of smuggling and considers that after the French wars smugglers had abandoned the use of sheer force and instead relied on ingenuity. There is a good deal of evidence in records that even in the second half of the eighteenth century, smugglers had adopted the method of sinking their contraband near the coast so that it could be collected at a suitable time by their confederates ashore. It was to combat this method of smuggling that in 1809 the Customs formed a new service known as the Preventive Waterguard which was intended to fill the gap between the Waterguard vessels at sea and the Riding Officers on land. Like the rest of the Customs service, this force was also assigned certain non-revenue functions such as assisting in the salvage and protection of wreck and in life-saving. To this end shipwreck stations were set up and were developed into Rocket Apparatus stations. After Waterloo the Coast Blockade was set up between Dungeness and the North Foreland and the Preventive Waterguard in this area was included in these arrangements. In 1822, however, the Customs preventive service was reorganised and the whole of it except the Coast Blockade was placed under the Board of Customs and renamed the 'Coast Guard'. At this time it was estimated that there were 59 revenue cruisers and 4,821 men engaged in revenue protection. When the Crimean War broke out in 1854, 3,000 men of the Coast Guard were 'called up' to the navy and two years later the whole of the Coast Guard and the revenue vessels, were transferred to the Admiralty. By this time the gradual advance of genuine 'free trade' was having its effect on the character of smuggling as also was the great increase in the type and size of ships. In general smuggling ceased to be the main object of a ship's voyage and usually occurred incidentally to the legitimate importation of cargo. Tubs of spirits were still sunk at places along the south coast and seizures of such contraband are frequently recorded, but as often as not no culprits were apprehended.

Although the Coastguard now came under the jurisdiction of the Admiralty, it was still required to carry out revenue protection duties. The Mounted Guard, later called the Land Guard, had already been disbanded and the main Customs revenue protection was now carried out by the Tide Waiters in the ports. After 1860 up to the end of the century smuggling was virtually confined to tobacco and spirits, the only commodities on which there was a substantial duty. Smugglers now took advantage of the fact that most articles were free of duty to introduce tobacco packed inside such articles. Also, with the development of steamships, they were able to use the bunker spaces and machinery for concealment purposes, not to mention numerous ingenious contrivances. The incidence of seizures of contraband by the Coastguard fell off as the century moved to its close while the numbers and quantities increased in the ports. Because of this the Customs set up, or rather reintroduced, the Waterguard in 1891 and early in the next century reinforced its detective service. The Coastguard remained responsible for the revenue protection of the coast until 1923 when it was replaced by a new force, the Coast Preventive Service under the Board of Customs and Excise and largely recruited from the Coastguard which was disbanded as a naval force, the name being transferred to a small force assigned to the Board of Trade for lifesaving, wreck salvage and the administration of foreshores.

Commander Shore lived long enough to see the disbandment of the Coastguard, for he lived until 1926. His enthralling account of smuggling days and ways has not been superseded and is likely to interest readers for many years.

MAY, 1972

SMUGGLING DAYS

AND

SMUGGLING WAYS;

OR,

The Story of a Lost Art.

CONTAINING SOME CHAPTERS FROM

The Unwritten History of Cornwall and other Counties,

TOGETHER WITH AN ACCOUNT OF

The Rise and Development of the Coastguard.

BY

LIEUT. THE HON. HENRY N. SHORE, R.N.,

AUTHOR OF "THE FLIGHT OF THE LAPWING; OR, JOTTINGS IN
CHINA AND JAPAN," ETC.

With numerous Plans and Drawings by the Author.

CASSELL & COMPANY, LIMITED:

LONDON, PARIS & MELBOURNE.

1892.

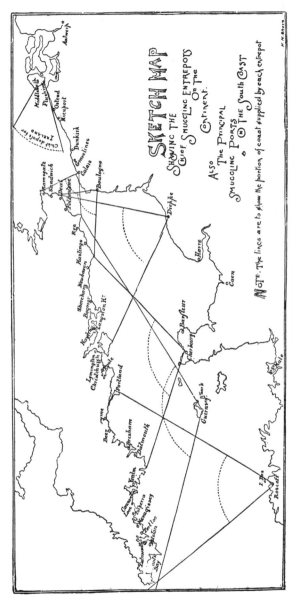

SMUGGLING MAP.

PREFACE.

IN view of the already overcrowded state of the book-market, the author of this little work feels that some apology is due to a much-enduring public for his temerity in adding yet another drop to the stream.

He deems it therefore necessary to explain that, while there are handbooks, guides, and manuals treating of almost every subject under the sun— from pie-making to governing empires—the student of sociology may search in vain for any reliable or authoritative work on a branch of industry which, if it contributed but little to the Exchequer, added largely, in the opinion of many people, to "the greatest happiness of the greatest number" in days gone by.

Thus, while of smuggling *fiction*, evolved chiefly from the fertile brains of the writers, we have an ample supply, there is a dearth of *facts*, and these are not always easy of access to the seeker after truth. If, therefore, this little book—the fruit of eight years' experience as inspecting officer of Coast-guard in England and Scotland—should contribute in any degree to the enlightenment of the public on a subject which is but little studied or understood at the present day, the author's utmost hopes will be realised.

CONTENTS.

———◆◆———

LIST OF ILLUSTRATIONS.

Smuggling Days

AND

Smuggling Ways.

———◆◆◆———

Part I.

THE "FREE-TRADE" DAYS.

———

CHAPTER I.

'The Good Old Times"—Smuggling, Past and Present—The "Free-Trade" Period—Smuggling in Kent and Sussex—Fights at Bulverhithe and Eastbourne—Fortunes made by Smuggling.

EVERYONE has a hazy sort of notion that in the "good old times" which the fervid imagination is apt to associate with the closing years of last century—or a still more remote and barbarous period—French brandy and claret, imported through other channels than those recognised by H.M. Customs, were favourite commodities with our "forebears," and, together with tea, lace, silk, and tobacco, figured largely in the staple of the contraband trader. But it is surprising how few people nowadays have any clear or accurate conception of the extent to which this traffic was carried on—the utter lawlessness which characterised it, or the support extended to it by the "masses and the classes" of the period during which it flourished. Still less acquaintance have they with the manners and customs of those who conducted the trade—the practical methods employed, or the measures initiated from time to time by the authorities for suppressing it.

In the following pages it has been the writer's aim to gather up the most interesting facts connected with the history of what might now be called a lost " art," and to place them before the reader in a more complete and connected form than has been attempted hitherto.

It must not, of course, be supposed for a moment because the " art " has been forgotten, that the smuggling instinct has vanished from the breast of the free and enlightened Briton of modern times—whether male or female : as witness the oft-repeated attempts to evade the vigilance of the Customs' searcher in the matter of cigars, scent, and other such commodities as can be secreted conveniently in the recesses of a trunk or the mysterious depths of a " dress-improver," not to mention occasional seizures on a much larger scale at the commercial ports of tobacco disguised in various forms, or certain notorious smuggling transactions in which H.M. ships, and even the Royal yachts, have played an important though unwilling part—all of which tend to show that although the flesh may be weak, the spirit is as willing as ever to avail itself of opportunities for turning a disreputable penny by defrauding the revenue of its dues.

But all these pettifogging attempts of modern times pale into utter insignificance when compared with the gigantic scale on which smuggling operations were conducted in the " good old times " aforementioned, and the modern smuggler can only be regarded as a contemptible cheat when measured by the heroic standard of other days.

For convenience of treatment, the history of

smuggling may be roughly divided into two distinct periods :—

First : The "free-trade" period, dating back to a very remote age, attaining its greatest prosperity about the middle of last century, and coming to a close during the early part of the present one, through the whole of which period the traffic—as implied by its name—was conducted with a freedom from interruption which must have excited the envy of later generations.

Second : The "scientific" period, dating from the conclusion of the great war, or about 1816, when the Government, being once more at liberty to give its attention to home affairs, struck the first really effective blow at the free-trader by the establishment of a properly organised and really adequate preventive force round the entire coasts of the United Kingdom.

As regards the first of these periods, it may be said generally that, so far as payment of duty was concerned, a quite peculiar elasticity of conscience universally prevailed throughout the kingdom. Everyone did what seemed good in his own eyes, with the result that commodities in general demand were imported wholesale, and in the most open and defiant manner, along the entire seaboard of Great Britain, with consequences to the exchequer which can be only dimly surmised. Thus, in a report to the Customs, under date December, 1703, Mr. Henry Baker, the supervisor for the counties of Kent and Sussex, where the contraband trade was prosecuted with the utmost activity, says : " For fine goods, as they call them (viz., silks, lace, &c.), I am well assured that trade goes on through both counties, though not in such vast quantities as have been formerly brought in—I mean in those days when (as a gentleman of estate in one of the counties has within this twelve months told me) he had been at once, besides at other times at the loading of a waggon with silks, lace, &c., till six oxen could hardly move it out of the place."

The measures suggested by Mr. Baker for the suppression of this trade proved utterly inadequate, for we learn that during the next forty-five years the daring of the smugglers in this part of England grew with the impunity which attended their operations. Large gangs of twenty, forty, fifty, and even one hundred, rode, armed with guns, bludgeons, and clubs, throughout the country, setting authority at defiance, and awing all the quiet inhabitants.

The Treasury papers contain many particulars of the daring and desperate acts of these companies, or gangs of men, in all parts of Kent and Sussex during the first half of the last century, principally in the smuggling of tea.*

---

* In 1736 a petition was presented to Parliament by the tea dealers, representing the serious losses they sustained by smuggling. They asserted that nearly half the tea consumed in England paid no duty. The duty at this time was 4s. per lb. on all teas alike. As an illustration of the vast proportions of the smuggling trade in tea, the following is worthy of note : In December, 1743, a pamphlet was published containing " A Proposal for Preventing of Running Goods," and the author observes, " Since an excise duty of 4s. per lb. was laid on tea, it has brought an average of £130,000 a year into the exchequer, which is but for 650,000 pounds weight of tea. But that the real consumption is vastly greater a single fact will prove. Some years ago the treasurer of our East India Company received a letter from Holland intimating that one person in the province of Zealand smuggled yearly for England no less than half a million pounds. Though this seemed incredible, the directors, upon inquiry, were convinced of the fact that such a person there was who, some few years before had been but an English sailor, was now married to a woman that kept a china shop, and had so well managed affairs that he had four sloops of his own constantly employed in smuggling ; that the quantity of tea which he was supposed to export had not at all been magnified, and that he had more guineas

Naturally, conflicts between the smugglers and officers of the Customs were of frequent occurrence, and, although in these affrays the officers were usually worsted, owing to the great numerical superiority and daring of their antagonists, who were thus enabled to save the whole or chief part of their goods, there were one or two notable occasions on which the free-traders received a severe lesson.

An interesting account of a fatal engagement which took place in March, 1737, at Bulverhithe, with one of the numerous gangs of Sussex smugglers, is given in a letter from a person writing under the assumed name of Goring to the Commissioners of Customs.*

" May it please your Honours,—It is not unknown to your Lordships of the late battle between the smugglers and officers at Bulverhide ; and in relation to that business, if your Honours please to advise in the newspapers that this is accepted off, I will send a list of the names of the persons that were at that business, and the places, names, where they are usually and mostly resident. Cat (Morten's man) fired first ; Morten was the second that fired ; the soldiers fired and killed Collison, wounded Pizon, who is since dead ; William Weston was wounded, but like to recover. Young Mr. Brown was not there ; but his men and horses were.—From your Honours'

Dutiful and most faithfull servant, GORING."

and English specie in his house than any banker in England." The remedy proposed by the author was a tax of from 5s. to 20s. on all families that drank tea, which will excite a smile on the part of modern political economists. The consumption of tea in the whole of Great Britain was computed at 1,500,000 lbs. a year, the price of which in bond was from 5s. 9d. to 6s. 10d. per lb.

* "Sussex Archæological Collection, vol. x., "Smuggling in Sussex," by Wm. Durrant Cooper, Esq., F.S.A.

" There was no foreign persons at this business, but all were Sussex men, and may easily be spoke with.

" This is the seventh time Morten's people have workt this winter, and have not lost anything but one half hundred of tea they gave to a dragoon and one officer they met with the first of this winter ; and the Hoo company have lost no goods, although they constantly work, and at home, too, since they lost the seven hundred-weight. When once the smugglers are drove from home they will soon be all taken. Note, that some say it was Gurr that fired first. You must well secure Cat, or else your Honours will soon lose the man ; the best way will be to send him up to London, for he knows the whole company, and hath been Morten's servant two years. There were several young chaps with the smugglers, whom, when taken, will soon discover the whole company. The number was twenty-six men. Marks' horse, Morten's and Hoads' were killed, and they lost not half their goods. They have sent for more goods, and twenty-nine horses set out from Groomsbridge this day, about four in the afternoon, and all the men well armed with long guns. . . . There are some smugglers worth a good sum of money, and they pay for taking. . . . The Hoo company might have been all ruined when they lost their goods ; the officers and soldiers knew them all, but they were not prosecuted. . . . Morten and Boura sold, last winter, someways 3,000 lb. weight a week." ·

And again in June, 1744. The officers of the Customs at Eastbourne having received intelligence of a gang of smugglers, went, with five dragoons mounted, to the sea-shore, near Pevensey ; but one hundred smugglers rode up, and after disarming the officers, fired about forty shots at them, cut them with their swords in a dangerous manner, loaded the goods on above one hundred horses, and made towards London.*

Having regard to the peculiarly favourable conditions under which the trade was conducted, no surprise will be felt at the statement that large fortunes were made by it. Warehouses and vaults were established in many districts by the smugglers for the reception of their goods, and large houses were built at Seacock's Heath, in Etchingham (by the well-known smuggler Arthur Gray, and called " Gray's Folly "), at Pix Hall, and the Four Throws, Hawkhurst, at Goudhurst, and elsewhere, with the profits of their trade.

Not only was smuggling carried on in the most open and defiant manner on shore, but in those days there was scarcely a fishing village—along the south coast, at any rate—which did not own a vessel, often several,† whose sole and peculiar employment was the importation of contraband articles for the use of the

---

* Even the streets of London were not exempt from occurrences of this nature. Thus, on May 13th, 1733, between 2 and 3 in the morning, the Watchmen of St Paul's, Covent Ga den, and St. Martin's-in-the-Fields seized 1,100 cwt. of uncustomed tea, together with three men and a boy, with the horses they rode. Two of the men were substantial farmers of Rye. There were nine men of the party, but five made their escape with drawn cutlasses in their hands.

And again on May 17th the Watch stopped two women in Whitecross Street with baskets on their heads containing 117 lbs. tea, which being taken to the Watch-house, two of the Watchmen went to be shown the house where the women said there was more, but being come into Bunhill Row, one of the women cried out, " Robbers, robbers !" upon which the smugglers came up, and so beat one of the Watchmen about his head with the handles of their whips that he died in a few hours.— See *Gentleman's Magazine* for 1733.

† The little Cornish village of Polperro owned at least five such vessels. See Couch's " History of Polperro."

B

adjacent populace. Many of these vessels were, moreover, heavily armed, and carried disproportionately large crews for the express purpose of resisting ill-considered attempts at interference; and in the

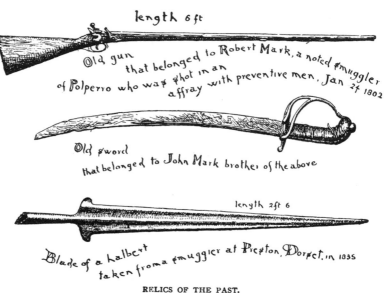

length 6ft

Old gun that belonged to Robert Mark, a noted smuggler of Polperro who was shot in an affray with preventive men. Jan 24 1802

Old sword that belonged to John Mark brother of the above

length 2ft 6

Blade of a halbert taken from a smuggler at Preston, Dorset, in 1835

RELICS OF THE PAST.

somewhat rare event of a coast officer, exciseman, or other base tool of a despotic government allowing his zeal for the interests of the revenue to get the better of his discretion, these free-and-easy traders would show their teeth in an unmistakably suggestive way. Occasionally, it is true, a capture on the high seas was effected by a king's ship, or by one of the few revenue cutters that attempted to keep watch and ward over our coasts, but the trade never languished for want of patrons or active sympathisers.

In these prosaic days one can hardly realise the

extent to which the country had gone wrong on this question of "free-trade"—which, by the way, we are taught to associate with the name and times of Richard Cobden—but now and again, when the local chronicler chances to lift the curtain a little, we obtain a glimpse of a state of things which seems almost as far off as the Druids and their mystic rites, and, so far as one can judge, as unlikely ever to return.*

CHAPTER II.

Why should the King tax Good Liquor?—The Smuggling Parson—A Long-felt Want—The Kentish Smugglers—The Hawkhurst Gang—Battle of Goudhurst—Thomas Kingsmill, Smuggler.

THE "misty glimpse of a moral sense," vouchsafed to our ancestors anent this free-trade business, is quaintly exemplified by an anecdote related by that eccentric genius the late Rev. R. S. Hawker, of Morwenstowe, *apropos* of unavailing attempts on his part to combat certain lax views current in his Cornish parish with regard to smuggling. He tells us that all his suggestions of morality, political economy, and finance were met by the unanswerable argument: "But why should the king tax good liquor? If they must have taxes, why can't they tax something else?"

Now, we may smile at all this, and even marvel at the moral obliquity of these simple folk of other days, but he would be a bold man who ventured the assertion that sentiments such as these formed no

---

* In the *Gentleman's Magazine* for 1735, under date September 3rd, a correspondent writes that "in several parts of Kent the farmers are obliged to raise wages, and yet are distressed for want of hands to get in their harvest, which is attributed to the great numbers who employ themselves in smuggling along the coast."

B 2

part of the moral stock-in-trade of many excellent Christians at the present day. We are all prepared to admit the necessity of paying taxes, but directly our own particular interests are affected, and the shoe begins to pinch, we cry out, "Why can't they tax something else," and discover all of a sudden that defrauding the exchequer is but a venial offence after all.

Even the clerical conscience is at fault sometimes, as witness the case of the Rev. ——, of Minnesota, who, on landing recently at New York, signed the usual declaration that he had no dutiable articles. But the Customs Inspector had his doubts, and on searching the reverend gentleman's trunks found, amongst other contraband goods, silk umbrellas, ladies' underclothing, perfumery, and 5,000 cigars. The reverend smuggler's trunks had false bottoms! It would be interesting to know what subject this erring shepherd selected for his next Sunday's discourse!

The truly Arcadian simplicity of manners which obtained up to within comparatively recent times in the parish of Morwenstowe—and doubtless in many other outlying districts—is thus quaintly sketched in by the chronicler we have already quoted from. Speaking of a wayward parishioner, Mr. Hawker says : " My efforts to soften and remove his doctrinal prejudice as to the unimportance, in a moral point of view, of putting the officers of His Majesty's revenue to death, were equally unavailing. ' There had been divers parsons,' he assured me, 'in his time in the parish, and very larned clargy they were, and some very strict, and some would preach one doctrine and some another, and there was one that had very mean notions about running goods, and said 'twas a wrong thing to do ; but even he and the rest never took no part with the exciseman.' "

With this quaint picture of Cornish men and manners before us, readers will be less surprised to hear that almost everyone was concerned in the illicit trade, while, far from experiencing any shame or remorse at practices, the bare mention of which wou'd make the hair of us moderns stand on end, the upper classes, landed proprietors, magistrates, members of parliament, and even in some instances—tell it not in Convocation—the clergy, were as eager to avail themselves of the cheap advantages thus brought within their reach—ay, and in many cases to share the profits of the trade, as the smugglers themselves.

Free-trade evidently supplied what the modern advertiser would call " a long-felt want " in the social economy of the age, and was prosecuted with a vigour and determination which baffled all the efforts of the authorities to cope with it.

One or two extracts from the chronicles of these old days will place the reader in a better position for appreciating not only the advantages enjoyed by our progenitors in the matter of liquor and baccy, but the enormous difficulties encountered by the authorities in their subsequent attempts to suppress the trade.

One of the most graphic and faithful pictures of the particular period when the high calling, or vocation, of smuggling was in its palmiest days, viz., about the middle of last century, is that given by the late G. P. R. James, whose historical romances most people are familiar with, and, as it bears evidence both of wide research and profound knowledge of the subject, the present writer ventures to reproduce it.

" Scarcely any one of the maritime counties was in those days without its gang of smugglers ; for if France was not opposite, Holland was not far off; and if brandy was not the object, nor silk nor wine, yet tea

and cinnamon, and hollands, and various East Indian
goods were things duly estimated by the British public, especially when they could be obtained without
the payment of Custom House dues. The system of
prevention also was very inefficient, and a few scattered Custom House officers, aided by a cruiser here
or there upon the coast, had an excellent opportunity
of getting their throats cut or their heads broken, or
of making a decent livelihood by conniving at the
transactions they were sent down to stop, as the peculiar
temperament of each individual might render such
operations pleasant to him. Thus, to use one of the
smuggler's own expressions, a 'roaring' trade in contraband goods was going on along the whole British
coast, with very little let or hindrance.

"As there are land-sharks and water-sharks,
so there were then (and so there are now) land-
smugglers and water-smugglers. The latter brought
the objects of their commerce either from foreign
countries or from foreign vessels, and landed them on
the coast ; and a bold, daring, reckless body of men they
were ; the former, in gangs, consisting frequently of
many hundreds, generally well mounted and armed,
conveyed the commodities so landed into the interior,
and distributed them to others, who retailed them as
occasion required. Nor were these gentry one whit
less fearless, enterprising, and lawless than their
brethren of the sea. . . . Each public-house was
supported by smugglers, and gave them in return
every facility possible. Scarcely a house but had
its place of concealment, which would accommodate
either kegs, or bales, or human beings, as the case
might be ; and many streets in seaport towns had
private passages from one house to another, so that
the gentleman inquired for by the officers at No. 1

was often walking quietly out of No. 20, while they were searching for him in vain. The back of one street had always excellent means of communication with the front of another, and the gardens gave exit to the country with as little delay as possible.

"Of all counties, however, the most favoured by nature and by art for the very pleasant and exciting sport of smuggling was the county of Kent. . . . The interior of the country was not less favourable to the traffic than the coast, and offered the land-smugglers opportunities of carrying on their trans-actions with the degree of secrecy and safety which no other county afforded. . . . Not a park, not a wood, not a barn, but did not at some period afford them a refuge when pursued, or become a depository for their commodities, and many a man on visiting his stable or his cart-shed early in the morning found it tenanted by anything but horses and waggons. The churchyards were frequently crowded at night by other spirits than those of the dead, and not even the church was exempted from such visitations.

"None of the people of the county took notice of or opposed these proceedings; the peasantry laughed at, or aided, and very often got a good day's work, or, at all events, a jug of genuine hollands from the friendly smugglers; the clerk and the sexton willingly aided and abetted, and opened the door of vault, or vestry, or church, for the reception of the passing goods; the clergyman shut his eyes if he saw tubs or stone jars in his way; and it is remarkable what good brandy punch was generally to be found at the house of the village pastor. The magistrates and officers of sea-port towns were in general so deeply implicated in the trade themselves that smuggling had a fairer chance than the law in any case that came before

them, and never was a more hopeless enterprise
undertaken in ordinary circumstances than that of
convicting a smuggler, unless captured in flagrant
delict."

Of the numerous smuggling companies roaming
at will through the counties of Kent and Sussex
at this period, the most notorious was that which
earned for itself the sobriquet of the "Hawkhurst
Gang." * Composed for the most part of a set of
brutal ruffians, who indulged in every sort of atrocity
in furtherance of their objects, and regarded the
murder of Customs officers as a perfectly legitimate
exercise of power, this gang exercised a species of
terrorism over a wide extent of country ; but their
daring and repeated attacks on the persons and
properties of the inhabitants, and the cruelties exercised on some who had opposed their extravagances,
brought matters at length to a climax. Driven to
desperation, and exasperated beyond measure, the
people of Goudhurst and neighbourhood determined
to submit no longer to a species of domination which
had become intolerable. At the instigation of a
young man of the name of Sturt, a native of the
place, who had recently been discharged from a foot
regiment, a paper expressive of their abhorrence of
the conduct of the smugglers and their determination
to oppose them was drawn up and signed by a con-

* In December, 1744, a reward of £50 was offered for appre-
hending and bringing to justice the persons concerned in assaulting
and wounding an officer and his three assistants belonging to the
Customs at Shoreham, in Kent, on 18th inst., and forcibly taking
from them their arms and horses, and carrying them away to Hawkhurst, in Kent. There the smugglers carried two of these four, who
had been formerly of their gang, to a wood, tied them to trees,
whipped them almost to death, and then clapped them on board a
vessel, and sent them to France.

siderable number of persons, who assumed the appellation of "The Goudhurst Militia," under the leadership of young Sturt. These proceedings coming to the knowledge of the "gang," who had captured a member of the Militia, and had tortured him into a full confession of the intentions of his fellows, the smugglers sent him back with a message that on a certain day they intended to attack the village, murder all the inhabitants, and burn it to the ground. On receipt of this news Sturt at once assembled his men, and made every preparation, with the somewhat limited resources at command, for the impending attack. The surrounding country was scoured in search of firearms; all the available lead was converted into balls for the muskets, while the members of the Militia were so disposed as to make the best use of their means of resistance. True to their word, at the appointed hour the smugglers, under the leadership of a determined character called Thomas Kingsmill, made their appearance before the hastily constructed defences, and after threatening the Goudhurst men with the consequences of holding out, and hurling curses against them, fire was opened by the smugglers, and as promptly returned by the Militia, by which one of the "gang" was killed, and after the loss of two more, besides several disabled with wounds, the smugglers retreated, pursued by the militia-men, who succeeded in making several prisoners.*

* The following brief reference to this extraordinary affair occurs in the *Gentleman's Magazine*, April, 1747 :—" Two smugglers, George Kingsman and Barnet Wolli·, both outlaws, the first of which formerly killed a man on Hurst Green, were killed in a skirmish with the townsmen of Goudhurst, in Kent, who found it necessary to arm against these desperadoes, who rob and plunder, and live upon the spoil wherever they come." The writer is indebted

Those who have read " The Smuggler" will remember that the author lays the scene of this attack at Goudhurst Church ; and the accuracy of this has been confirmed by another writer,* who states that his great-grandfather, who was residing in the place at the time, gave a similar version of the affair.

Apropos of this extraordinary conflict, Mr. James —who wrote in 1840—observes :—" The reader will probably ask, with a look of surprise, ' Is this a scene in North America, where settlers were daily exposed to the incursions of savages?' And he may add, ' This could not have happened in England.' But I beg to say this happened in the county of Kent, less than a century ago ; and persons are still living who remember being sent with the women and children out of the village that the men might not be impeded by fear for those they loved while defending the spot on which they were born."

The maxim that " he who fights and runs away lives to fight another day," held true in the case of the leader of this attack on the Goudhurst men— Thomas Kingsmill, who, however, was no coward, for we are told that he "was a native of Goudhurst, and had been a husbandman ; but, having joined the smugglers, was distinguished and daring enough to become captain of the gang—an honour of which he was so proud that he sought every opportunity of exhibiting specimens of his courage, and putting himself foremost in every service of danger."

to the courtesy of the Rev. James Clarke, Vicar of Goudhurst, for the following extract from the parish register :—" 1747, Ap. 20, George Kingsmill, Dux sclerum glaude plumbeo emisso, cecidit."
    * William Durrant Cooper, Esq., F.S.A.

CHAPTER III.

Attack on Poole Custom House—The Centre-tree in Charlton Forest—The Hawkhurst Men again—Breakfast at Fordingbridge—Widow Payne— How the Smugglers treated the King's Officers—The "Red Lion" at Rake—Galley's Grave.

THOMAS KINGSMILL'S next escapade, for which he ultimately forfeited his life, was a daring attack on the Custom House at Poole, and the rescue of thirty-seven hundredweight of tea, valued at over £500, a proceeding which the Crown counsel at his trial spoke of as "the most unheard-of act of villany and impudence ever known." This tea was intended to have been run on the coast of Sussex, but, acting on information, the commander of the revenue cutter stationed at Poole intercepted the vessel which was bringing over the cargo, and, after a long chase, captured her, took her into Poole, and handed the cargo over to the collector of Customs ; the tea and other goods being placed for safety in the King's warehouse or Custom House.

The smugglers, to whom the cargo belonged, being much exasperated at this unlooked-for diversion of their goods, resolved not to sit down contented with their loss, but, after consultation, agreed to go and forcibly remove the tea from the warehouse where it was lodged. Accordingly, a body of them, to the number of sixty, well armed, assembled in Charlton Forest, and from thence proceeded on their enterprise, to accomplish which they agreed that only thirty of them should proceed to the attack, the remaining thirty being placed as scouts upon the different roads leading to Poole to watch

the motions of the officers and soldiers, and to be
ready to assist or alarm the main body.

In the night-time, between the 6th and 7th of
October, 1747, they went to Poole, broke open the
Custom House, secured their tea, which was placed
on the horses which they rode, and next morning
returned with their booty through Fordingbridge, in
Hampshire, where some hundreds of people were
assembled to view the cavalcade.

More than eighteen months elapsed before the
men concerned in this outrage were brought to justice, and the evidence of one of the witnesses for the
Crown on the occasion of their trial supplies such a
curious picture of the times that it is well worth
quoting. On being told by the Court to give an
account of what he knew of the business, he said :—

" The first time I was with them (the smugglers)
about it was in Charlton Forest, belonging to the
Duke of Richmond. There was only one of the
prisoners at the bar there then. We set our hands to
a piece of paper to go and broke open Poole Custom
House, and take out the goods. Some of them met
there a Sunday, but I was not then with them ; when
we met of the Monday, at Rowland's Castle, the
prisoners were all there, except Kingsmill and Fairall,
and were all armed, when they met, with blunderbusses, carbines, and pistols ; some lived thereabouts,
and some towards Chichester ; so we met there to set
out altogether. When we came to the Forest of
Bere, joining to Horndean, the Hawkhurst gang met
us, the prisoners Kingsmill and Fairall being with
them, besides the horses they rode on, a little horse,
which carried their arms ; we went in company after
we were joined till we came to Lindhurst ; there we
lay all day on Tuesday ; then all the prisoners were

there, and we set out for Poole in the glimpse of the
evening, and came to Poole about eleven at night."

In reply to a question by the Court as to whether
the prisoners were all armed, the witness continued—

"To the best of my knowledge all the prisoners
were armed, both at Horndean, in the Forest of Bere,
and at Lindhurst, and when we came to the town of
Poole we sent two men forward to see if all things
were clear for us to go to work in breaking the warehouse. One of them came back to us and said there
was a large sloop lay up against the quay ; she will
plant her guns to the Custom House door, and tear
us in pieces, so it cannot be done. We were turning
our horses to go back, when Kingsmill and Fairall
and the rest of their countrymen said, 'If you will not
do it, we will go and do it ourselves.' This was the
Hawkhurst gang. We call them the east-country
people ; they were fetched to break open the Custom
House. Some time after this, while we were con-
sulting what we should do, the other man we had
sent on returned and said the tide was low, and that
the vessel could not bring her guns to bear to fire
upon us. Then we all went forward to Poole. We
rode down a little back lane on the left side the town,
and came to the sea-side. Just by this place we left
our horses."

From another smuggler who had turned king's
evidence the following curious facts were elicited :—
That the meeting in Charlton Forest took place at "a
noted tree that stood there called the 'centre-tree,'"
and that on setting out for Poole "all the Hawkhurst
men had long arms slung round their shoulders, and
Fairall, alias the Shepherd, had a hanger. . . . We
all looked at our firearms to see if they were primed."
The little horse that accompanied the Hawkhurst

men for the purpose of carrying their arms "would follow a grey horse one of them rode on." On arriving at Fordingbridge next morning with their booty, the smugglers breakfasted, fed their horses, and then " went for a place called Sandy Hill, but at a place called Brooke we got a pair of steelyards and weighed the tea, and equally divided to each man his share ; it made five bags a man, about twenty-seven pounds in a bag."

A large reward was offered for the apprehension of any of the men who had taken part in this daring outrage ; but some months elapsed before the slightest clue could be obtained by the king's officers, and then only through a chance word let fall in a spirit of bravado by one of the throng of spectators who had witnessed the cavalcade passing through Fordingbridge the morning after the attack.

A striking commentary, surely, on the state of merry England in the year of grace 1747 ! Here was a body of thirty armed men riding into a seaport town, storming the " king's warehouse," and passing openly and undisguised the following morning with their booty through a portion of the most civilised and thickly-populated part of England, and yet not a single individual of the many who witnessed the passage of the strange cavalcade, and were acquainted with many of those composing it, could be induced to come forward and assist the authorities in bringing the offenders to justice.

Some clue to this extraordinary state of things will be found in the following narrative.

Having once embarked on a career of crime, the down-grade is usually a rapid one, and the present case proved no exception to this rule. With a view to preventing evidence being brought against them, as well as to intimidate intending witnesses from coming forward on behalf of the Crown, the smugglers perpetrated a series of the most barbarous and revolting murders that ever disgraced the annals of a civilised country.

One Sunday morning in the February following the attack on the Poole Custom House, an aged tide-waiter in the service of the Customs at Southampton, who was travelling in company with a shoemaker of Fordingbridge named Chater, arrived at the little village of Rowland's Castle near the borders of Sussex, and after inquiring the way to Stanstead, drew up their horses at the "White Hart" Inn for the purpose of getting refreshments. The fact of these men travelling with a letter for Major Batten, a justice of the peace for the county of Sussex, at once raised the suspicions of widow Payne, who kept the inn, and she lost no time in sending for her two sons of smuggling repute and telling them her belief that the strangers were intent on doing harm to the smugglers, who at that time formed no inconsiderable part of the inhabitants of the place.

Bad news flies apace, and in a very short time the chief smugglers of the neighbourhood flocked in to ascertain the truth. After drinking and chatting in a friendly way with the strangers for a short time one of the men induced Chater to come outside, and elicited from him that he was on his way to swear against one of those concerned in the outrage at Poole. Galley, the tide-waiter, fearing that the witness was being tampered with, came out to bring him back, but was promptly knocked down by one of the smugglers. On remonstrating and informing his assailant that he was a king's officer, the man replied with an oath, "You a king's officer? I'll make a

king's officer of you, and for a quartern of gin I'll
serve you so again." Some of the others interposing,
the quarrel was patched up. and they all turned in
again to drink; the two men Galley and Chater being
made drunk and put to bed, from whence they were
taken when darkness set in, and tied on to one horse
with their legs fastened together under the belly, and
in company with a party of the smugglers on horseback set off on a journey from which they were
never destined to return.

The first intention of the smugglers appears to
have been simply to keep the two men secreted till
after the noise of the affair had blown over, and then
to send them across to France, a practice, it seems,
which was very often resorted to at this particular
time as a means of removing over-zealous officers out
of harm's way. But this, it seems, was far too mild a
way of disposing of them to suit the wives of some of
the smugglers who had come in to see the fun, and
who cried out " Hang the dogs ! for they came here
to hang us." So it was eventually decided to carry
the men to some place of safe keeping till it was
known what was to be the fate of one of their own
number who had been arrested on suspicion, and
against whom Chater was going to give evidence,
and in the meanwhile a contribution of threepence a
week was to be levied all round for the maintenance
of the two men.

The party had no sooner started than the real
character of the men, into whose hands these two
unfortunates had fallen, discovered itself, for with a
coarse oath Jackson, the leader, began to "lay on"
to them with his heavy whip, calling out "Whip
them, cut them, slash them, d——n them !" an injunction which was instantly acted on by the whole

body of smugglers, who continued thus to ill-use the
two unhappy men, until, no longer able to endure
the agony, they rolled over with their heads under the
horse's belly, in which position they were driven some
distance, the horse striking their heads with his feet
every step he took. They were then set upright
again, and the brutal usage was commenced afresh,
the smugglers applying their long whips with brutal
ferocity, over the head, face, eyes, and shoulders indis-
criminately, until, worn out and from sheer exhaus-
tion, the poor creatures once more rolled over with
their heads downwards; when, finding them too
weak to keep upright, the smugglers cast adrift their
lashings and laid them separately across the horses
behind two of the party.

All through this dark February night did the
ghastly cavalcade continue its course through the
narrow lanes and rough tracks which at that time
intersected the country along the border of Hampshire and Sussex, for ten weary miles, poor Galley's
sufferings being increased by a system of torture
which cannot here be described, the wretched man
murmuring the while "barbarous usage, barbarous
usage ; for God's sake shoot me through the head."

Becoming at last unconscious, the two men were
secured with lashings, and in this condition arrived at
an early hour the following morning at the village of
Rake, near Liss, where, after some difficulty, the landlord of the "Red Lion" was persuaded to admit the
party. After drinking for some time, Galley's body
was taken out to the wood near by and buried in a
sandpit, though whether he was actually dead or not
seems uncertain, for on the corpse being exhumed
some months later his hands were found held over
the face as if to protect it.

C

THE OLD
RED LION INN
at RAKE

H. Shore

The particular spot in the beautiful valley of Hart-ingcombe, where the closing scene in the first act of this ghastly tragedy was enacted, is still pointed out by the old people of the neighbourhood as " Galley's grave." The whole aspect of this country has under-gone many changes since the period in question, but the old " Red Lion " Inn at Rake may still be discovered by the curious, very much as it was on the morning when its landlord was disturbed out of his sleep and forced to admit the gang of murderous ruffians with their ghastly freight. Though no longer an inn—has never, indeed, been used as such within the memory of the oldest inhabitant—there it still stands, pro-bably the sole connecting link between the present day and the events herein described.

CHAPTER IV.

The Turf-house at Trotton—Smugglers' Revenge—Harris' Well—Last Act of a Bloody Tragedy—" He'd Whipped many a Rogue "—How poor Hawkins was done to Death—A Garment rolled in Blood—Merry England—Terrorism—William Fairall and the Sussex Magistrate.

WHILE Galley's body was being disposed of in the manner described, poor Chater, with blood pouring down him from the brutal treatment he had ex-perienced during his ten miles' journey, was taken by some of the party to the house of a well-known smuggler, whose services could be depended on, residing some four miles off, at the village of Trotton, where the poor wretch was chained by the leg like a wild beast, to a post, in a " turf house," two of the smugglers remaining by him as a guard. In this condition, with just sufficient nourishment ad-ministered to keep body and soul together, he was

C 2

kept for two entire days and nights, while his inhuman captors were arranging how to dispose of
him.

After Galley's body had been put under ground,
the smugglers reassembled at the "Red Lion," where
they spent the greater part of the day carousing and
discussing their future plans, agreeing to disperse to
their homes at nightfall, and after rallying up some
more of their gang, to meet again at the same house on
Wednesday night.   They had already tried to drown
suspicions concerning their doings by telling the
landlord a plausible story about having had a fight
with the king's officers, in course of which some of their
number had been killed and their goods taken, while
still further to avoid giving cause of alarm it was
agreed that they should drop in at the next meeting one after another, as if by accident ; so that it
was late on Wednesday night before they were all
assembled.

And now commenced the second act of the
tragedy.   The smugglers had already agreed on the
necessity of destroying Chater, and the question that
remained to be settled was the choice of methods that
were least liable to discovery.   First it was proposed
to shoot him by tying a string to the trigger of a
gun, and then by all taking hold of it and pulling
together equalise the share of guilt in his murder.
But this was objected to as being far too expedi-
tious a method of dispatching him, the aim of these
ruffians being to prolong the poor man's sufferings as
long as life would last, "as a terror to all such
informing rogues (as they termed them) for the
future."

Ultimately, they decided on carrying him to Lady
Holt Park and throwing him into "Harris' Well,"

where at one time they intended dispatching poor Galley. The whole body of smugglers accordingly repaired to the house at Trotton, where the miserable Chater had been chained up since an early hour on Monday, and proceeded to put their plans into execution. But here a fresh scene of barbarity was opened, for some of the party going into the " skilling " where Chater lay in chains upon some turfs, one of them, named Tapner, immediately pulled out a large clasp knife, and with horrible oaths addressed him in the following manner : " Down on your knees and go to prayers, for with this knife I will be your butcher." The poor man being terrified at this dreadful menace, and expecting every moment would be his last, knelt down upon a turf as he was ordered, and while in the act of repeating the Lord's Prayer, another ruffian got behind him and kicked him, and with the most bitter taunts upbraided him for being an informing villain. On venturing to ask what had become of his friend Galley, Tapner replied, " D——n you, we have killed him, and we will do so by you ; " and then, without the slightest provocation, " drew his knife aslant over the wretched man's eyes and nose with such violence that he almost cut both his eyes out, and the gristle of his nose quite through. Not satisfied, however, with this wanton act of cruelty, in another sudden fit of frenzy Tapner aimed another stroke at his face, designing to cut him again in the same wound, but happening to strike a little higher, made a terrible gash across his forehead, from which the blood flowed in abundance."

To cut short these revolting details, the poor creature was at length set upon Tapner's horse, and the cavalcade started off for Lady Holt Park, a distance of about five miles, Tapner telling him with

a coarse oath that " if he blooded his saddle he would
destroy him that moment, and send his soul to hell."
Arrived at the well, an attempt was first of all made
to hang Chater, but the rope being too short to admit
of a sufficient drop, the body hanging half-way over
the edge of the well, the rope was cast adrift from the
railing, and Chater pitched in head first. But even
then life lingered on in this poor mangled body, and
so, by way of completing their fiendish job, the
smugglers threw down large stones and pieces of
timber, until every sign of life was hushed, and then,
mounting their horses, dispersed to their homes ere
break of day.

It may be observed that before the smugglers and
their prisoners set out from Rowland's Castle on the
Sunday night, one of the leaders of the gang took the
precaution to pull out his pistol in the presence of
the whole company, and swore that " whoever should
discover anything that passed at that house he would
blow his brains out," and the whole business from
beginning to end had been managed with so much
secrecy and care, that the smugglers believed themselves to be entirely free from all risk of discovery.

There were, however, two witnesses still living
who, though dumb, might prove extremely incon-
venient, namely, the horses which the unfortunate
men had ridden. It was therefore decided to make
away with them, and accordingly Galley's horse was
knocked on the head, flayed, and his skin cut up into
small pieces and effectually disposed of ; but the
horse which Chater rode managed to get away, and
was eventually returned to its owner.*

* For a full account of these brutal murders see a curious and
little known pamphlet originally published in 1749, now long out of
print, entitled " A full and genuine history of the inhuman and un-

Having thus, as they believed, effectually disposed of the only evidence which the authorities had been able to secure in connection with the attack on Poole Custom House, the smugglers felt themselves perfectly secure, especially as the fate that had befallen Galley and Chater, though screened from the knowledge of the authorities, would be sure to act as a deterrent in the rare event of any of their own party being tempted to act the traitor.

Before going on to describe the way in which the authorities at last got a clue to the fate of the unhappy men, it may be as well, perhaps, by way of giving a still more realistic picture of the state of the country at this time, to relate the circumstances of another atrocious murder perpetrated by the same gang of smugglers within a very few miles of the place where the other victims met their doom.

Some bags of "run" tea, deposited in a barn at Yapton, near Chichester, having disappeared, suspicion fell on a labourer called Hawkins; accordingly, one afternoon in January—a few weeks before the events above described—two of the smugglers, namely Mills, son of the man in whose turf-house at Trotton poor Chater had been chained up, and Curtis, a butcher belonging to Hawkhurst, went over to Yapton, where they found Hawkins at work with his master threshing corn, called him out, placed him on a horse without further explanation, and carried him away to the "Dog and Partridge," an ale-house on Slindon Common, threatening to shoot him through the head if he offered the least resistance.

paralleled murders of Mr. William Galley, a Custom House officer, and Mr. Daniel Chater, a shoemaker, by fourteen notorious smugglers, with the trials and execution of seven of the bloody criminals at Chichester," by a "gentleman of Chichester," containing many quaint illustrations.

On arrival here he was taken into a back parlour, Mills coolly observing that he "had got a prisoner." They then began questioning Hawkins about the tea, the whereabouts of which he professed complete ignorance, upon which Curtis said, "D——n him, he did know, and if he would not confess, he would whip him till he did, for, d——n him, he had whipped many a rogue, and washed his hands in his blood." But nothing would move the man from his declaration of innocence ; so the ruffians, after striking him in the face, made him strip to his shirt, and then, with their heavy riding-whips, belaboured him furiously over the face, arms, and body, until out of breath with the exertion. Then, stripping to their shirts, they began again, continuing the ill-treatment till the unfortunate man fell down, crying out that he was innocent, and begging them to spare his life for the sake of his wife and children. But appeals of this nature were thrown away on these inhuman monsters, who only redoubled their efforts, taking advantage of his position to inflict a species of torture which cannot now be described, besides kicking him violently in the belly. In his agony the poor man let fall some words about his father and brother, which his tormentors, interpreting into a declaration of their guilt, at once proceeded to act on. Calling for their horses Mills and Curtis set off once more for Yapton, where they found the two men they were in quest of, and making them immediately mount behind them on the horses they rode, started back for the "Dog and Partridge," with the full intention of treating them in the same way as they had already done by poor Hawkins.

In the meantime poor Hawkins rapidly sank under the injuries he had received, and as soon as it was seen that life was extinct, those who had

remained with him mounted their horses and set off
to meet Mills and Curtis, who, on being informed of
Hawkins' death, were persuaded with difficulty to let
their prisoners go. They then all returned to Slindon,
and after threatening the landlord to burn his house
down if he told anything, they consulted together and
decided on carrying Hawkins' body to a pond in
Parham Park several miles away, where, after tying
stones to it in order to sink it, they threw it in. And
thus was consummated another of those brutal outrages by which the smugglers sought to terrorise the
country side.*

" The only reason these villains had to commit
this murder on the poor wretch, who left behind him a
wife and many children," says a contemporary writer,
" was on a supposition only, that he had concealed a
small bag of tea from them ; though the villains on a
second search, after they had murdered the man,
found the tea where they had hid it."

The non-return of Galley and Chater after a
reasonable lapse of time led the authorities to suspect
some misfortune had befallen them ; and when it was
reported that the great-coat worn by the former had
been picked up on the road near Rowland's Castle in
a bloody condition, the day after they had set out on
their journey, there was no further room for doubt that
they had fallen into the hands of the smugglers, and
either been sent across to France, as was their custom,
or brutally murdered. A proclamation was therefore
issued offering a reward and free pardon to anyone

* One more instance of the brutalities practised by these men may
be mentioned. In the month of March, 1745, at Beccles, in Suffolk, a
gang of them entered a house, pulled a man out of bed, whipped him
most barbarously, forced him out of doors, and tied him naked upon a
horse, and then rode off with him. The man was not afterwards
heard of.

who should discover what had become of them. Six
or seven months, however, elapsed before the Government could obtain the least clue to the affair; and
then a full discovery was gradually made, and the
whole gang of murdering ruffians brought to the bar
of justice.

The remarks of a contemporary writer, styling
himself a "gentleman of Chichester," help to explain
the long immunity enjoyed by the smugglers, and
are on that account worthy of reproduction.

"The terrible executions committed by the
smugglers on these poor men, and the dreadful
menaces which they uttered against any person that
should presume to interrupt them, so terrified the
people everywhere, that scarce anybody durst look at
them as they passed in large bodies in open daylight.
And the Custom officers were so intimidated that
hardly any of them had courage enough to go on their
duty. Some of them they knew they had already
sent to France, others had been killed or wounded in
opposing them, and Galley, in particular, had been
inhumanly murdered by them.

"The smugglers had reigned a long time uncon-
trolled; they rode in troops to fetch their goods,
and carried them off in triumph by daylight; nay, so
audacious were they grown, that they were not afraid
of regular troops that were sent into the country to
keep them in awe, of which we have had several
instances. If any one of them happened to be taken,
and the proof ever so clear against him, no magistrate
in the county durst commit him to gaol; if he did,
he was sure to have his house or barns set on fire, or
some other mischief done him if he was so happy to
escape with his life."*

* As a further illustration of the terrorism exercised by these

As an example of the species of terrorism exercised by these ruffians over the magistracy take the following case :—

About a year previous to the events above described, William Fairall, a member of the Hawkhurst gang, and one of the principals, as will be remembered, in the attack on the Poole Custom House, a native of Horsendown Green, in Kent, of no occupation, but " a man of brutal courage, and inured to smuggling from his infancy," was apprehended in Sussex on account of some smuggling transactions, and brought before Mr. James Butler, who sent him under a strong guard up to London to be tried. He was taken to an inn in the Borough, from whence, during the night, he managed to give his guards the slip—quite possibly by arrangement—and seeing a horse standing in the street, mounted it and rode off in the presence of several people to join his gang in Sussex ; who, knowing of his committal, were surprised to see him back again so soon. After explaining the fortunate circumstances of his escape, he at once vowed vengeance against Mr. Butler, and various proposals were submitted and discussed. It was agreed first to destroy all the deer in his park, and all his trees, but Fairall and the more reckless of the gang declared that this was far too mild a punishment for daring to interfere with them, and vowed their intention of setting fire to his seat, one of the finest in Sussex, and burning it to the ground with

ruffians over peaceful citizens, the following may be mentioned :— Under date August 14th, 1747, a correspondent writes : " About twenty smugglers, well-armed and laden with prohibited goods, rode through Rye, Sussex, and stopping at the " Red Lion " to refresh, fired several times to intimidate the inhabitants, and observing James Marshall, a young man, too curious of their behaviour, carried him off, and he has not been heard of since."

him in it. But at this point a disagreement arose, some of the party objecting to the taking of life or the destruction of the house, and they parted without coming to any definite arrangement. But Fairall, Kingsmill, and some others, determined not to be baulked of their revenge, agreed to shoot Mr. Butler, and to this end laid in waiting for him one night when he was returning home from Horsham. By a fortunate chance their intended victim was detained, and they were thus foiled in their ruffianly designs, but were overhead swearing that they would have his life if they had to watch for a month together, which being told to Mr. Butler, steps were taken to have the men apprehended if they came into those parts again, and the conspiracy thus happily fell through.

CHAPTER V.

A Clue to the Murderers—The Special Assize—Retribution at Last—"A Popish Relique"—Confessions of a Smuggler—Busy Times for the Hangman—A Couple of Desperadoes—Last Moments of Fairall, the "Shepherd"—Break up of the Hawkhurst Gang.

THE way in which a clue was at length obtained to the fate of poor Galley and Chater was by some person who was cognisant of the whole affair sending an anonymous letter to the authorities, in which a hint was dropped as to Galley's probable resting-place. Acting on this, a search was instituted with the result of finding the body in the spot indicated. Another letter was then received from the same source, giving the name of a man who was concerned in the murder, and stating where he was to be found. The accused was arrested, and he immediately offered himself king's evidence, to make a full discovery and disclosure of the whole transaction, as well as of the persons concerned therein.

To quote once more from the "Gentleman of Chichester's" narrative, "The body of smugglers was now increased to a prodigious number, and the mischiefs they did wherever they came were so enormous that the whole country were afraid of them, and even the Government itself began to be alarmed, and to apprehend consequences that might be fatal to the public peace, in case a speedy check was not put to their audacious proceedings.* His Majesty, therefore, being perfectly informed of their notorious villanies, and informations being given of many of the names of the most desperate of their gangs, particularly those who broke open the Custom House at Poole, issued a proclamation, with lists of their several names, declaring that unless they surrendered themselves to justice at a day appointed they should be outlawed ; promising a reward of £500 for the apprehension of everyone who should be afterwards convicted."

---

* That the British Government was not alone in its difficulty with regard to the suppression of smuggling is shown by the following :— In the course of the debate in the House of Commons on the Smuggling Bill, brought in and passed in 1736, it was stated by one of the speakers that "in France, where the punishment of every sort of smuggling is death or the gallows, where they keep up a particular sort of army called *Les Maltotiers* for that very purpose, yet smuggling is in that kingdom almost as frequent as in England, and their smugglers much more desperate than ours ; for they march in little armies, are well-armed and disciplined, and often engage in battle with the Custom House officers and their guard of *Maltotiers*." And eighteen years after it was reported from the south of France that a body of 6,000 smugglers were assembled in the neighbourhood of Lyons. and. that a general with a like number of soldiers were to be sent against them, though it was hoped that such a display of force would be the means of avoiding a conflict, and that many of the smugglers might be induced to enlist in the army, being mostly fine, active fellows.

The result of the information furnished by the
anonymous correspondent, as well as the energetic
measures initiated by the Government, was that
within a short time seven of the murderers were
lodged in gaol, and by special request of the gentry
of Sussex, who were, doubtless, thankful to have
these scoundrels safe at last within the law's grip, a
special assize was held at Chichester for their trial on
January 16th, 1749—nearly a year after the perpetration of the murders. The whole were found guilty
and sentenced to execution the following day;
the bodies of five, including Jackson, who, as will
be remembered, commenced the barbarous treatment of poor Galley and Chater, to be hung in
chains.

Accordingly, on the 19th of January they were
taken in a cart, under a strong military escort, to a
place called the Broyle, near Chichester, where, with
the exception of Jackson, who died in gaol shortly
after sentence of death had been pronounced upon
him, they were executed in the presence of a vast
concourse of spectators.

The body of one of the smugglers was hung in
chains close to the scene of poor Galley's resting-
place, on the roadside, near Rake, another on Rook's
Hill, near Chichester, and the other two on the sea-
shore near Selsea Bill, from whence they could be
seen a great distance, and where they had often
landed their goods.

Jackson, who, from being the ringleader in the
barbarities practised on the two men, was the more
worthy of death than any, had, it seems, professed the
Roman Catholic religion a few years previously, and
the local chronicler tells us that a printed paper,
"supposed to be a Popish relique," was found care-

fully sewn on a linen purse in his waistcoat pocket, containing the following words in Latin :—

> "Ye three Holy Kings,
> Gaspar, Melchior, Balthasar,
> Pray for us now, and in the hour of death."
> "The papers have touched the three heads of the Holy Kings at Cologne. They are to preserve travellers from accidents on the roads, headaches, falling sickness, fever, witchcraft, all kinds of mischief and sudden death."

This man had been very ill all through the trial, and on being told that he was to be hung in chains was seized with such horror and confusion that he died in two hours, and thus escaped the indignities to which he had been sentenced. He was undoubtedly the worst ruffian of the gang, and bore a bad character even amongst the smugglers, who declared that if he knew them to have run goods he would contrive to steal them away.

What hardened villains these men had become may be gathered from the fact that after sentence had been passed two of them declared they "thought it no crime to destroy such informing rogues."

Two more of the gang implicated in the murders were arrested soon after, tried at East Grinstead, and sentenced to be hung. One was executed at Rake and afterwards hung in chains. The other, who was concerned also in the murder of poor Hawkins at the "Dog and Partridge," was executed on Slindon Common, and afterwards hung there in chains.

At the same assizes five other smugglers were tried for highway robbery and housebreaking, and, with one exception, sentenced to be hung. They were executed at Horsham. Two of these men belonged to the Hawkhurst gang, and had previously been rescued from Newgate by a party of smugglers,

who overpowered the turnkey.*   Of the latter party
was Thomas Potter, also a member of the Hawkhurst
gang, who, with three others, also smugglers, and
natives of Kent, were tried in the April following at
Rochester for various robberies, and convicted. Their
method was to go to houses at night, disguised and
armed, bind all the occupants, and then rob them.
After sentence was passed Potter admitted that
although he had committed crimes sufficient to have
hanged him by law for many years past, he had never
been guilty of murder, though he did design to
murder the turnkey at Newgate when he effected the
rescue of his fellow-smugglers.   One of the men hung
with Potter had been concerned in the murder of
Mr. Castle, an excise officer, who was shot on Sel-
hurst Common while seizing some run goods.   Just
before their execution one of the men declared they
had taken to highway and other sorts of robbery
from sheer necessity, as, being outlawed smugglers,
they dare not show themselves at their homes, and he
further declared his conviction that the fear of being
seen and apprehended was the cause of nearly all the
villanies and murders which had been committed by
the smugglers.

When we learn that three other criminals were
hung at the same time and place for various offences,
it must be clear that the public executioner was kept
pretty busy.

And now we come to the closing scenes in this
ghastly chapter of crime.   And no doubt it will have
been noticed how, as is so often the case, one outrage

* Arthur Gray, who escaped with another smuggler from Newgate
by knocking down the turnkey, and was retaken and sentenced to
seven years' transportation, was reputed to be worth £10,000 (June,
1748).

led to another, beginning with the rescue of goods from the king's warehouse at Poole, and ending with the barbarous atrocities for the perpetration of which so many suffered the extreme penalty of the law.

On April 4th, 1749, five men, apprehended on the sworn evidence of the two smugglers who had turned king's evidence, were tried at the Old Bailey for what was spoken of by the Crown counsel as "the most unheard-of act of villany and impudence ever known,"* namely, breaking into the king's Custom House at Poole, and stealing out thence thirty-seven hundredweight of tea, value £500. Of these, Thomas Kingsmill and William Fairall were "reckoned two of the most audacious, wicked fellows amongst the smugglers," and were both equally concerned in the long list of atrocities with which the notorious Hawkhurst gang were credited, and in all of which these two men were the moving spirits. Though only twenty-eight and twenty-five years old respectively, they were the most hardened and defiant criminals of any who had been brought up for trial, and preserved their dauntless attitude up to the moment of their death, maintaining that they had committed no crime in rescuing the goods from the Custom House, as these were "the property of no one but of those who had sent their money over to Guernsey for them." It was elicited in evidence that both Fairall and Kingsmill had been instrumental in

---

* The same offence was committed the following year in the county of Essex, when thirty smugglers, armed with blunderbusses and pistols, at 2 A.M. broke open the king's warehouse at Colchester with a large blacksmith's hammer and crowbar, and carried off sixty oil bags, containing about 1,514 pounds of tea.—See *Gentleman's Magazine* for the year 1748.

D

carrying several officers of the Customs and Excise out of the country, for no other reason than for having displayed too great zeal in detecting smugglers, and seizing their goods.

Of the two, Fairall carried off the palm for utter recklessness and brutal courage, and even his own countrymen were glad when he was removed from amongst them, because he was known to be a desperate fellow, and "no man could be safe whom Fairall should once think had done anything to offend him." His behaviour at the trial was quite in keeping with the character he bore; he stood the greater part of the time with a smile, or rather a sneer, on his countenance, laughing at some of the witnesses, and making threatening signs at others. On sentence being passed, he said, "Let's have a pipe and some tobacco and a bottle of wine, for as I am not to live long I am determined to live well the short time I have to be in this world." The evening before his execution he smoked his pipe very heartily, and drank freely, and on being ordered into his cell for the night, said, "Why in such a hurry; cannot you let me stay a little longer, and drink with my friends, I shall not be able to drink with them to-morrow night?"

On the morning of their execution neither of the men showed the least fear of death, and when one of the others who was to be hung at the same time commiserated them on having to be hung in chains afterwards, Fairall replied, smilingly, "We shall be hanging in the sweet air while you are rotting in your grave." All three were conveyed to Tyburn under a strong guard of soldiers, and then executed, the bodies of Fairall and Kingsmill being afterwards taken to a smith's shop in Fetter Lane, where they were fitted with chains, and afterwards conveyed to the places where they were to be hung up, viz., Fairall on Horsendown Green and Kingsmill at Gowdhurstgore, the places where they had lived. And thus one of the most notorious bands of criminals that ever figured in the annals of crime was " smashed up," and effectually put an end to, to the relief of all peaceful and law-abiding citizens.

CHAPTER VI.

Drink the Cause of Crime—The Woman Tempted Me—Master-Smugglers and their Men—Smuggling Methods—Tub-Carriers—How the Tubs were Slung—The Reverse of the Medal—*Nous sommes trahis*—The Unpardonable Sin—Activity of the Smugglers—Ruxley's Crew.

AFTER an impartial survey of the facts so far recorded, the reader will probably incline to the opinion—any previous bias notwithstanding—that in spite of the modern Briton's tendency to grumble at his surroundings, dwellers in England in the nineteenth century— especially in rural England—enjoy many advantages which were denied to their predecessors of a century ago, and that if rates are high, the ratepayers are at least free from the exactions and persecutions of desperadoes such as those of the Hawkhurst gang.

It is not without interest to note that, even at this somewhat remote period, over-drinking was at the root of many of the outrages committed by the smugglers, one of whom, previous to his execution, admitted " that all the smugglers, both masters and riders, drank drams to great excess, and generally kept themselves half drunk, which was the only thing that occasioned them to commit such outrages as they did sometimes." *

* The journals of this particular time teem with reports of outrages

D 2

This witness further declared that, to the best of his belief, there was no intention of hurting either Galley or Chater until some of the smugglers' wives proposed hanging them. Amongst other curious facts elicited in the course of these trials were certain details connected with the methods and practices of the smugglers which are worth noting, helping as they do to a better understanding of the whole system of smuggling, both then and in more recent days.

A witness, in the course of examination, said that "the master smugglers contract for the goods either abroad, or with the master of a cutter that fetches them, for a quantity of teas (called 'dry goods') and brandies, and the master of the cutter fixes a time and place where he designs to land, and seldom or never fails, being pretty punctual as to the time, if the weather permits. As the master smugglers cannot fetch all the goods themselves, so they hire men whom they call 'riders,' and they allow each man half a guinea a journey, and bear all expenses of eating and

---

perpetrated by the outlawed smugglers on people who gave them cause of offence. A correspondent writing from Horsham, under date August 23rd, 1748, says: "I have frequently conversed with many gentlemen of fortune about these dangerous men, and they assure me that the outlawed and other smugglers in this and the neighbouring counties are so numerous and desperate that the inhabitants are in continual fear of the mischiefs which these horrid wretches not only threaten, but actually perpetrate all round the country. The outrageous proceedings which you see in the public papers are not a tithe of what they really commit, and, to be quite familiar with you, I cannot better describe the terror which they strike than by quoting Milton :—

'Oh, what are these?
Death's ministers, not men, who thus deal death,
Inhumanity to men, and multiply
Ten thousand fold the sin of him who slew
His brother ; for of whom such massacre
Make they, but of their brethren, men of men.' "

drinking, and horse, and allowance of a dollop of tea, which is forty pound weight, being the half of a bag, the profit of which dollop, even of the most ordinary sort, is worth more than a guinea, and some 25s., and some more ; and they always make one journey, sometimes two, and sometimes three in a week, which is indeed such a temptation that very few people in the country can withstand, and which has been the cause of so many turning."

The medal has its reverse, the witness adding that it was very hard work going down to the seaside to fetch the goods—and taking into consideration the risks, not only of capture, but to their own persons, as they were obliged to ride at night, and through all the byways, avoiding the public roads as much as possible—people would not be so ready to take up with the smuggling were it not for the great profits that arose.

As regards the profits on a successful " run," it was a common tenet amongst smugglers, so late as even the first half of the present century, that if they could save one cargo out of three the business paid them.

One other point remains to be noticed. It was given in evidence by the captain of the " privateer "* who captured the goods, afterwards rescued from Poole, that the casks of brandy were slung with ropes, ready to sling over the horses, "as smuggling brandy commonly is." Now this practice of "slinging" the casks before shipping them continued up to the final suppression of the trade, or well into the present century, for, though in later times horses were no longer used

* The fact of a " privateer" being engaged in looking after the interests of the revenue shows the heterogeneous nature of the force entrusted with this particular duty at the time.

for carrying the casks, which were conveyed by
"porters," or "tub carriers," as the men were called—
the size of the cask being greatly reduced to meet
the change—it was still of the utmost importance to
get the goods away from the coast with the least
possible delay, and this was greatly facilitated by
having the casks ready slung for throwing over the
men's shoulders.

These matters have been gone into at some length
for the reason that to arrive at a proper understanding
of the subsequent history of smuggling—in the southern counties, at any rate—it is essential that the
peculiar state of things prevailing during the halcyon
days of the free-trader should be clearly realised.

It must be confessed, moreover, that the condition
of England, or a considerable portion of it, at this
particular time was somewhat different to the picture
not infrequently presented to our gaze by erudite
ladies and gentlemen, who lay themselves out to describe it for us, but who carefully avoid all reference
to this dark chapter in the annals of our land. That
the informer should be held in the utmost abhorrence
by the smugglers one can easily understand, and
we have seen something of the sort of treatment extended to these individuals when unlucky enough to
fall into the grasp of their foe. Many old smugglers,
indeed, have assured the writer that the informer had
more to do with the suppression of the trade than any
other agency ; a pardonable exaggeration, when the
very natural antipathy of the free-trader to the preventive man, and his disinclination to recognise any
good or useful qualities in his old enemy, are considered. "*Nous sommes trahis*" has been often pleaded
by the beaten side in extenuation of defeat, and that
the smuggler should resort to the same excuses rather

than admit having been beaten by fair and open means
need excite no surprise.

The obliquity of vision sometimes manifested by
the rustic conscience in matters affecting the informer
has been quaintly illustrated by a writer already
quoted. Speaking of one of his predecessors in the
parish of Morwenstowe, the Rev. R. S. Hawker tells
us how on one occasion, when "he presided, as the
custom was, at a parish feast, in cassock and bands,
and presented with his white hairs and venerable
countenance quite an apostolic aspect and mien, on a
sudden a busy whisper among the farmers at the
lower end of the table attracted his notice, interspersed
as it was by sundry nods and glances towards himself.
At last, one bolder than the rest addressed him, and
said that they had a great wish to ask his reverence a
question, if he would kindly grant them a reply ; it
was on a religious subject that they had dispute,
he said. The bland old man assured them of his
readiness to yield them any information or answer in
his power. 'But what was the point in dispute?'
'Why, sir, we wish to be informed if there were not
sins which God Almighty would never forgive?' Surprised and somewhat shocked, he told them 'that he
trusted there were no transgressions, common to themselves, but if repented of and abjured they might
clearly hope to be forgiven.' But with a natural
curiosity, he inquired what kind of iniquities they had
discussed as too vile to look for pardon. 'Why, sir,'
replied their spokesman, 'we thought that if a man
should find out where run goods was deposited, and
should inform the gauger, that such a villain was too
bad for mercy ! "

Although the infamous Hawkhurst gang had been
broken up, and its power for evil destroyed by the

death of its moving spirits, it must not be supposed
that the practice of smuggling had received any serious
check throughout the counties of Kent and Sussex.
With profits of a hundred per cent. within the reach
of the enterprising merchant, and a guinea or more
to be earned by unskilled labour over a night's outing,
the temptations were far too strong for average human
nature to resist, and through the remainder of the
century, and well into the present one, the free-trade
was prosecuted with amazing activity and success.

But, while the land smugglers had to content themselves with the profits arising from their own particular line of illicit trading, the sea smugglers varied
their business by indulging in occasional acts of piracy
on the high seas, which made the honest seafarer's
vocation almost as risky and exciting as that of the
fair-trader on shore during the Kingsmill and Fairall
régime. A gang of these sea ruffians, known as
" Ruxley's crew," belonging chiefly to Hastings, are
said to have continued their depredations afloat for
seven years or more before they were brought to
justice, and the particular act which brought the
myrmidons of the law on to their track, and resulted
in the capture of the greater part of them, was committed in 1768, when they boarded a Dutch vessel,
and chopped the master down the back with an axe.
But even in this case the perpetrators of this dastardly
outrage would probably never have been discovered
had they not openly bragged to one another how the
Dutchman wriggled when they cut him down the
backbone.

CHAPTER VII.

FOR the purpose of completing our survey of the frec-trade period, we must now turn our attention to what was going on in other parts of the United Kingdom, not only in the most distant portions, such as Scotland and Ireland, but in what was then, though not so far removed from the seat of Government, almost equally remote and difficult of access, namely, Cornwall. For it would be casting an unwarrantable reflection on the smuggling fraternity generally to suggest, even by inference, that the smugglers in the more remote parts of the kingdom were any less daring or active than their fellow-traders of the southern counties.

As regards Cornwall, the learned Dr. Couch, in his interesting, though little-known, history of his native village of Polperro—lying in a cleft of rock about sixteen miles west of Plymouth—gives us a very graphic sketch of the state of things existing there towards the close of last century :—

" On one occasion intelligence had been received at Fowey that a run of goods had been effected at Polperro during the previous night, and several men of a cutter's crew were accordingly sent as scouts to get all the information they could. Meeting with a farm labourer, who, it was suspected, had been engaged in this particular transaction, they tried to extract information from him by stratagem, but finding that

POLPERRO.

he was not to be entrapped, they tried the opposite
plan, and threatened him with immediate impressment
into the king's service if he did not tell them where
the goods were hidden. They succeeded in frightening
him, and he informed them that a large number of
kegs were stowed in a certain cellar, which he promised
to point out by placing a chalk-mark on the door.
Having from the opposite hill seen this done, a portion of the crew returned to Fowey to get a reinforce-
ment. Headed by the Custom House officers they
soon returned, and proceeded in the direction of the
cellar. The arrival of the force and their object were
discovered ; and a band of desperate smugglers, armed
with cutlasses and pistols, assembled on Newquay
Head, which place commanded an open view of the
cellars which contained the kegs. A large gun was
drawn down, and loaded and pointed, while a man
with a match stood by, waiting the command of the
skipper to fire. The revenue men were then defied
and threatened in a loud and determined voice. They
consulted their prudence, and resolved to send for a
still stronger force. In a few hours a well-armed
band arrived and rushed into the cellar, but found to
their great disappointment that, although the place
had been watched from the outside, the kegs, which
had really been there, had been removed they knew
not whither."

Of the Polperro smuggling fleet our author remarks, that "in these vessels were perpetrated so
many overt acts of defiance against the law, and so
much contempt of authority was shown as to lead one
to doubt that the circumstances could have occurred
within so recent a date."

One more sketch of Cornish free-trade times,
and our survey of the English coasts must be con-

sidered sufficiently complete for the purpose of this history.

"It was full six in the evening of an autumn day," writes Mr. Hawker, "when a traveller arrived where the road ran along by a sandy beach just above high-water mark. The stranger, who was a native of some inland town, and utterly unacquainted with Cornwall and its ways, had reached the brink of the tide just as a 'landing' was coming off. It was a scene not only to instruct a townsman, but to dazzle and surprise. At sea, just beyond the billows, lay the vessel, well moored with anchors at stem and stern. Between the ship and the shore boats, laden to the gunwale, passed to and fro. Crowds assembled on the beach to help the cargo ashore. On the one hand a boisterous group surrounded a keg with the head knocked in, for simplicity of access to the good cognac, into which they dipped whatsoever vessel came first to hand ; one man had filled his shoe. On the other side they fought and wrestled, cursed and swore. Horrified at what he saw, the stranger lost all self-command, and, oblivious of personal danger, he began to shout, 'What a horrible sight! Have you no shame? Is there no magistrate at hand? Cannot any justice of the peace be found in this fearful country?'

"'No ; thanks be to God,' answered a hoarse, gruff voice. 'None within eight miles.'

"'Well, then,' screamed the stranger, 'is there no clergyman hereabout? Does no minister of the parish live among you on this coast?'

"'Aye! to be sure there is,' said the same deep voice.

"'Well, how far off does he live? Where is he?'

"'That's he, sir, yonder, with the lanthorn.'

"And sure enough there he stood on a rock, and

poured, with pastoral diligence, 'the light of other days' on a busy congregation."

Well might Mr. Hawker observe, *apropos* of this and other scenes, that "the life and adventures of the Cornish clergy during the eighteenth century would form a graphic volume of ecclesiastical lore. Afar off from the din of the noisy world they dwelt in their quaint gray vicarages by the churchyard wall, the saddened and unsympathising witnesses of those wild, fierce usages of the west, which they were utterly powerless to control."

Turning now to Scotland, where, by reason of the sparseness of population over a great part of the country the demand for "run" goods was not so great as in the southern portion of the kingdom, we find a pretty brisk trade carried on, nevertheless, along the shores of the Solway Firth and neighbouring counties.* Thus, speaking of Port William, on the Wigtonshire coast—a noted smuggling rendezvous in free-trade days—a writer observes :—

"My friend, Mr. James McWilliam, formerly officer of excise at Wigtown, in a letter which I received, dated Wigtown, September 28th, 1840, says, in answer to some queries which I had put to him on the subject of smuggling : ' I remember in the year 1777, being then a boy of about twelve years of age,

---

* To the credit of the Scots let it be recorded that the annual committee of the Convention of Royal Burghs of Scotland (October, 1736), having in a circular letter represented to each burgh the pernicious consequences of smuggling in its clearest light, and earnestly exhorted their countrymen to desist from so infamous a trade, several of the burghs, in their corporate capacity, came to the strongest resolutions to discourage it for the future, viz., they would not be directly or indirectly concerned in running foreign goods, or in purchasing or in vending any goods knowing them to be run, but will lay themselves out to get intelligence, and assist the officers in seizing and condemning the same.

counting 210 horses, laden with tea, spirits, and tobacco, accompanied by about half that number of "Lingtowmen," passing within a mile of the town of Wigtown, in open defiance of the supervisor, two excise officers, and about thirty soldiers, stationed at Wigtown, to assist the revenue officers in the suppression of smuggling. I recollect this circumstance particularly from four of the smugglers' horses falling down dead in the road, as was supposed from the heat of the day and the strong smell of the tobacco.

"'I recollect that about the same time I accompanied my father, who was then excise officer in Wigtown, and the supervisor, with about twenty-five soldiers, to Port William, where two luggers were lying ready to discharge their cargoes of contraband goods. One of these luggers mounted twenty-two guns, the other fourteen, and each had a crew of about fifty men. Upon our arrival at the beach the commander of one of these vessels came on shore, and said if the party did not instantly retire he would cause a broadside to be discharged from the ships, and would land a hundred armed men to clear the beach of us; but if the party would retire quietly to a distance of three or four miles, so as not to disturb the landing of their goods, he would leave thirty or forty ankers of spirits for us on the beach. Our party retired, and the captain of the lugger fulfilled his promise by leaving thirty-six casks of spirits for us at the place appointed.

"'The smugglers evinced great ingenuity in the construction of cellars for concealing the contraband property. I remember my father going several times with a party of soldiers to the farm of Drumtroddan, in consequence of having received information of there being a cellar for the reception of smuggled goods, either below the barn floor or about the kiln; but though he caused the floor and every place about the house to be trenched, he could not find the entrance to this cellar. It was, however, discovered afterwards by another officer immediately under the fire of the kiln, which fire had always been kindled as soon as my father and his party made their appearance. There were generally two cellars at the same place, one over the other, for the sole purpose of deceiving the officers, who, when they found one, never thought of searching for another, till the plan was discovered by Mr. Reid, the Inspector-General of Customs, who brought out from Edinburgh with him, in December, 1777, two men who understood draining so well that they discovered so many of these under-cellars, both at the Clone and at the Mull of Galloway, that in the course of a few days his party seized about eighty chests of tea and one hundred and forty ankers of gin and brandy, with nearly as many bales of tobacco.'"

Mr. Samuel Robinson, in his "Reminiscences of Wigtonshire," tells the story of the suppression of the illicit traffic in the following words :—

" It had its rise in a struggle which took place for the representation of the Wigtonshire Burghs in the House of Commons between Sir William Maxwell, of Monreith, and Commodore Stewart, of Glasserton. At that time it seems to have been the practice for candidates to parade the streets at certain times, attended with large bodies of their adherents by way of display and bravado. Sir William's followers were chiefly his Clone tenants—who were all smugglers— and on meeting the Commodore on the street of Whithorn, the old sailor, who could not let slip the chance of having a hit at the Baronet, exclaimed, 'You are very active to-day, Sir William, with your smugglers at your back!' 'Yes,' replied the Baronet, 'if you had been as active when you allowed the Dutch fleet to pass you off the Dogger Bank, it would have been telling the Crown of Britain many thousand pounds.' 'I'll suppress the smuggling,' was the retort of the Admiral. He laid the case before the Government, and a barracks was built at Port William, a party of soldiers quartered there, and the trade and those who conducted it were ruined."

Sometimes there was a humorous side to these transactions, as the following story shows :—

" A few miles from Lochnaw is the little harbour of Dallybay. Here, one day in last century, some smugglers had landed a cargo of their usual wares, such as brandy, wines, and tobacco, and these were carried up the hill of South Cairn, waiting till a band of volunteers arrived with a string of pack-horses to transport them inwards for distribution. The Custom House officer in charge of the district received information of their doings, and hurrying to the spot with the only coastguardsman* disengaged, he promptly effected a seizure of the whole of the goods. The smugglers skulked off, and the one coastguardsman was sent back to press men and horses in the king's name to convey the precious treasure to Stranraer. The officer, pluming himself not a little on his alacrity, sauntered sentry-fashion round and round his prize, which lay heaped before him in rich profusion, his sword and a brace of formidable pistols by his side. Presently Maggie McConnell approached the great man, wishing him a good morning, to which he affably replied, and accepted Maggie's proferred hand. He had unwittingly sealed his own fate. His arm was thrust upwards, and at the same instant he

* This is a common mistake. There was no such service as the coastguard till after the peace in the early part of this century.

was encircled by the siren's arms, and with a heavy fall was thrown helplessly upon his back. Maggie then sat coolly down upon her victim, and having placed her apron over his eyes, she held him firmly down as if bound in a vice. In vain he struggled; he coaxed and threatened her by turns; he shouted for help in the king's name, and for a moment his hopes ran high; footsteps approached; he roared louder and louder, but no friendly voice replied. At last, but only when it suited her pleasure, Maggie released him from her grasp. But oh, the vanity of human hopes! When he looked up not one of the articles lay in its old place, as he had himself seen them just before upon the ground. By-and-by his companion reappeared, but only to find the head officer *tête-à-tête* with this Galloway matron, who, bidding them adieu, disappeared without further loss of time, wishing them both a pleasant ride into Stranraer." *

The mention of Scotch smuggling will, of course recall to the mind of the reader Sir Walter Scott's novel, " Guy Mannering," in which, with an unerring eye for incident, the great writer has seized on some of the most daring escapades of the free-traders as a foundation on which to build a very graphic picture of this particular period; and if, in some parts, colour has been applied with a degree of license only permissible to a great artist, the picture, as a whole, may be accepted as a pretty accurate reflex of the time.

With reference to the character of Dirk Hatterick, Sir Walter Scott informs us that his prototype " is considered as having been a Dutch skipper called Yawkins, well known on the coast of Galloway and

* " History of Wigtownshire."

E

Dumfriesshire as sole proprietor and master of a bucklar or smuggling lugger called the *Black Prince*, often
employed by French, Dutch, Manx, and Scottish
smuggling companies. Sure of active assistance on
shore, Yawkins demeaned himself so boldly that his
mere name was a terror to the officers of the revenue.
He availed himself of the fears which his presence
inspired on one particular night, when, happening to
be ashore with a considerable quantity of goods in his
sole custody, a strong party of excisemen came down
on him. Far from shunning the attack, Yawkins
sprang forward shouting, 'Come on my lads! Yawkins is before you!' The revenue officers were
intimidated, and relinquished their prize, though
defended only by the courage and address of a single
man. In his proper element Yawkins was equally
successful. On one occasion he was landing his cargo
at the Manxman's Lake, near Kirkcudbright, when
two revenue cruisers, the *Pigmy* and the *Dwarf*,
hove in sight at once, on different tacks, the one
coming round by the Isles of Fleet, the other between
the Point of Rueberry and the Muckle Row. The
dauntless free-trader instantly weighed anchor, and
bore down right between the luggers, so that he
tossed his hat on the deck of the one and his wig on
that of the other, hoisted a cask to his maintop to
show his occupation, and bore away under an extraordinary pressure of canvas, without receiving injury.*
To account for these and other hairbreadth escapes
popular superstition alleged that Yawkins insured
his celebrated bucklar by compounding with the devil
for one-tenth of his crew every voyage. The *Black
Prince* used to discharge her cargo at Ince, Balcarry,

---

* The reader is advised to take a pinch or two of salt with this
astonishing narrative.

and elsewhere on the coast, but her owner's favourite landing-places were at the entrance to the Dee and the Cree, near the old castle of Rueberry. A large cave near here, often used by Yawkins, is now called Dirk Hatterick's cave."

Sir Walter Scott further observes that "the trade was entirely destroyed by Mr. Pitt's celebrated commutation law, which, by reducing the duties, enabled lawful dealers to compete with the smuggler. The statute was called in Galloway and Dumfriesshire by those who had thriven upon the contraband trade, 'the burning and starving act.'"

Doubtless the "trade" was hard hit, but with all respect to so high an authority, the writer would submit that the word "destroy" is hardly applicable to the situation, for, in spite of the statute, smuggling, as is well known, went on merrily for many years after.*

---

* Let it be recorded to the credit of all concerned, and as a set-off to the above, that, in the month of July, 1744, a smuggling vessel having landed a quantity of French brandy on the coast of Angus, it was discovered by some gentlemen and farmers, who immediately informed the officer of the revenue, and assisted in the seizure, and upon the ships still hovering near the shore, they went armed in boats to search her ; and though they were fired upon with small arms by the crew, they returned the fire, overpowered the smugglers, and brought the vessel into port. It was also stated at the time that several seizures of a like nature were made in other parts of the country, and that three or four smugglers were killed in their obstinate attempts.

CHAPTER VIII.

An Armed Smuggler—Shot by Mistake—The "Smugglers Act"—Advice
to the Unwary—Where the Gin Came From—How the Farm Hands
were Employed—Napoleon's Opinion of Smugglers—Cheap Liquor
and Starvation—The Archbishop Exercises Self-Denial.

IN the sister isle, as elsewhere, the free-traders drove
a roaring trade and, if there was less of armed resistance in connection with it, and, consequently, less
bloodshed, the absence of these disagreeable accom-
paniments must be attributed in great measure to
the immunity from interference with which the trade
was conducted along the greater part of the Irish
coast. There were exceptions, of course. Thus, in
the biography of a recently deceased officer of distinction, we read that in the year 1790, when General
Chesney's father was " coast officer " at Mourne, co.
Down, a famous armed smuggling craft, called the
Morgan Rattler anchored in Glass Drummond
Bay for the purpose of landing contraband goods.
The vessel being recognised, and her intention
divined, the revenue men were at once called out to
prevent a landing, and their boat manned and sent
afloat, upon which the vessel landed sixteen of her
crew for the double purpose of driving the revenue
men off and capturing their boat. But the revenue men
at once opened fire, and beat the smugglers off.
Twelve more men were then landed at a point about
half a mile away, with the object of taking the king's
men in the rear, and these had now to retreat, while
the smugglers, being in the proportion of three to
one, succeeded in landing their cargo.

None of the revenue men were hurt in this affair, but
while it was in progress the smugglers were heard calling
to each other to " fire at the man on the white horse,"
meaning Captain Chesney, the officer in command.

It seems that, in consequence of this officer's activity in suppressing the free-trade along this part of the coast, the smugglers and boatmen conceived a grudge against him, and determined to waylay him with a view to taking his life. In the darkness of a winter's night, however, they mistook their victim, and killed the chief boatman instead.

Stories such as these of the old free-trade days might, of course, be multiplied indefinitely, for there is scarcely a village round our coast but has its traditions of the good old times, when the smuggler bold was elevated into the hero of romance, clothed with all the manly virtues, and regarded as a noble benefactor of his race, while the excise man, poor fellow, though doing his duty—sometimes, strictly enough, according to his lights—was invariably made to play the part—well, if not exactly of the villain, certainly the fool of the piece. Such a curious inversion of the moral order of things supplies a quaint commentary on the times.

Enough however has been advanced to establish the fact that not only were the times sadly out of joint, but, moreover, that if the arm of the law reached to the uttermost parts of the realm, it was extended in a very attenuated form, and its action in many parts completely paralysed by the attitude of the inhabitants. The popular cry of " Where is the policeman?" must have gone up from many hearts in those days with far more reason than exists at the present time, and with less chance of a satisfactory reply, for the representative of law and order was a very different being to the stalwart blue-coated and helmeted individual of our own day, and over wide tracts of country he was conspicuous simply by his entire absence, with results which stand out so plainly that all who run may read.

If, after all that has been stated, anyone is still so blind as to cherish a belief in the harmlessness of smuggling, in so far as concerns its effect on the morals of a nation, the writer would commend to his earnest study, with an open mind, the words of a contemporary observer of men and manners. In opening the case against the prisoners indicted for murder at the memorable assizes held at Chichester in January, 1749, Mr. Banks, the Crown counsel, made use of the following words :—

" I cannot here omit taking notice of the unhappy cause of this fatal effect now under your consideration. Everyone here present will, in his own thoughts, anticipate my words, and know I mean smuggling. Smuggling is not only highly injurious to trade, a violation of the laws, and the disturber of the peace and quiet of all the maritime counties in the kingdom, but it is a nursery for all sorts of vice and wickedness ; a temptation to commit offences at first unthought of ; an encouragement to perpetrate the blackest of crimes without provocation or remorse; and is, in general, productive of cruelty, robbery, and murder.*

" It is greatly to be wished, both for the sake of the

* The fact is not generally known, and therefore worthy of remark, that the famous Porteous riot in Edinburgh had its origin in the execution of a smuggler " who had, heedless of his own fate, saved the life of a brother criminal by springing upon the soldiers around them, and by main force keeping them back while his companion fled, who never afterwards was heard of " (1736). The violent deaths of no less than nine persons, including Captain Porteous, were the far-reaching consequences of this act. The following particulars concerning the smuggler aforesaid are worthy of note:—" Every gentleman has heard of the execution of that noted smuggler, Andrew Wilson, whence all this mischief has flowed. That deluded man main-

smugglers themselves, and for the peace of this county, that the dangerous and armed manner now used of running uncustomed goods was less known and less practised here.

"It is a melancholy consideration to observe that the best and wisest measures of the Government calculated to put a stop to this growing mischief have been perverted and abused to the worst of purposes. And what was intended to be a cure to this disorder has been the means to increase and heighten the disease.

"Every expedient of lenity and mercy was at first made use of to reclaim this abandoned set of men. His Majesty, by repeated proclamations of pardon, invited them to their duty and their own safety. But instead of laying hold of so gracious an offer, they have set the laws at defiance, have made the execution of justice dangerous in the hands of the magistracy, and have become almost a terror to Government itself."

It may be as well to state here for the information of those who are not *au courant* with smuggling matters, that the famous "Smugglers Act" was passed in 1736, modified in 1779 and 1784, and a

---

tained to the hour of his death that he was most unjustly condemned, and died with great tranquillity, so firm, so fixed was he in the belief of his own innocence. When a minister was endeavouring to undeceive him and bring him to a sense of his guilt, he admitted having taken money from a collector of the revenue by violence ; that he did it because he knew no other way of coming at it ; that the officers of the revenue had, by their practice, taught him this was lawful, for they had often seized and carried off his goods by violence, and so long as they had goods of his of greater value in their hands than all the money he took from them, they were still in his debt, and he had done no wrong." (See speech in the House of Commons on the Scotch Riot Act, May 16, 1737).

review of all the statutes relating to the subject made
in 1826.

Some idea of the extent of the trade in 1779—the
date of the passing of the second Act—may be
gathered from a pamphlet entitled, "Advice to the
Unwary," published with a view to making the new
law known, wherein it is stated that the practice of
smuggling had made such rapid strides from the
sea-coasts into the very heart of the country, per-
vading every city, town, and village, as to have brought
universal distress on the fair dealer ; that the greater
part of the 3,867,500 gallons distilled annually at
Schiedam was to be smuggled into England ; that a
distillery had lately been set up for making geneva,
for the same purpose, at Dunkirk ; that the French
imported five or six millions of pounds of tea, the
greatest part of which was to be smuggled here ; that
the trade of Dunkirk (where, and at Flushing, the
Sussex and other smugglers had regular resident
agents) was mostly carried on by smugglers, in vessels
not only large, but so well constructed for sailing that
seldom one of them was captured ; that in many
places near the sea the farmer was unable to find
hands to do his work, whilst great numbers were
employed in smuggling goods from one part of the
country to another. Even the war with France in
1793 caused no appreciable diminution in the import
trade, which was carried on all through the war, even
from the French ports, the smugglers betaking themselves to the still more discreditable practice of conveying letters and correspondence to the enemy, concerning which there will be more to be said in its
proper place.

Of the enterprise and activity with which these
vocations were conducted we have curious evidence

from so unexpected a quarter as the Emperor Napoleon, who, in course of conversation with Dr. O'Meara, concerning which there will be more to say later on, said, " They (the smugglers) have courage and ability to do anything for money. They took from France annually forty or fifty millions' worth of silks and brandy."

A writer describing the closing years of last century tells us that "smuggling was carried on to an astounding extent, and it was calculated that one half of the spirits as well as a great quantity of tobacco and other articles consumed in Kent and Sussex had never paid duty." But as there is no rose without a thorn, so this enticing picture of free-trade days has a dark side, for the writer goes on to inform us that "there was a terrible scarcity of bread, and numerous measures were suggested to mitigate the deficiency ; while the royal family abstained from the use of pastry—a course which the Archbishop of Canterbury urged for general adoption." The times were sadly out of joint! History, indeed, affords no more touching picture of Christian resignation and self-sacrifice than this of his Grace of Canterbury eating his humble pie without any crust. So much for the good old days of free-trade !

CHAPTER IX.

Why the " Free-Trader" Prospered—" They Won't be Happy till They Get It "—Corrupt Officers—The Country's Extremity the Free-Trader's Opportunity—The "Scientific Period" of Smuggling—Forty Years of Coercion—Plot and Counter-plot—A Lost Art—"They Haven't the Heart for It."

IT will naturally be asked at this point why no steps were taken by the authorities ere the evil had assumed the gigantic proportions we have seen, to put an end to a state of things so detrimental to the national interests. That the Government was fully alive to the existence of the evil has been already shown. The very losses sustained by the revenue, to say nothing of the risk to life and limb continually incurred by the servants of the Crown in their efforts to guard its interests, must have kept the matter *en évidence*, and the reader may well wonder why the authorities allowed things to drift on in the way they did.

The explanation is not altogether so simple as might be supposed. Various circumstances combined to favour the free-trader, and, indeed, we have only to bear in mind the popular feeling on the subject of smuggling, and the violent opposition to repressive measures invariably displayed by that large section of the public interested in the maintenance of it, to recognise the almost hopeless task which the Government had undertaken in endeavouring to suppress it.

The very instruments by which it was sought to combat the evil were too often corrupted and perverted to the furtherance of the very ends they were intended to suppress,* and we all know that when the

---

* That there was some excuse for the little weaknesses displayed at times by these excellent public servants will be clear from the following:—In the course of a debate in the House of Commons on the Smuggling Bill (1736) it was given in evidence that "in some parts of the maritime counties the whole people are so generally engaged in smuggling that it is impossible to find a jury that will, upon trial, do justice to an officer of the revenue in any case whatever. In those counties where smuggling is become general, the majority of the coroner's inquests always consists of smugglers, so that it has been found by experience that these inquests *always bring the officer and his assistants in guilty of murder*, even though it be made clearly appear, by the most undoubted testimonies, that the killing happened *de uefendendo.*"

bulk of a nation make it evident by their action with reference to the object of their heart's desire, that " they won't be happy till they get it "—no matter whether to their own or to the national advantage, the struggle will be a bitter one.

As a matter of fact there was no really adequate force available for the suppression of the trade, and certainly during the later free-trade period—from the commencement of the war with France till the return of peace, in 1816, the Government had no means of raising such a force. The reader need scarcely be reminded that the country just at this time was passing through one of the most momentous crises of her history. She was engaged in a desperate struggle, on the issue of which not only her independence, but her very existence as a nation depended. The greatest general of modern times was carrying on a game of political skittles, in which dynasty after dynasty had succumbed to his unerring strokes. Britain alone, amongst the powers of Europe, had survived this wreck of empires, and continued to present an undaunted front. Blow after blow had been parried and returned with interest ; but the strain was intense, for the population of these islands was then but small, while, in the absence of conscription, the difficulty of keeping the fighting line intact was, of course, almost insurmountable ; for no matter how brave and patriotic a nation may be, there is no disguising the fact that the mass of the populace are far more intent on minding their own affairs at home than in going abroad to fight the enemy. Happily for most countries, great crises usually produce the men capable of meeting them, and though the means by which England's difficulty was met and overcome may seem harsh and tyrannical to what we

are pleased to call the "enlightened opinion" of
modern times, they were admirably adapted to the
end, and, what is of more importance, proved entirely
successful. Briefly, every able-bodied man that
could be got hold of, whether in the service of the
Crown or of private individuals, was packed off to
fight the king's enemies, and thus, while the utmost
efforts of a press-gang only just sufficed to keep the
fleet manned—batches of convicts, actually, in some
instances, being drafted to fill up vacancies in his
Majesty's ships—the most desperate expedients had
to be resorted to for the purpose of swelling the ranks
of the army. When we read of bounties of from
thirty to forty pounds being paid for the enlistment
of boys of fifteen, in the thick of the Peninsular
war, and of actual gaol deliveries to make good
deficiencies that no other means could supply, some
faint conception may be formed of the difficulties
which a harassed executive had to contend with at
this particular juncture of our history.

Obviously, under such conditions, there was little
chance of a properly organised preventive force being
called into existence, and the reader will now understand why, so far, at any rate, as concerns the later
period of its existence, the hydra-headed monster of
free-trade was never fairly grappled with. The
country's extremity was the free-trader's opportunity,
and we have seen how eagerly this enterprising individual availed himself of it.

With the termination of the struggle with France
we come to the second, or, as it has been called, the
"scientific period" in the history of smuggling—a
period which in many ways is by far the most interesting, if somewhat less sensational in its developments, from the fact that being nearer to the present

day, and therefore within the recollection of people now living, we have more precise and detailed information in regard to it, while a far higher degree of intelligence and ingenuity, not to say science, was brought to the business than was ever displayed, or indeed required, in the pre-scientific or free-trade days.

The Government being at liberty to turn its attention once more to home affairs, lost no time in

REPRESENTATION OF AN ENGAGEMENT BETWEEN THE "PIGMY" REVENUE CRUISER AND A SMUGGLING VESSEL IN 1822, CARVED ON THE HEADSTONE OF A SMUGGLER WHO WAS SHOT ON THIS OCCASION, IN WYKE CHURCHYARD, NEAR WEYMOUTH.

initiating active measures for the suppression of a trade which had proved so inimical to the best interests of the country. But the very immunity which the smugglers had enjoyed so long not only made them extremely loth to give up so profitable a business, but had utterly demoralised the coast population along the entire seaboard of the United Kingdom. Defrauding the revenue had come to be looked on as a perfectly justifiable means of asserting a Briton's indefeasible right to buy his goods in the cheapest market, rather

than as a practice to be eschewed by honest citizens
and loyal subjects, while the enforcement of the law
against smugglers was regarded as a piece of un-
justifiable tyranny.   And no doubt when a smuggler
shot a brutal king's officer in defence of his goods,
and was called on to pay the penalty, his friends and
admirers would charge the authorities with having
provoked a breach of the peace by their unwarrantable interference with an old-established industry—
a nice, simple way of looking at things which never
struck these jolly free-traders as in any way repre-
hensible.

The evil was far too deeply rooted, however, to be
eradicated by a mere Government enactment; and it
required the sustained efforts of the executive enforcing its measures by means of a numerous and
zealous body of officers and men through a period of
nearly forty years—forty years of coercion! to effectually suppress it.   And old smugglers will tell you
that the trade would never have been put down even
then had it not been for the informer, together with
great reductions in the duty on foreign spirits.

That the free-traders and their allies should bitterly
resent Government interference was, of course, only
natural, and although *open* defiance of the authorities
was no longer practised—the risk of armed resistance
being far too serious to be lightly incurred, except in
very special cases, several desperate conflicts took
place along the south coast, and many lives were lost
on both sides ere the spirit of resistance was finally
quelled.

The smugglers now found themselves treated to
an amount of attention which they certainly never
courted, and would fain, it is believed, have dispensed
with; while the altered circumstances of the trade

necessitated a complete revolution in its methods, for, whereas formerly the smugglers were content simply to overawe the officers of the revenue by a display of superior force, their efforts were now chiefly directed to circumventing them. Each move of the executive was met by a corresponding move on the part of the smugglers, and in the game of plot and counterplot which ensued a marvellous amount of ingenuity was displayed on both sides, though certainly the palm must in all fairness be awarded to the illicit traders, whose fertility of resource, daring, and enterprise—worthy, it must be confessed, of a nobler cause—cannot but command our admiration and even respect.

The contraband trade was no longer a question of mere brute force ; it had become a science, a handicraft, which called into play the highest faculties, and gradually deve'oped a species of craftsmanship which stands unrivalled in the annals of trade. It had its own nomenclature, its own peculiar lore, and " trade secrets," which are already more than half forgotten, and must ere long, in the very nature of things, pass away, never to be recovered. Nearly half a century has elapsed since a " run " of goods in the old style has been attempted on any part of our coasts, and smuggling with most of us is a mere tradition, while nearly all who took a prominent part in the business have vanished from the stage. Here and there along the southern seaboard, in out-of-the-way nooks, one may still come across some old " sheer hulk," tottering along with feeble steps, or sunning himself on a bench by the sea, gazing with dimmed eye at the restless play of the element associated with some of the most stirring scenes of his life, and which even now, in old age, exercises over him an indescribable power, conjuring up before his mental vision, with almost

realistic force, events and days which have long gone
by. And yet it is quite likely that this old man in
his day was one of the most famous smugglers on the
coast, whose strength of limb, activity, keenness of
vision, nerve, and fertility of resource, was unequalled
by any of the craft.   Occasionally, it is true, you may
meet with an old smuggler who would fain bury his
past under a veneer of affected respectability ; but the
most of them delight in nothing better than a good
" crack " about the old smuggling days and the part
they played in them ; and if you catch one of these
old fellows on the right "lay" his yarn is sure to be
worth listening to, and, as he warms to the subject,
his eyes sparkle, he fidgets on his seat, and the old
fire of youth flickers up fitfully once more.   And then
when the tale is done, and the old man shakes your
hand with something of the grip of old, he says regretfully, " Ah, well, neither you or I will ever see *those*
times again," adding, with a touch of irony, " Why,
bless you they haven't the heart for it nowadays ! "

CHAPTER X.

Sources of Information—Smuggling Class nearly Extinct—Similarity of
    Methods along the Coast—Skill of the Cornish Smugglers—Cornwall,
    the Smuggler's " Paradise "—Chivalrous Smugglers—Coastguard and
    Contrabandists—The Suppression of Smuggling.

IT has been the writer's lot, in the course of profes-
sional duties, to be thrown a good deal amongst that
particular class of the populace which in former days
supplied the most numerous and efficient recruits to
the smuggling ranks ; and having made it an invariable
practice to follow the well-known and much-to-be
commended "Cuttle-ian ' system of notation—" when
found "—he has succeeded, by dint of searching out

old smugglers and coastguard pensioners, in rescuing a mass of curious information from the oblivion to which modern indifference and respectability would fain have consigned it. From the interest manifested in the subject by many people it has occurred to the writer that some attempt to gather up these scattered threads of unwritten history, and to weave them into the form of a connected narrative, might prove not altogether unacceptable to the general reader.

It may be as well, perhaps, to observe that the sources from which this particular sort of information is to be obtained are becoming scarcer year by year; indeed, many of the writer's old smuggling friends have passed away since these lines were penned, and the number of real smugglers still living may soon be counted on the fingers of one hand, a fact which renders their reminiscences all the more interesting and valuable.

It would be easy, of course, to fill volumes with anecdotes of the old smuggling days; but, interesting as these would no doubt prove to residents near the particular localities described, they could scarcely be other than tedious to the general public. One may easily have too much of a good thing, and it has therefore been deemed better to limit the scope of the following history of nineteenth century smuggling as far as possible to one portion of the kingdom, supplementing it by such references to other localities as may seem necessary for the elucidation of the subject, and for imparting to the reader as comprehensive a view of smuggling ways as can be acquired without undue effort.

Confining ourselves, therefore, to the south coast of England, which from its proximity to the Continent offered the greatest facilities to the contrabandists, we find a certain similarity of method distinguishing the

F

smuggling systems all along the seaboard, though
when we come to examine these a little more closely
we shall find many local peculiarities, which give interest to the inquiry, and preserve it from the reproach
of monotony.

As regards the skill and enterprise displayed by
those who conducted the trade, it is difficult to award
the palm to any one county, though on the whole,
perhaps, and after a careful consideration of all the
circumstances of the case, the writer is inclined to
give it to the Cornishmen. Not that the East
countrymen were one whit behind them in point of
courage or activity; but the very fact of having to
travel a far greater distance for their goods exposed
them to increased risks, and to many dangers from
which the trade elsewhere was tolerably exempt, thus
giving scope to the highest faculties, and developing
seamanlike qualities of no mean order. As an instance
of the desperate risks that are sometimes willingly
incurred in the pursuit of high profits, it may be stated
that when smuggling was at its height the Cornishmen
were in the habit of running over to France—a distance of about a hundred miles—in open boats, in
mid-winter too, for their supplies of spirits.

The adventurous disposition of the inhabitants of
"far Cornwall" seemed to mark them out as peculiarly suited to the prosecution of a trade fraught with
so many dangers; while the comparative isolation of
this quaint corner of England, with its rugged coast
line, its fine natural harbours with their infinite
ramifications of creeks and "pills," that seemed
to have been ordained by a special providence for
the smugglers' behoof, offered facilities which could
be matched in no other part of England. To these
natural advantages the Cornish smuggler brought

in his own person an amount of skill, cunning, and enterprise which was scarcely equalled, certainly unsurpassed, elsewhere, and which, combined with the remoteness of his home, enabled him to pursue his vocation for many years after the trade had been suppressed in more accessible parts of the kingdom.

To the credit of Cornishmen let it be recorded that smuggling was conducted—during the present century, at least—in a far more "chivalrous" spirit than characterised the trade further east. There was none of that reckless disregard for life which produced so much bloodshed along the coasts of Kent and Sussex ; while Cornish smugglers never disgraced their manhood by acts of brutal and ruffianly outrage, such as those which from earliest times have, alas ! disfigured the annals of certain eastern counties.

No history of smuggling would be complete without some reference to that splendid body of public servants which performed such yeoman service in the final suppression of the trade, and concerning whom the most lamentable ignorance very widely prevails at the present day. Smuggling history is, in fact, so closely bound up with the rise and development of that branch of the public service known now by the appellation of coastguard, while the spheres of action of smuggler and preventive man are so intertwined that the two can hardly be considered apart. It has, therefore, been deemed expedient to present the reader with a brief account of the force which has played so important a part in the social and economic history of our country during the last seventy years, and to whose existence at the present day the nation is indebted to an extent but little appreciated for the happy immunity from smuggling which now very generally prevails.

F 2

Part II.

THE SCIENTIFIC PERIOD.

TRADE ROUTES AND SHIPPING.

CHAPTER I.

Chief *Entrepôt* of the Trade—Peculiar Privileges of the Channel Islands—
Effect of Smuggling on the Revenue—Futile Attempts to Introduce a
Custom House—Diversion of the Trade to French Ports—The Import-
ance of Roscoff—Dependence of Guernsey on the Smuggling Trade.

THE chief *entrepôt* for the smuggling trade with
England during the greater part of last century and
the early years of the present one was at the Channel
Islands ; and of this very lucrative business Guernsey
monopolised by far the larger share. Thus, in describing the islands at the commencement of the 18th
century, the historian Duncan* tells us that "the
English smuggler resorted to Guernsey for his cargoes
of spirits, tobacco, tea, and other high taxed commodities, for which he found a ready and profitable
sale on his own coast." And again it was stated in
evidence before the committee of the House of Commons which sat in 1845 to inquire into the causes of
the "most infamous practice of smuggling," that in
January of that year nine smuggling cutters sailed
from Rye for Guernsey, in order to take in large
quantities of goods to be run on the coast. It was
from here, also, that the smuggling vessel, *The Two*

* "The History of Guernsey." Jonathan Duncan. 1841.

Brothers, procured her cargo of tea and spirits which was captured and placed in " The King's Warehouse " at Poole, and thence afterwards rescued in the manner described. The means by which the trade became diverted from the Island of Guernsey into other channels and the disastrous consequences which ensued therefrom to the inhabitants forms one of the most curious if little known chapters in the history of smuggling ; and as some knowledge of the facts pertaining thereto is necessary to a proper understanding of the course which the trade took in subsequent years, the most salient points will be briefly sketched in for the benefit of those who are not already cognisant of them.

It must be premised that the Channel Islands, by reason of certain charters, dating back to a some-what remote period, were secured the enjoyment of special and peculiar privileges, comprising, amongst others, exemption from the excise laws and various Customs regulations enacted from time to time for the protection of the revenue of Great Britain.* Consequently, up to the time of the suppression of the trade by means of certain legislative enactments which will be presently described, the English smuggling vessels could lay there and load in perfect security from interference on the part of British cruisers ; while the inhabitants of the islands were not slow to avail themselves to the fullest extent of the peculiar advantages thus conferred on them. " Up to the period of the first American war, in 1775, the trade of

---

* Amongst other curious privileges, was that of being looked upon as a harbour of refuge, and considered neutral in times of war, so that a prize made by either of the belligerents could be declared to be illegally made. According to a high legal authority this privilege "has never been formally abolished, but has fallen into disuse."

the island," says Duncan, " was chiefly confined to the import of spirits and tobacco to supply the wants of the English smugglers."*

It was scarcely to be expected that with money tight all round—the annual loss to the revenue being estimated by the Commissioners appointed during George III.'s reign to inquire into the matter, at £350,000— the British Government would look favourably on the peculiar manner in which the loyal inhabitants of Guernsey were using, or as some might consider it, abusing their privileges. On the contrary, the Government, through a long course of years, had been seriously contemplating the suppression of this njurious trade, and on several occasions, viz., 1709, 1717, 1720, and 1722, attempts were made to impose Custom House officers on the islands, but without effect. In 1767, however, the " Registrar's office," or Custom House, was actually established in Guernsey, and one Major appointed to the command of a schooner of fourteen guns, with a cutter, four or five boats, and forty men to assist in carrying on the duties, and with full powers of examination and seizure within the harbours and ports of Guernsey, Jersey, etc. The instructions were full and precise, and amongst other matters they were enjoined " to see that no brandies or spirits be imported into or exported from these islands in casks of less than sixty gallons, or in vessels under fifty tons burden."

The gist of the whole matter lay in these few words, which aimed a deadly blow at the existing methods of the trade, conducted as it was then by means of handy little vessels conveying the spirits in

---

* It was no uncommon occurrence at this time for a merchant at Rotterdam to receive an order from Guernsey for 1,000 pipes of geneva or gin. (*See* Tupper's " History of Guernsey.")

small casks of ten gallons—ankers as they were called—which could be conveniently handled and carried about.

The operations of Major and his coercionists—for in that light did the loyal islanders regard their efforts to obstruct trade—were, however, but short-lived, and for some not very clearly-explained reason the measures above described were allowed to fall into abeyance, and Major and his staff vanished from the page of history.

But even this half-hearted attempt to check the trade was not without important, though little suspected consequences to the future of the islands, as will now be seen. Writing in 1841 the historian already quoted observes, " The object of the British Government in framing this restrictive Act (1767) was evidently to protect her own revenue by putting a check to smuggling, but the scheme was not as successful as anticipated. High duties will operate as a bounty and encouragement to illicit trade, and if one opening be stopped another will soon be discovered. Thus it happened with the attempt of the British Government to secure its revenues by depriving the Channel Islands of their chartered rights conceded by many sovereigns and guaranteed by several Acts of Parliament. A large share of the illicit trade was transferred to Roscoff, a small village on the coast of Brittany, within a few hours' sail of the island. This insignificant hamlet, for it deserved no higher appellation, immediately became an interesting object to the French Government, and it is worthy of observation that no sooner were the officers of Customs established in Guernsey and Jersey than the question of making Roscoff a free port or *port d'entrepôt* was discussed in the French councils and immediately agreed to.

The edict of the king of France was promulgated on the 3rd of September, 1769. Its effect was soon felt. Roscoff, till then an unknown and unfrequented port, the resort only of a few fishermen, rapidly grew into importance, so that from small hovels it soon possessed commodious houses and large stores, occupied by English, Scotch, Irish, and Guernsey merchants. These on the one hand gave every incentive to the British smugglers to resort there ; and on the other hand the French Government afforded encouragement to the merchants. England added nothing to her revenue, while France was enriched."

These remarks supply a clue to a mystery which puzzled the writer for a long time, and which none of his smuggling acquaintances were able to explain, namely, why the insignificant Brittany town of Roscoff suddenly became, and continued to be until the suppression of smuggling, the chief *entrepôt* for the illicit trade with the western counties of England. During the first half of the present century Roscoff was a household word amongst west-countrymen of all classes ; and the volume of trade that streamed into the counties of Cornwall and Devonshire from this remote French port must have far exceeded anything of the same description that passed through the legitimate and duly authorised channels of H.M. Customs. What it amounted to will be seen in due course.

That the trade of Guernsey was but little injured by the Order of 1767 is shown by the following : " During the first American war," says Duncan, "and the French revolutionary war, especially the latter, the trade of Guernsey flourished more extensively than at any antecedent period of her history. The island became the principal depository of spirits, eagerly purchased by the smugglers, and so great was the traffic that many fortunes were realised simply by the manufacture of casks. Such was the excessive import demanded by the illicit trade that the vaults and stores, numerous and capacious as they were, were totally inadequate for the lodgment of the various supplies." *

The inquiring mind will probably wonder why Guernsey enjoyed this advantage over her sister islands. It may be as well, therefore, to explain that, owing to certain climatic conditions, the island had become a favourite place with the merchants of Bordeaux and elsewhere for the storage of wines, which here developed certain qualities of excellence unattainable elsewhere, and this led to the construction of the enormous cellars which were subsequently utilised for the storage of spirits for the smuggling trade with England.

Though England was the chief it was by no means the only sufferer by reason of the peculiar privileges enjoyed by the Channel islanders. Thus, it was given in evidence that during the year preceding the last French war the amount of manufactured tobacco brought into Guernsey by French vessels amounted to above one hundred thousand pounds, the whole of which was smuggled back into Normandy and Brittany, and in a report made to the French Government

---

* One family alone are currently reported to have amassed by this means a fortune of £300,000, which was still further increased by judicious speculations in French rentes. The vaults which played such an important part in the commercial economy of Guernsey in days gone by are still to be met with in different parts of the town of St. Peters Port, and by their vast proportions enable one to realise in some measure the volume of trade that passed through the island. The greater number of them are situated on the quay facing the old harbour and are now chiefly used for the storage of coal.

in 1781 by the Governor of Cherbourg, the Channel Islands and their inhabitants are thus referred to: " Good neighbours during peace, closely united by the contraband trade, which enriches them with the inhabitants of the neighbouring coasts of Normandy and Brittany . . . They are always in a state of warfare ; now against the Custom House officers of the two kingdoms; now against the French commercial marine."

CHAPTER II.

Determination of Government to Suppress the Trade—Correspondence between the Commissioner and the Royal Courts—Results of Diverting the Trade to France—Encouragement of Smuggling by the French Government—Value of the Trade to France—Privateering in the Channel Islands—The Guernsey Merchants' Best Customers.

AT length, after nearly thirty years had elapsed since the passing of the Order of 1767, the British Government became thoroughly aroused to the importance of suppressing a traffic which had not only increased to an enormous extent, but had proved so highly injurious to the revenue. Accordingly, in 1800 the Government sent over to Guernsey a Mr. Stiles, in the capacity of Commissioner, who, besides entering into personal explanations with the chief civil authorities of the island with regard to the views and intentions of the English Government on the subject of the illicit trade, addressed a lengthy communication to the Bailiff. Amongst the points touched on in this document, the following are most worthy of our notice :—

" . . . I beg leave to acquaint you more particularly that the fraudulent trade carried on from this island is in its consequences so highly detrimental and injurious to the revenue and fair trade of Great Britain that the Lords Commissioners of H.M.'s Treasury feel the necessity of recommending to his Majesty in Council some measure for the prevention thereof.

. . . It must be presumed, sir, from your long residence in the islands and high station you are well aware that the illicit commerce in question has increased to a very great and alarming extent, insomuch as to affect the interests and lessen the revenue of Great Britain most materially, and that at a time, too, when she is labouring under the pressure of unusual burdens, which have been necessarily imposed for the maintenance of her constitution, her dearest interests, and even her very existence as an independent state. The inhabitants of this island are so highly favoured as to be excused from bearing any of these burdens, and indulged in the consumption of many articles of commerce infinitely cheaper than the inhabitants of Great Britain.

" It is but reasonable to hope that an injury of such magnitude as the one complained of need only be pointed out and impartially considered by the inhabitants who may directly or indirectly be concerned therein, to induce them cheerfully to acquiesce in any measures which Government may deem expedient for the suppression of this illicit commerce altogether ; and as such measures must necessarily occasion a great alteration in the trade of the island, and may eventually affect a good deal the interests of some of the inhabitants thereof . . . they are therefore unwilling to decide suddenly on the plan so intended to be submitted. . ."

Accompanying this letter was a document setting forth the measures contemplated by the English

Government for the suppression of the contraband trade, in which the following observations occur:—

"Smuggling from the islands of Guernsey and Alderney having increased to a great and alarming extent, and the offenders having, in some instances, committed murder on the revenue officers on the coast of England, Government has it in contemplation to put a stop to such growing and serious evils, so highly prejudicial to his Majesty's revenue and fair trade, to effect which it is not only intended to enforce the several rules, regulations, and restrictions contained in his Majesty's Order in Council of February 12th, 1767, but to add others for the better carrying the said Order into execution. . . "

Mr. Stiles' letter and the Memorandum by which it was accompanied created the utmost consternation amongst the inhabitants of Guernsey, and every effort was made to stave off measures which could not but prove disastrous to a trade by which they all so amazingly throve. Accordingly, a petition was drawn up by those principally concerned, and presented to the Bailiff. The following extracts will suffice to show the importance of the trade to the island, as well as the views of the islanders on the subject of its suppression:—

". . . They cannot but feel alarm at the plan proposed to the Royal Court to suppress the trade of this island—a plan pregnant with ruin to thousands of industrious inhabitants, who have carried on the respective trades, etc., without any interference than that which arose from his Majesty's Order in Council of 13th February, 1767, which, being forcibly registered but never enforced, could not be expected to be made the sudden instrument of the ruin of this island after a lapse of thirty-three years. . . . There is more than conjecture to warrant the belief that the trade, when suppressed here, would be transferred to other ports, since there is already one port on the Continent more resorted to by smugglers, and from which a trade more extensive and more injurious to the trade of Great Britain is carried on. . . . The wealth gained here reverts to the mother country, and helps to support the public funds, promotes the navigation of the country, and affords, in time of war, the means of fitting out numerous privateers, to the great annoyance of the enemy's trade.

"That in the other case all the advantages cease for the mother country, and are thrown with double weight in the scale of a rival country. The payments are made in specie, which never returns; and a great accession of wealth and still greater activity of circulation is infused into the commercial interests of the country.

"That the suppression of the trade of this island would be productive at all times of the most fatal consequences to the inhabitants . . . . would annihilate large capitals, and diminish the property of every man in the island to one-half of its value, and reduce thousands of innocent and industrious persons to beggary and ruin."

The reply of the Royal Courts of Guernsey to Mr. Stiles' letter of August 31st, dated 27th September, 1800, is too lengthy to give here; but the following passages will serve to indicate the line of argument adopted, besides throwing an interesting light on this particular chapter of smuggling history. Adopting a lofty moral standpoint, the reply begins— "As to smuggling, we should hold it unworthy of our station as magistrates to countenance, or encourage it in any manner whatever; and we would readily

concur in any measure or regulation to put a stop to
it from this island "—the descent from this lofty ideal
pedestal to the standpoint of expediency is somewhat rapid!—" had it not been evinced by facts upon
trial that the suppression of it here was shifting it to
the enemy. . . . We therefore humbly submit
our doubts as to the expediency and efficiency of
shutting up the ports of this island to smugglers . . .
at least in time of peace. We can now speak from
facts . . . the Order of 13th February, 1767, was,
by the subsequent ones of 9th October, 1767, the
16th December, 1768, and 13th March, 1769, for a
time enforced, but what had been foreseen was very
soon evinced.

"The French Government was no sooner apprised
of the measures than it opened several of its ports
to the smugglers, and made those ports free to
smugglers; among those was the port of Roscoff,
to which several English, Scotch, Irish, and Guernsey
merchants resorted, and there erected several dwelling-
houses and warehouses, receiving every incitement
from the French minister, who not only declared it
a free port, but allowed rum and Spanish brandies
(notwithstanding the rivalship with theirs) to be
deposited there by *entrepôt*, for sale to the smugglers,
and in proof thereof, we shall beg leave to refer to a
publication in the year 1771, now delivered to you,
in which, at the appendix, are two edicts of the King
of France—No. 1, dated the 14th March, 1768, and
No. 2, dated the 3rd September, 1769; the last
issued in consequence of a letter written by the
intendant of the finances at Paris, and whose answer
is inserted at page 34, all of them evincing
the importance the French Government attached to
drawing the smugglers to that port; and also after-

wards to that of Fécamp, fronting the Sussex coast, and of the measures taken to that end in consequence of the above-named Orders in Council. We shall not repeat what is inserted in the pamphlet, further than to observe the importance to which the measure raised the port of Roscoff—the advantage which resulted therefrom to the produce of the French West India Isles, and the encouragement it gave to their Newfoundland fisheries, and thence to the raising of seamen for the fleet, besides increasing the population of the province, and drawing from England some thousands of guineas, which were carried to Paris, which, when brought to this island, they were at all times returned to England ; in proof of which we can adduce, that one of our Southampton traders, which had twelve hundred guineas concealed on board, being taken in a former war by the French, and purchased after peace by our merchants, the whole were found on board, and returned to whom they belonged ; and if we are rightly informed, the port of Flushing receives, at this very time, from nine to ten thousand guineas per week from the smugglers who resort thither . . . It may be proved that from such measures (shifting the illicit trade from Guernsey to the enemies' ports) they have been enabled to fit out privateers against our trade. Whereas, on the contrary, every acquisition of wealth to these islands is in war launched out in privateers, and with such success in the American war, that the captures of French and American vessels by the privateers of these islands amounted to about *one million and a half sterling ;* * and Mr. Burke is

* In reply to inquiries, a Guernsey gentleman remarked to the writer, "I remember hearing when at St. Malo that during the old war there was an understanding between the merchants there and in

reported to have said in Parliament that he could almost call these islands naval powers. . . The spirits which are brought here and sold to the smugglers are all low hollands proof. . . If we are rightly informed what is smuggled from this island, or Roscoff, *is generally sent to Cornwall or Devonshire, and mostly disposed of to some thousands of miners of those counties, who mostly live underground, to whom spirits are beneficial, but who, nevertheless, could not afford to pay for entered spirits.* (The italics are the author's).

" In this island the governor and magistrates have been particularly attentive to prevent smuggling vessels being armed, which has not been, and certainly would not be attended to at Roscoff, or any other French port. Nevertheless, it must be granted, that in a few instances some have been wicked enough clandestinely to carry muskets and use them against his Majesty's Custom House cruisers, and with them to have wounded or killed some of the crews ; but on an information given here that the perpetrators of such enormities had sheltered themselves in this island, the magistrates have been diligent in securing and delivering them up to proper officers, that they might be sent to and tried in England, which would not have been done in France."

Jersey, by which they exchanged information concerning movements of the privateers of their respective countries, with a view to escaping loss by capture. I was even told the names of the Jersey merchants concerned."

CHAPTER III.

The Trade Doomed—The Bill in the House of Lords—Extension of the
"Smuggling Limits" to the Channel Islands—Loyal and Self-denying
Conduct of the Guernsey Men—Methods of the Trade—Characteristics
of the Smugglers.

IF the Guernsey men had reason for alarm at the
prospect of the extinction of their trade, they had
certainly no cause to complain of any undue haste on
the part of the British Government in giving effect to
the contemplated measures for its suppression, for
the question dragged on another five years before any
definite steps were taken in the matter, and when at
length the time arrived for the final discussion of the
proposed measures in Parliament, the people of
Guernsey gave expression to their views once more
in a petition to the House of Lords.

The debate took place on July 9th, 1805, on which
occasion Lord Holland spoke eloquently and argu-
mentatively on behalf of the islanders. "The
object of the Bill," said his lordship, "is to prevent
smuggling, and so far the measure is wise and
expedient. The only question that remains is,
whether the provisions it contains are likely to be
generally effectual. I ask whether these provisions
will be equally effectual with respect to the smuggling
from France and Holland, as they will be with
respect to that from Guernsey. . . In case the
regulations are insufficient to prevent the smuggling
from France and Holland, the only effect of this Bill
will be to transfer this trade from British subjects
to foreigners, and the additional powers given to

G

Custom House officers for the extent of one hundred leagues will certainly complete this mischief. My lords, I call it a mischief, for though I am aware I cannot speak of smuggling here as a fair trade, yet, if it is the necessary consequences of high duties that smuggling should be carried on more or less, it is better it should be carried on by subjects than by foreigners." After recapitulating the consequences arising from former attempts to interfere with the natural course of this trade, his lordship concluded his speech with the following remarkable words:—
"It is impossible totally to prevent smuggling; the interested motives of mankind will always prompt them to attempt it, particularly when taxes are extremely high, and the hope of large profit is a temptation sufficient to make light of any risk; all that the legislature can do is to compromise with a crime which, whatever laws may be made to constitute it a high offence, the mind of man can never conceive as at all equalling in turpitude those acts which are breaches of clear moral virtue."

Whatever opinions may be held by the more enlightened moral sense of the present day, there can be no doubt that the speaker merely gave utterance to sentiments that were very widely entertained at the time, while his forecast of the probable result of the measures proposed by Government was verified in every particular, as will be shown in the subsequent chapters of this history.

The other side of the question was ably handled by Lord Hawkesbury, who pointed out that "the vicinity of Jersey and Guernsey to this country and the Continent gave them great facilities for smuggling . . . and it was found easy from the vicinity of the coast of Hampshire and Sussex to bring spirits in small barrels—in vessels of small burdens—and roll them on shore in the night. . . . And it was the opinion of those best acquainted with the matter that the only effectual mode of remedying the evil was to take care that none but packages of a proper size should be made use of in the islands, and that their trade should be carried on in vessels of a certain burthen. . . . If they (the islanders) were not prevented from fitting out smuggling expeditions in their own ports, it was impossible to prevent the success of these expeditions here." It will be observed, however, that the main objections to the measure, from the islanders' point of view, remained untouched ; namely, its inefficacy in really checking the trade. In fact, they argued that the measure would simply divert the trade to a foreign port, and thus ruin the islanders, without bringing any resultant benefit to the revenue of Great Britain.

But the British Government was inexorable, and, in spite of all argument, held to the view expressed many years before by Lord North, the then minister, who, in reply to the pleading of one of the Guernsey magistrates, deputed by the Royal Courts to lay the case before Government, said, " We have no authority in the ports of France, but we have in your islands, and therefore we must make the trial."

By a majority in the Lords of nineteen to six the " law to prevent smuggling " was extended to a distance of one hundred leagues from the United Kingdom, by which the Channel Islands were brought within its operations ; and the islanders, seeing that the Government was inflexibly resolved to put down the illicit trade, wisely bowed to the inevitable, and as a proof of their loyalty to the British Crown, and their repentance for the evil ways of the past, " the people

G 2

of Guernsey," to quote the historian, Duncan,
"established a Chamber of Commerce, the condition
of membership being a promise to discountenance all
illicit traffic."

Before bringing this chapter to a close the writer
ventures to reproduce some further remarks on the
smuggling trade from the pen of the historian,
Duncan.   He writes :—" Previous to its suppression
the smuggling trade was carried on in cutters and
luggers, of from 80 to 130 tons, built at Hastings,
Mevagissey,* Polperro, and other English ports, and
the greater part were owned in England, as the
inhabitants confined themselves chiefly to the sale of
goods to the smugglers, and on the outbreak of a war
either purchased these vessels or fitted out their own
as privateers, for which they were admirably adapted.
The smuggling crews were almost entirely English,
well acquainted with their own and the Irish coast,
and almost every man of whom was the *beau idéal* of
a British sailor—active, daring, and prodigal of their
dangerous gains.   They forgot in the pleasures of the
day the risks of the morrow, as the favourite season
for their vocation was the winter."

It remains now to be shown in what manner the
extension of the "hovering limits" to the Channel
Islands affected the flow of spirits into Great Britain.

---

* The Mevagissey-built vessels enjoyed an especially high reputation,
and were often purchased by East-country smugglers.

CHAPTER IV.

THE value of the goods imported annually into Great Britain without payment of duty during the first quarter of the present century would be an interesting subject of inquiry, but as, for obvious reasons, no reliable data on which such calculations could be based are forthcoming, we can only make a vague guess on the subject from such material as can be obtained. The old records are, unfortunately, not very explicit on this point, but such as they are, they enable us to realise, at least in some degree, the vast proportions attained by the illicit trade, as well as the marvellous energy with which it was conducted. The general condition of the trade at the commencement of this period was fairly well depicted by a pamphlet, in which it was stated that the greater part of the 3,867,500 gallons distilled annually at Schiedam was to be smuggled into England; that a distillery had lately been set up for making geneva, for the same purpose, at Dunkirk; that the French imported five or six millions of pounds of tea, the greatest part of which was intended to be smuggled over; that the trade of Dunkirk was mostly carried on by smugglers in vessels not only large but so well constructed for sailing, that seldom one of them was captured; and that the smugglers paid for what they bought in cash, or by the illicit exportation of English wool. It was further given in evidence by the Royal Courts of

Guernsey, in the year 1800, that "there is no doubt that from ten to twelve thousand guineas are every week carried by smugglers to the Continent."

A correspondent of a Glasgow paper gives the following very graphic picture of the state of smuggling in the North :—" Howsoever much the regular commerce of the country is impaired by the present pressure, there is no question the smuggling trade continues with extreme vivacity. This extraordinary traffic appears to be conducted with a publicity which could scarcely be credited by the testimony of one's own sight. The smugglers—or, as they are called from the manner of conveying whisky, "flaskers"—go in large bands on the high roads in open day, and laugh at the traveller who, in his looks, expresses wonder at contraventions of law so undisguised, and yet so undetected. One Monday night, for instance, a gang of twenty-four, with the order of so many soldiers, marched through Springbank to Cowcaddens, in the suburbs of Glasgow, where, in the face of numbers of persons, some of whom bawled out, ' Success to smuggling !' they entered a house, and deposited their laden flasks until night enabled them to penetrate safely to their resetters in Glasgow." (1816.)

Some curious evidence on the same subject is furnished by the Emperor Napoleon, who, doubtless, had good authority for his statements. Speaking of the English smugglers, he said : " They did great mischief to your Government ; they took from France annually forty or fifty millions of silks and brandy."

It would be only reasonable to suppose that the war with France would have very materially affected this trade. As a matter of fact, however, it went on very much as before, the French Government, for reasons of its own—which are not hard to divine—offering every facility and encouragement to the English smugglers to frequent their ports. " During the war," observed the Emperor Napoleon, " they had a part of Dunkirk allotted to them, to which they were restricted ; but as they latterly went out of their limits, committed riots, and insulted everybody, I ordered Gravelines to be prepared for their reception, where they had a little camp for their accommodation. At one time there were upwards of five hundred of them in Dunkirk." * After the close of the war the trade in tea, silks, tobacco, and spirits, was carried on with greater activity than ever, more especially from the French ports, the partial restrictions on intercourse, which had necessarily rather cramped the smugglers' movements during the war, being now removed. By degrees tea became difficult to get, while the reduced duties on silks left little profit to the smuggler ; but spirits increased in value, by being some 40 per cent. over proof, while tobacco still gave large profits. The particulars that will now be presented may be accepted as perfectly authentic, having been supplied by agents on the spot, or gathered from old records, and they certainly furnish a curious commentary on the revenue laws of the period concerned.

In 1819 the following vessels were reported to be fitting out at Flushing for smuggling purposes with the British coast, viz. :—

	Tons.
Vlunix lugger	200
Idas (No. 1) cutter	157
Idas (No. 3) cutter	180
Jane cutter	207
Folkestone lugger	140
(also a cutter building).	

* " Napoleon at St. Helena." By Barry O'Meara.

1823, October.—The *Hopewell* lugger of 80 tons sailed from Flushing with 1,200 five-gallon casks (half ankers) of brandy and geneva, intended to be run at Truro in Cornwall for a person called Sleeman.

From Jersey it was reported that on March 17th a Cawsand Bay boat of 15 tons took in at St. Brelade's Bay upwards of 300 ankers of brandy and several bales of tobacco. On March 31st a cutter of 25 tons from near Plymouth took in at the same place upwards of 600 tubs of brandy and geneva, besides a quantity of other goods ; and on June 10th a cutter of 25 tons from East Looe in Cornwall took in at the same place 690 casks of brandy, and during the same month a Cawsand Bay boat took away a large cargo of spirits.

Evidently the inclusion of the Channel Islands within the " hovering limits " had not had the desired result of suppressing the illicit traffic ; indeed, it is a well-known fact that a very brisk smuggling trade went on with the Channel Islands in spite of all Government measures and " self-denying ordinance " on the part of the Guernsey men, up to within comparatively recent times, the only difference lying in the fact that, instead of being carried on in the free and undisguised manner which had obtained formerly, the operations were conducted clandestinely, and that tobacco very largely took the place of spirits.*

---

* Readers of the " Life of Sir Charles Napier " will doubtless remember that when, as a young officer, he was crossing to Guernsey with his regiment, an alarm was raised during the night that a French privateer was chasing them. The stranger sailed round them, and on receiving a volley sheered off, answering their hail with " Guernsey smuggler." This occurred in 1807, two years after the "self-denying ordinance " had been passed.

The reader will doubtless recollect the pathetic picture of the "underground men" of Cornwall and Devonshire, which the Guernsey men touched in by way of extenuating their evil ways in regard to the liquor traffic when threatened with Government interference ; how they spoke of them as a class "to whom spirits were beneficial, but who, nevertheless, could not afford to pay for entered spirits." Now it is quite possible that there are honest souls who will experience a painful shock of surprise at the levity of these Guernsey men in referring to spirits as "beneficial" even to "underground men," and we all know how opinions differ on this point ; but on one subject at least there can be no difference of opinion in view of the facts stated, namely, that beneficial, or not beneficial, the Cornishmen were intent on having a real good time of it.

During 1824 several persons who were deeply concerned in the smuggling carried on from Flushing had a difference, with the result that they separated, and one party established itself at Ostend on a very extensive scale under the firm of Trueman and Co., erected several tobacco presses, and placed two very large luggers on the stocks to be used for smuggling. Another party, under the firm of Phillipson and Co., established itself at Nieuport with three luggers, making frequent trips to the English coast with tin cases of snuff, and tubs of brandy and gin.

A correspondent, writing from Ghent in October, reported a great increase having taken place in the smuggling establishments there, that additional tobacco presses had been erected, and that the produce was sent over in tin waterproof cases, which were taken by the large fishing "doggers" belonging to the place, and exchanged for fish or money with

the Harwich and other boats at sea. On approaching
the coast the cases were sunk, and afterwards picked
up by small boats as opportunity offered.

Shortly after information was received of a large
armed smuggling craft from Flushing, expected on
the coast of Devon or Cornwall "the first easterly
wind."

In November a correspondent at Roscoff supplied
the following information concerning certain well-
known smuggling boats and their probable destination :—

Maria (1st) of Cawsand ...	West of the Deadman in Cornwall, where it is intended to run the goods.	
Maria (2nd) of Cawsand ...	West of the Deadman in Hemmick Cove, at the Dodman.	
Cruizer ... of Polperro ...	St. Austell Bay (N.B. — She landed her last crop at Mevagissey, Oct. 24.)	
Ant ... of Mevagissey	St. Austell Bay, near the Blackhead.	
Arethusa ... of Cawsand ...	St. Austell Bay, near the Blackhead.	
Exchange of Polperro ...	St. Austell Bay, near the Blackhead.	

The St. Austell Bay mentioned here comprised an
extensive stretch of coast on the south of Cornwall,
bounded by Mevagissey on the west, and the Gribbon
on the east, in those days very imperfectly guarded,
and consequently a favourite place for landing goods.

Curiously enough, about this time a notation
occurs in the old records to the effect that "several
runs having taken place in the Fowey district, the
officers and crews are reprimanded, and all promotion
is stopped," from which it may be inferred that the
"underground men" had succeeded in saving their
Christmas supplies of liquor.

One result of these "runs" was the establishment
of additional coastguard stations for the more efficient
protection of this portion of the coast ; and as, later

on, the coastguard made some very valuable seizures hereabouts, let us hope they removed the stigma which had attached to them.

From this time forward Roscoff assumed a position of extraordinary importance in smuggling annals, and, judging from the facts which have come down to us, did a larger volume of trade with the West of England than almost any other foreign port, a striking confirmation of the views expressed by the Royal Court of Guernsey.

Next year, 1825, a French sloop with two Polperro men on board besides her crew sailed from Roscoff with a cargo of spirits for some place near the Land's End. Information was also received that the *Venus*, of Rye, 80 tons, had worked three voyages lately, of 800 casks of spirits each time, in the "London river;" that a schooner of 122 tons and a crew of thirty men was taking in a cargo of hollands, brandy, tobacco, and tea, at Flushing, for Ireland, while the *Whiting*, *Two Brothers*, and *Fox* smacks, of London, were loading at the same port with geneva, brandy, etc., for the West of England, and the cargoes were being prepared for sinking.*

CHAPTER V.

Smuggling from Jersey—Reconnoitring off Roscoff—Fighting over the Spoil—Activity of the Revenue Cutters—"Our Own Correspondent"—French Smuggling Vessels—"French Jack"—Halcyon Days at Roscoff—Narrow Escape of Smuggling Boats.

EARLY in 1826 a thirty-feet galley to row ten oars was reported to be building at Jersey for the purpose

* This operation will be described later on.

of smuggling between that island and England. Boats of this description played a most important part in the smuggling economy of olden days, and this importance rather increased than otherwise as time went on, and speed became a greater *desidera-tum* than ever in the successful prosecution of the trade. We shall hear more of these galleys as the history proceeds.

In consequence of several well-known smuggling boats being absent from Cawsand, and supposed to be taking in cargoes at Roscoff, the revenue cutter *Harpy*, of the Plymouth station, was sent across to look them up (June, 1826), and on reconnoitring outside Roscoff, discovered there the *Little Henry*, of Portsmouth, the *Bee, Jane*, and *Friend's Endeavour*, of Cawsand, and *Hope*, of Polperro—all no doubt on smuggling intent, though safe in a French port at present. This information was coupled with a note to the effect that "these boats being outside of their limits are liable to seizure on attempting to return to the English coast," from which we may anticipate an exciting game of hide and seek, the first "darks," or moonless nights, with a southerly breeze.

Sometimes the good cognac was diverted into quite other channels than its owners intended, and, to judge by the graphic little picture of the times presented below, we may infer that the crews of the revenue cutters were as much on the alert, and, as eager to participate in the spoils of the trade as their fellow preventive men on shore. It is recorded (Feb., 1827) that "the commander of the *Lion*, revenue cutter, was reprimanded for allowing his boat's crew to take by force part of a 'seizure' made by the boats of the Looe and Polperro stations." It seems that the *Lion's* men, in their anxiety to share in a seizure, endeavoured to carry off some of the tubs "crept" up by the Polperro boat's crew, under command of the chief officer of the station, who, in consequence of the reckless way in which the *Lion's* men used their knives in cutting off the tubs from the sinking rope, had several of his fingers severely cut. A pretty state of things, indeed! Evidently these untamed young lion cubs wanted licking into shape.

The following case affords a curious illustration of the proverbial slip 'twixt the cup and the lip:—"The *Lively* was captured in Lundy Roads (Nov., 1831) with 300 tubs of spirits on board, having been twenty-six days at sea." Nearly four weeks "battyfagging" about, waiting a chance to run her cargo, and then to be taken! Hard luck, indeed! The records further state that "two of her crew were sent into the navy and one to gaol" to repent at leisure!

It must be understood, of course, that these cases are merely selected as representative ones out of a very large number that have drifted to the surface, and can by no means be accepted as affording any real indication of the volume of the trade that poured into the country during the period in question, or of the activity with which it was conducted. The records are often silent when we are most in want of information, and we have need to read between the lines to get a true measure of the energy brought to bear on this particular branch of industry.

Next year (March, 1832) "a well-informed correspondent" reported from Roscoff that "smuggling had not been carried on so extensively at any time during the last twenty years as it is now." At the same time several boats were reported taking in cargoes of spirits under the Isle of Bass (outside

Roscoff), which said news had the effect of putting the revenue cruisers on the *qui vive*—and to some purpose, as the sequel shows : for soon after (April) we read that the revenue cruisers *Harpy* and *Arrow*, belonging to Plymouth, made three Cawsand boats and one from Yealm throw over their cargoes to escape capture—a waste of good liquor which must have brought sorrow to many a household.

More news from Roscoff in September that "the *Good Intent* is carrying on a successful contraband trade in brandy and tobacco between the Isle of Bass and Plymouth. Also that the *Daniel and William*,* passenger vessel, of Portsmouth, is occasionally employed in the same trade ; and that a boat had arrived at Roscoff with her name covered over with canvas, and that Mallabay,† a merchant, was preparing sixty tubs of spirits to put on board her during the following night. Further, that another cutter called the *Jean Baptiste* had been purchased for smuggling tobacco, and that the *Aurore* had been altered so as to admit of her cargo being placed on deck when nearing the shore, ready to land ; also that a long 'clincher-built' boat to draw but little water was being built for her."

The attractions of Roscoff seemed to grow stronger as time rolled on ; the bare mention of the name, indeed, being enough to bring an anticipatory gleam of delight into the face of a properly-constituted Cornishman of those days, for was it not synonymous with cheap liquor and baccy ? Thus, for many years, the produce of Roscoff, or Rusco, as it was called, proved as indispensable to the men of the west country as their daily bread, and while they

---

* A celebrated smuggling craft.

† One of the chief spirit merchants patronised by the smugglers.

poured their gold into the laps of the Roscovites like water, the latter repaid them with the water of life they loved so well.

In November, 1832, information was received from the same source of the sailing of the *Rose* from Roscoff with 100 tubs of brandy for Fowey; and a little later of the following vessels being there, viz., the *Eagle*, 35 tons, and *Rose*, 11 tons, both of Fowey, and bound to Fowey with spirits.

Just picture the scare in smuggling circles at Roscoff, had a little bird whispered " a chiel's amang ye taking notes and faith he'll ——! " We can understand now why so many of their nice little schemes " went aft agley." For the sake of the revenue—to say nothing of his own person, let us hope " our correspondent " never fell into the hands of the Philistines, or there would have been rough work to report from Roscoff.

In January, 1833, some interesting information is given concerning the movements of French smuggling vessels, further to the eastward, viz.: " The following from Cherbourg are in the habit of visiting the English coast, chiefly about Weymouth; they range from 27 to 37 tons :—

Betsey		Louise	L'Espoir
Phœbe	} just built.	Sisters	Argus
Eliza		L'Amité	Bien Aime
		Arthur Eugène	L'Aimable Virtue

" The following mostly frequent Dartmouth—

Jeune Eliza   L'Argus
Two Sisters   L'Active Eugenie
Louisa (The master of this vessel formerly sailed in the *Two
        Brothers*. He is called " French Jack," and has
        lately been released from Bodmin gaol)."

The enterprising smuggler known by the sobriquet

of "French Jack" was a rather celebrated character in his way, and was well known to the revenue cutters on the Dorsetshire coast. There are old pensioners living still who have a lively recollection of "French Jack" and his good old cognac, a bottle of which was always kept in the binnacle expressly for the boat's crews that boarded his vessel—a considerate act on his part, for many was the dance he led them. He was said to be very popular amongst the cutter's men! Can we be surprised?

In February we find the *Daniel and William* back again at Roscoff, also the *Eagle, Laura,* and *Help.* "They are to sail the first fair wind."

And again in March—"Information from a private source" at Roscoff, of the sailing of the following smuggling vessels, which are working under feigned names :—

Love, with 250 tubs of brandy destined for Coverack (Cornwall).
Help „ 110 „ „ Plymouth.
Rough,, 260 „ „ Dartmouth.
Eagle ,, 300 „ „ Fowey.

To which is appended a note that "The *Rough* is a fine cutter of 28 tons, and her master's name is Smooth. It is her first trip to Roscoff." This sounds like a *jeu d'esprit* on the part of the skipper : and so it is, for later on comes "information" from the same source that the *Help* is really the *Dove*, of Cawsand, and the *Rough* the *Sun*, of Cowes.

The extraordinary activity with which the smuggling trade between Roscoff and the coast of Cornwall was being conducted may be gathered from the list of sailings and arrivals for the month of March, 1833, furnished by the correspondent above-mentioned :—

ARRIVALS BETWEEN 13TH AND 31ST MARCH.

YAWL.			TONS.		
Goldfinch	...	...	14	...	From Plymouth.
Four Brothers		...	12	...	,, Plymouth.
Goldfinch	...	...	17	...	,, Dartmouth.
Supply	...	...	9	...	,, Dartmouth.
Rose ...	...	...	13	...	,, Lizard.
Dove ...	...	...	18	...	,, Cowes.
Eagle ...	...	...	35	...	,, Fowey.
William	...	...	13	...	,, Falmouth.
Love ...	...	...	26	...	,, Coverack.
2nd Trip { Goldfinch	...	...	14	...	,, Plymouth.
Eagle ...	...	...	35	...	,, Fowey.
Love ...	...	...	26	...	,, Coverack.

DEPARTURES BETWEEN 15TH AND 27TH MARCH.

*Goldfinch	with	90 tubs...	...	For Plymouth.
Four Brothers	,,	20 ,, ...	...	,, Plymouth.
Goldfinch	,,	120 ,, ...	...	,, Dartmouth.
Supply	,,	60 ,, ...	...	,, Dartmouth.
Rose	,,	80 ,, ...	...	,, Lizard.
Dove	,,	125 ,, ...	...	,, Cowes.
*Eagle	,,	150 ,, ...	...	,, Fowey.
*Love	,,	125 ,, ...	...	,, Coverack.
William	,,	80 ,, ...	...	,, Falmouth.
Total		850		

" Note—The three boats marked thus * have been very successful; especially the two last, on board of which are the two Dunstans.* They sailed on the 27th, landed their cargoes, and were back to Roscoff on the 31st. A tobacco voyage will now take place ; Mallabay is conducting the preparations with the greatest secresy, and is trying to get authorised by the Customs to load in the roads of the Isle of Bas."

Next month comes the following information from Roscoff :—

DEPARTURES BETWEEN 13TH AND 20TH APRIL.

Goldfinch	with	100 tubs ...	...	For Plymouth.
Love	,,	150 ,, ...	...	For Fowey.

* The two Dunstans above-mentioned belonged to a celebrated smuggling family, one of the survivors of which was living until quite recently, and was well known to the writer, to whom on various occasions he imparted some curious smuggling reminiscences.

H

Eagle	with	180 tubs ...	...	,,	Coverack.
Fox	,,	70 ,, ...	...	,,	Dartmouth.
Friends	,,	150 ,, ...	...	,,	Plymouth.
Goldfinch	,,	100 ,, ...	...	,,	Teignmouth.

Total   750

"Note.—The first three boats put back twice since their arrival on March 31st, having been chased by a revenue cruiser. They were fired at, and the *Eagle* was in the greatest danger, having only escaped by good sailing."

CHAPTER VI.

Where are the Coastguard?—Prize-money Galore—Roscoff Again—Activity of the West-country Smugglers – Fate of Smugglers—Hovering Limits —Terrors of the Middle Passage—The *Two Brothers*—Eventful Lives of Smugglers.

WHAT, it may be asked, were the coastguardmen doing all this time? And where were the revenue cruisers? From the scant information supplied by the records, it might be supposed that little was being done by H.M. servants to stop the flow of cheap liquor. As a matter of fact, however, both coastguard and revenue cruisers were busy enough, and prize money was plentiful. A casual entry here and there gives one an inkling of what was going on. Let the reader judge for himself.

Here are some of the entries for 1833 :—

"July. Forty-two tubs, the *Dove's* cargo, are taken by the boats of the *Harpy*, revenue cruiser, and Cawsand and Yealm stations."

"Twenty-one tubs are taken by the Cawsand crew in the galley *John*, of Cawsand; the remainder are still sunk off the Eddystone. They are part of a 'crop' belonging to John A——, of Downderry, 'who was seen near Craft Hole, lying by a hedge, drunk.'"

Poor John A——, to what a pass did the good old cognac bring thee! Not an exceptional case, though, by any means. It may be remarked, in passing, that our friend was a noted smuggler, some of whose adventures were recounted to the writer by a member of the family.

"August. One hundred and fifteen tubs belonging to the *Dove* were taken by the Looe coastguard.

"September. Five tubs washed ashore near Looe, and a boat marked *Fox*, of Plymouth, found on the beach a mile west, and another tub in the cliff close by.

"Fifty-seven tubs belonging to the *Elizabeth* are crept up by the Looe boat off Seaton.

"October. Fifty-eight tubs out of sixty, forming the cargo of the *Dove*, are crept up off Downderry by the Looe boat.

"November. A new boat without name is found on Lantivet beach, and sixty-nine tubs of spirits are found in the cliff near Lantivet beach, which are believed to have been landed from the *Daniel and William* on the morning of the 14th inst., and the boat afterwards removed to Lantivet.

"December. Some tubs belonging to the *Four Brothers* are taken near Plymouth breakwater by the Cawsand crew. The Admiral's tender chased the *Daniel and William* near the Eddystone, but lost sight of her in a fog." And so on.

But all these captures were a mere drop in the ocean to the stream of liquor that flowed in, and evidently had no damping effect on the trade, for news comes from Roscoff again of the departure of an English schooner with 300 tubs, which "she took

in one night, and sailed again at 4 next morning."
Also of the following :—

Jane with   135 tubs   ...   ...   For Plymouth.
Active ,,   190 ,, ...
William }
Goldfinch } detained by fine nights and N.E. winds.

And so the game went merrily on, with varying
success on both sides ; the smugglers being eager and
willing to risk the crossing so long as freights were
high, while the freighters considered themselves amply
recompensed so long as they could save one cargo
out of three. And we may be sure the coastguardmen
enjoyed the fun, and seldom grumbled at overwork
while seizures were plentiful.

As a matter of fact, during no period was smuggling carried on with more energy or success in the
West of England—not excepting even the free-trade
days, than during that comprised between 1825—35.
And in this trade no one took a more prominent or
active part than the inhabitants of the quaint little
village of Cawsand, on the western shore of Plymouth
Sound. Their boats were in demand all along the
south coast of Cornwall, while the men who sailed
them enjoyed a reputation for skill, daring, and enterprise which was unequalled in any part of the kingdom.*

As for the authorities, they were at their wits' ends
how to stop the trade. The extension of the hovering
limits to one hundred leagues from the British coast
—which was to have proved the death-blow to

---

* The writer has succeeded in compiling, from authentic sources, a
list of no less than fifty-two boats and eighty-one men belonging to
Cawsand in the habit of making occasional runs across to Roscoff for
contraband during the ten years, 1832—42. Not a bad record for a
fishing village !

smuggling—had only driven the trade to French ports —as foretold, without sensibly diminishing the imports. The Government had played its trump card and here was the result.

However, a smuggler's luck could not last for ever, and there was something chilling to say the least in the spectacle of a fine boat—the smuggler's own property may-be, and on which his chances of earning a livelihood depended—being slowly and solemnly sawn through into three separate portions, while the cargo of good old cognac, with which, alas! at an unfortunate moment it had been freighted, was diverted into altogether unlooked-for channels. Such, however, was the fate of a smuggling boat when taken *in flagrante delicto;* while for the crew their fate was five years' service in a man-of-war, or a term of imprisonment on shore, all of which must have rubbed a good deal of the gilt off the gingerbread of a smuggling transaction.

The extension of the "hovering limits" had proved advantageous to the preventive men in one respect, insomuch as they had now the power of arresting any vessel or boat discovered outside of the limits specified on her licence, viz., three leagues from the English coast, in the case of vessels not engaged in the foreign trade, and all boats. The very fact of being outside the three league limit was regarded as *ipso facto* proof of being on smuggling intent, and sufficient to warrant seizure and detention, if not condemnation. Still, the sea was wide, the revenue cutters were few and far between, while the crossing was always made at night in a strong breeze, for choice; and so far as sailing qualities were concerned, the smuggling boats were notoriously capable of showing their heels to every cruiser on the coast.

The chances of capture were not, however, the only risk attaching to the smuggling trade, there were the dangers of the "middle passage," no light ones either, when it is remembered that the winter was the time when the trade was prosecuted the most actively.

Crossing the hundred miles of water intervening between Roscoff and the Cornish coast in the bitter gales of a hard winter was no child's play in a decked vessel, and we can only dimly surmise what must have been gone through in the open boats, to which the more adventurous souls trusted their persons and their cargoes. Many a "neat little crop" had to be sacrificed in mid-channel to the safety of the boat, and tales are still handed down from father to son of these "battering times," and of boats and men that sailed, but never returned. One such story the writer remembers well, in which it was related of a well-known Cawsand smuggling boat, how she was lost on the Mewstone with all her crew; the head of one man, a very celebrated smuggler, whose brother was holding high rank in the royal navy, being found afterwards in the cabin.

An entry the writer chanced on in some old records affords another picture of these stirring days:

"March, 1834. — The *Arrow*, revenue cruiser, chased the *Two Brothers* on shore on Plymouth breakwater at one a.m., when she became a total wreck. The crew saved themselves with great difficulty by lashing themselves to the cranes, and were taken off at daylight by the crew of the light-vessel. The *Harpy* and *Arrow* secured the wreck together with 101 full tubs. The Bovisand coast-guard boat got four more, and the rest went to pieces."

A smuggler's life was by no means all beer and skittles, as the saying goes. It was exciting, no doubt, if not particularly glorious, and had its ups and downs like every other walk in life—rather more so in fact than most. Still, it seemed to possess attractions to the coast population of those days, and certainly never wanted for patrons..

CHAPTER VII.

East Coast Smuggling—Smuggling Galleys—New Developments of the Trade—A Run of £20,000 Worth of Goods—A Famous Smuggling Craft—Busy Times at Boulogne—Smuggling in French Boats—The Cawsand Fleet—A Curious Instance of Reversion.

SO far, this history has been chiefly concerned with the West of England. A few particulars which it is now proposed to submit to the reader will show that the contraband trade was conducted with equal assiduity further East, if with somewhat less variety of incident. As a matter of fact there had been scarcely any break in the trade, or any diversion of the stream from one port to another, as was the case in the West of England; while even the war with France, as we have seen—thanks to the fostering care of Napoleon—scarcely effected any change in the annual volume of imports. Certainly the "blockade" * had necessitated certain adaptations in the methods of the trade, and of these the most important was the more extensive employment of smuggling galleys and "tub-boats." Luggers and decked boats still did a large business from Deal, Margate, Ramsgate,

* The "coast blockade" along the Kent and Sussex coast, described further on.

Folkestone, Hastings, and Rye, from the latter
especially ; while on the other side of the Channel the
chief smuggling *depôts* were at Flushing, Nieuport,
Dunkirk, Calais, Harfleur, Boulogne, Gravelines, and
Fécamp, and lastly Cherbourg.   The galleys were
constantly running from the latter port, as well as
from Calais, Dunkirk, and Boulogne, and the records
are full of references to the activity displayed at these
notorious smuggling centres.   Thus, in 1831, the
coastguard stations were cautioned that "smuggling
in open boats from Boulogne and other ports opposite
Kent and Sussex is carried on as actively as ever by
some secret mode," which they are enjoined to discover—if they can !

The galleys were usually manned by English
smugglers, though built and owned by Frenchmen.
They would dash across from the French coast, and
sometimes even from the Channel Islands, to Portland and places further east, being timed to reach the
English coast soon after dark, where they would
" run " or more usually sink their cargoes, and be
back by daylight next morning.   It was a common
practice with the crews of smuggling vessels lying at
Cherbourg waiting for a fair breeze, to make a trip
over to Portland or the Isle of Wight in one of these
galleys—*pour passer le temps*—receiving £1 per man
for the trip from the freighter.

The establishment of the coastguard on the
south-east coast in place of the " blockade " soon
made itself felt in smuggling circles ; and in 1832 the
following warning was issued :—" The smugglers being
disconcerted along the coast of Kent and Sussex in
the more open mode of smuggling, intend trying to
import their goods in partly-laded colliers."   This
method of smuggling continued in high favour for

many years, and several large seizures were made by active officers.

The following piece of information from a "private source" gives a curious insight into the trade methods of the period. The letter was dated from Bombay, and ran as follows (June, 1832):— "The chartered ship *Orwell* will be on the coast of England with a valuable contraband cargo to be distributed among small trading craft, previous to our arrival in London river in May or June, 1833. We have Gravesend watermen on board, who are to conduct the trade in the river. In this manner £20,000 worth was smuggled last voyage by one of these ships. Even the gunbreechings were 'sick,' and crape shawls 'served' over them, and we have many men on board who have made fortunes by this trade."

Dry goods were still smuggled from the Continental ports on a very large scale when opportunity offered. Thus, in 1834, we find "a cutter of about 80 tons is expected on the Sussex coast from Nieuport with dry goods, worth from three to four thousand pounds, supposed to be the *Eliza*. There are three other cutters there, of 35 to 40 tons."

The *Eliza*, it may be remarked, was a celebrated armed smuggler that chiefly frequented the Irish coast.

Four years later (1838) a correspondent wrote from Boulogne:—"Smuggling has been carried on from here to a great extent these three months past; over twenty vessels of various sizes have left with cargoes."

The practice of crossing in English boats became at length, through the vigilance of the coastguard on shore, and revenue cruisers afloat, fraught with too much risk to be any longer indulged in. A caution, dated March, 1839, will explain matters more clearly :—

"In consequence of the large number of Cawsand and other English boats that have been recently taken, lost, and made to throw overboard their cargoes, the coastguards are warned of the probability of the smugglers employing French boats to bring over their cargoes."

This warning was not uncalled for. As a matter of fact the employment of foreign vessels had become pretty general amongst English freighters, who were thus enabled to conduct their operations without exciting the suspicions of the home authorities, a result which it was almost impossible to avoid in the case of English craft, whose absence from their accustomed haunts, together with their crews, had the effect of putting the coastguards on the *qui vive.*

The famous Cawsand smuggling fleet now vanished from the stage, having long played its part with a degree of skill, energy, and industry that seems little short of marvellous. But if the activities of the Cawsand men had been driven into other channels, let it not be supposed that the traffic had been suppressed —far from that ! Here, for instance, is an entry which throws light on the matter (October, 1843) :—

"A new mode of smuggling is discovered, viz., cargoes are brought over in French vessels, and when within a convenient distance from the shore, the tubs are rafted, and towed to the place appointed, to land by a 'tub-boat,' which is carried on board the vessel for that purpose. To prevent the discovery of an assemblage of persons waiting for the arrival of the vessel, the tubs, on being first landed, are deposited in caves, or buried in the sand. The carriers are then collected,

and early the following night led to the spot where
the tubs are secreted."

The French smuggling vessels whose names most
often occur at this time are :—

Le Pierre.	*Letitia.*	*La Grande Favella.*
Le Oif.	*Le Annie.*	*La Petite Emilie.*

Le Anna (French Jack, master). — This vessel
traded mostly between Guernsey and the western
parts with tobacco, and often brought across one or
two of the notorious Cawsand and other smugglers as
" spotsman," or freighter. Increased energy was
now devoted to the smuggling of tobacco, from which
large profits could still be realised. Thus (December,
1843) it was reported that large quantities of smuggled
tobacco were selling in London and other large towns,
and in January following, " great energy is shown by
the smugglers at Flushing and Guernsey in sending
over cutters with tobacco."

Although the illicit trade was now, as a matter of
expediency, chiefly conducted in foreign " bottoms,"
English vessels and boats often made clandestine
trips across to the French coast, while *en route* from
port to port—sometimes taking in cargoes of contraband in mid-channel, from vessels sent to meet them.
The worst offenders in this line of business were the
pilot vessels and trawlers—notably the Cowes pilot-
vessels ; while of the trawlers, the *Place, Boconnoc,* and
*One and All,** of Fowey, are most worthy of mention.

---

* This curious name calls for explanation. The Cornish arms and
the motto, " One and All," are said to have originated during the
crusades, when a certain Duke of Cornwall was taken prisoner by the
Saracens, and held to ransom for fifteen bezants. On the news reaching Cornwall the whole of the population subscribed the necessary sum,
and their Duke was liberated. The fifteen bezants are represented by

In this way smuggling dragged on a fitful sort of existence for a number of years, with occasional bursts of activity—consequent, doubtless, on the relaxed vigilance of the coastguard, who now began to lack the stimulus of prize-money, seizures becoming scarcer every year.   Thus, in July, 1850, there is an entry to the effect that "smuggling has greatly increased again," and the year after a correspondent, writing from Plymouth, observes :—"I am credibly informed that the funds for smuggling on this part of the coast are larger than they have ever been for five years."

Curiously enough, just before the final extinction of the trade we meet with the names of several old revenue cruisers figuring amongst the lists of smuggling vessels.   Thus, in February, 1850, "The *Childers*, 201 tons, late a revenue cruiser, and formerly captured as a smuggler in the Bristol Channel, has been bought by her former owner—a barber by trade, residing in Guernsey—and sailed from Plymouth with five suspicious characters, who have been in constant communication for the last ten days with well-known Plymouth smugglers, with whom the master is in frequent company."   Also the *Rob Roy*, late revenue cruiser, which "has been fitting out at Ramsgate for smuggling, has sailed with some notorious smugglers on board, two of whom were previously captured and imprisoned."

Again, in April, the *Secret*, of Poole, one of the revenue cruisers, "lately sold out of the service," is reported to have arrived at Pentewan, near Mevagissey, in Cornwall, where Richard K——, of smuggling

the fifteen balls in the shield of the Cornish arms, and the motto, "One and All," was chosen to commemorate the fact that *all* subscribed. Of course, other explanations are offered.

notoriety, appeared, and was in constant communication with the master.

And last of all, the *Eliza,* " late coastguard tender at Fowey, and formerly captured by the Cawsand crew as a smuggler, is expected with a cargo of spirits from Roscoff."

And, having thus come back once more to the place we started from, this chapter must close, observing that this is the last mention of Roscoff in smuggling annals.

CHAPTER VIII.

The Scilly Islanders—Sunday Diversions—Warm Reception of a Coast-guardman—Occupations of the Inhabitants—Condemnation of Smuggling Boats—Annie L—— —King Log and King Stork—"A Complete Nest of Smugglers "—Daffodils and Pota·oes.

THE Scilly Islands are so intimately associated in the minds of most people at the present day with the cultivation of early vegetables and flowers for the London market, that it must come as a rude shock to their admirers to hear that during the early years of the century the energies of the worthy islanders were chiefly devoted to a branch of trade which brought more profit than honour to all concerned in it. As a matter of fact, this interesting group of islands were at that time extensively used as *depôts* for contraband goods imported from France, or landed from homeward-bound vessels, to be smuggled as opportunities offered across to the English coast. Consequently, when the preventive service was established in the western counties, it was soon found necessary to extend the sphere of its activity to the adjacent islands, as a means of checking the depredations on the revenue which had become so flagrant. Thus, in 1828 we find an " inspecting commander" located here, with a force of twenty-three officers and men, distributed between St. Mary's, St. Agnes, St. Martin's, and Tresco. That the presence in their midst of so many servants of the revenue should not have proved altogether congenial to the simple tastes of the islanders can easily be understood, if the fact was not emphasised by a curious record of the times, which chance has fortunately preserved, and which throws an interesting light on the improving manner in which these simple folk spent their Sabbaths—sometimes :—

" *St. Mary's, Scilly, 9th September*, 1828.

" I beg to report that Cornelius Oliver, a commissioned boatman, stationed on the island of Bruger, having represented to me that several boats belonging to that island went off alongside of several ships in the offing on Sunday, the 7th inst., and as the said boats were returning to Bruger the said officer (and his son, a boy about fourteen years old) went on the landing-place in order to search the said boats. There were several of the islanders assembled, one of whom threw a stone at the officer, and the men threatened him most severely if he would attempt to rummage the boats. The officer, in return, threatened that if they continued to pelt him with stones he would fire amongst the crowd. About seven p.m. the boats *Pigeon* and *Howe* landed nearly the same time, and on the officer attempting to board the latter boat, a man named Stephen I———, belonging to the island (and on board the *Howe*), prevented him, and afterwards shoved the boat off from the beach, and held up a bottle of spirits, and holding forth the most awful threats if the said officer again attempted to board. On the boat again attempting to land, Oliver ran into the water, and jumped into the boat, on which the said Stephen I—— seized the officer in his arms (so that he was not able to disengage his pistol), and threw him overboard into the water, and before he could recover himself the boat's crew ran on shore with what contraband goods they had in the boat. After Stephen I—— landed on the beach, he seized the boy (Oliver's son), and threw him down and kicked him most severely, the marks of which are quite visible. The officer, also, has been hurted, his watch, commission, arms, etc., wetted, and the pistol lost out of his belt. I therefore humbly beg leave to recommend that the said Stephen I—— may be prosecuted for assaulting the officer, and made an example of to the rest of his colleagues."

Certainly it was desirable that the good people of Bruger should be taught respect for the majesty of the law, as represented by Mr. Cornelius Oliver!—— though it seems unfair to have expected a solitary officer to turn the inhabitants of Bruger aside from their evil ways.

Alas! poor Cornelius! It appears that his nerves never recovered from the rude treatment he received on that Sunday night, for we find the inspecting commander shortly after advising his removal to another station, "as he appears to be intimidated ever since the assault was committed on him." Writing under date, 11th October, 1828, the inspecting commander reports that "in consequence of the stir which I made relating to the rig, navigation, etc., of the boats belonging to these islands, I have entirely prevented them from going to France for the purpose of effecting runs about these islands and the main.   I further beg leave to report that these islands were never known with so little smuggling as this year, and the greatest part of the inhabitants are reduced to great distress in consequence, for hitherto it used to be their principal employment, and a strong guard will be always advantageously employed here, otherwise they will smuggle to a great extent, and run the goods to the main, and dispose of the same to the numerous vessels which gain shelter there."

It may be some satisfaction to the Guernsey men to know that they are not the only people who suffered from interference with what they had always regarded as a natural and perfectly legitimate branch of industry.

One of the reasons for the Scilly boats discontinuing their visits to Roscoff was, it seems, an impression that "parties were looking out for them there to report their movements," and this impression must have been matured into something very like conviction by an affair which took place at this time, viz., the arrest on "information" of two boats belonging to Tresco, the *Speedwell* and *Mary Ann*, for having been seen at Roscoff, and for running their cargoes at the Land's End and Mount's Bay.   Both were convicted and condemned to be cut up (March, 1830).

A long and curious correspondence took place at this time concerning a certain Annie L—— who, with that fine solicitude for the interests of the revenue which is so marked a trait of her sex, had furnished the coastguard with several valuable "informations," by means of which some important seizures were said to have been effected, and who now

complained of the reward being out of all proportion
to the value of the services rendered.*

" 'Tis an ill wind that blows nobody any good," as
the old proverb says, and the islanders hoped great
things from a change in the *personnel* of the coastguard. Thus, the inspecting commander reports
(June, 1829) that " the smugglers have recommenced
with great energy, as they expect my removal
shortly." But these gentry reckoned without their
host, for they soon made the unpleasant discovery
that it was merely a change from " King Log" to
" King Stork."

Allusion has already been made to the system of
smuggling from homeward-bound ships. A case in
point was that of the *Thames*, East Indiaman, which
attracted some attention at the time, and led to
a Customs prosecution, in which the chief officer
was heavily fined. It seems that on arrival of the
vessel off the Scillys, a pilot boat came alongside
with six or seven men, who betook themselves
to the mate's cabin, where a rich display of silks,
etc., was ready prepared for their inspection. These
draperies were at once deftly disposed round the
persons of the visitors by a process of winding;
and a further supply, neatly packed in cases, was

---

* A curious instance of the conscientious scruples sometimes entertained by ladies in regard to the rendering of dues is supplied by the
Postmaster-General in his Report for the current year. It seems that a
lady residing in Siam forwarded to London several parcels, declared to
contain walking-sticks and stationery of the value of £7 10s.; " but the
vigilant eye of the Custom House officer promptly detected a brilliant
collection of diamonds and jewellery worth upwards of £25,000. The
postage, at the registered letter rate, would have amounted to about
£30, and it may be assumed," adds the report, " that the course
adopted was prompted by the desire to save the difference between the
ordinary parcel rate and this amount."

I

rapidly passed down into the boat, which thereupon returned to the islands. Unfortunately, as it proved for the mate, some inquisitive outsider had watched the proceedings, and actuated, let us hope, by lofty motives, promptly informed against him on arrival of the vessel in the Thames.

Smuggling continued for many years after the advent here of the coastguard ; in fact, the islanders had thriven too long on this precarious means of livelihood to turn their hands readily to a more respectable calling. Thus, in January, 1831, the inspecting commander writes :—"Foreign spirits, tea, and tobacco, may be had in any quantities at two or three days' notice, but not without despatching a vessel to France, which illegal traffic the vessels and boats are at all times ready to engage in that belong to these islands, as they are a complete nest of smugglers."

And so matters dragged on, but without any incidents worth recording. The transition from the smuggling habits of yore to the present-day cultivation of daffodils and potatoes was necessarily a slow one, and alogether devoid of interest for the student of smuggling history.

Part III.

THE COASTGUARD.

ITS ORIGIN AND DEVELOPMENT.

CHAPTER I.

Punch's Idea of the Coastguard—Good Times for the Smugglers—The Coast Blockade—Origin of the Coastguard—Unsatisfactory Nature of the Blockade—Preventive Boats' Crews—A Cutter Man's Ruse—Preventive Water Guard—Composition of the Force—'Longshoremen Afloat.

ALMOST everyone is familiar with the trim paths, well-tended gardens, and whitewashed walls of a coastguard station, and may even have a vague sort of notion that this little centre of order and good discipline is connected in some mysterious kind of way with the prevention of smuggling, but as for any clear ideas concerning the duties pertaining to the officers and men of the coastguard at the present day, or how the force came into existence in the first instance, such a pitch of knowledge is rarely attained by the free and independent tax-payer. And when this worthy person beholds a sturdy tar marching up and down with a big telescope, the cynosure of admiring rustics at a popular watering-place, he is apt to assume that this jolly mariner's lot has fallen in pleasant places.

The popular ignorance concerning this branch of the public service was curiously exemplified some time ago by our old friend *Punch*, who, in a moment

I 2

of forgetfulness let us hope, so far deviated from the
standard of good taste which usually characterises his
remarks on men and manners, as to define coastguard
stations as "castles of idleness, where able-bodied
men spend their time in looking through long glasses
for imaginary smugglers." A short experience of
coastguard work during the winter months would
have considerably modified the opinions of the author
of this impudent libel.

To discover the germ from whence the coastguard
originally sprung, we must go back to the very early
years of the century. It has been shown how the
unsettled state of the country during the wars with
France enabled the free-trader, as he was called, to
follow his vocation with an audacity which could
scarcely have been tolerated under more settled
conditions, and how, with the return of peace, the
Government turned its attention once more to domes-
tic affairs with the result that the free-trader found
himself all of a sudden the object of the profoundest
solicitude, and his calling threatened with extinction.

It must not be inferred, however, that the smuggler had been allowed to indulge his tastes hitherto
without interference of any sort, or that there was no
force in existence for the protection of the revenue
before the coastguard was called into being. As a
matter of fact this duty had been entrusted hitherto
to the officers of Customs and Excise on shore, while
afloat the revenue cutters, when not engaged in
smuggling on their own account, had done what little
they could to cope with an evil which had acquired
proportions far beyond their powers of control.

But, unfortunately, the Customs officer and his
minions had become, through no fault of their own,

the laughing-stock of the countryside, while as for
the revenue cutters they had long ceased to have any
terrors for the intrepid mariners who gained their
living by defrauding the revenue of its dues. But the
halcyon days of the free-trader were drawing to a
close. The very lawlessness which characterised his
operations could be regarded in no other light than as
a disgrace to any country calling itself civilised;
while the heavy losses sustained annually by the
revenue showed the necessity of strictly enforcing
the various statutes enacted from time to time for
coping with such depredations.

The authorities having determined on putting
down their feet in the matter, lost no time in giving
effect to this resolution, and commenced operations
by establishing a thorough blockade of the coasts of
Kent and Sussex. For this purpose a man-of-war
was stationed in the Downs,* another at Newhaven
in Sussex,† and their crews landed, broken up into
detachments, and quartered in the Martello towers
along the coast. Where towers were not available
a sort of barracks was built, and these " blockade
stations," altered in accordance with modern require-
ments, are used for coastguard quarters at the present
day. Here, then, we have the germ of the modern
coastguard station along the coasts of Kent and
Sussex. The various stages of development will
now be traced.‡

---

* The *Ramillies.* This fine old seventy-four had last seen service
in the American war under command of Sir Thos. Masterman Hardy,
during which she narrowly escaped destruction by torpedoes on two
occasions.

† H.M.S. *Hyperion,* forty-two guns.

‡ In a volume of the " Family Library," published in 1840, the
following curious passage occurs :—" Captain Hanchett, C.B , R.N.,

The blockade stations were commanded by lieutenants of the Royal Navy, of whom, at the close of the war, there were a large number out of employment, and with but small prospect of obtaining it afloat. A station comprised so many towers, which, with their complement of men, were in charge of petty officers with the rating of quartermaster. The entire force was under naval discipline, and in the event of misconduct the offenders were liable to be sent on board the old *Ramillies* to be " dusted down "—an occurrence which, if tradition is to be relied on, was by no means infrequent, " Old Jock McCulloch," as the worthy Scotsman who commanded that fine old seventy-four was somewhat irreverently called, having a decided *penchant* for this particular method of " moral suasion."

The " coast blockade" lasted a number of years, but the system was never altogether satisfactory. The service was unpopular with the men of the fleet, the better class of whom held off from joining it, and those who were induced to enter connived with the smugglers, got drunk, and often deserted, and there was a very general complaint amongst them that the quartermasters were entrusted with too much power.

The blockade was broken up in 1831, the men withdrawn, and their places taken, partly by men from the revenue cutters and partly by civilians, the designation of the force being altered to "coastguard." Long before this, however, the principle of the blockade had been extended gradually, and in a modified form

who proposed the constitution of the coastguard, and was appointed to its head with emoluments of £2,000 a year or more, was accused of attempting to sell his appointments, and without trial dismissed his post, degraded of his Companionship of the Bath, and stripped of his commission."—" The Mutiny at Spithead and the Nore," page 322.

under another name, round the entire seaboard of the kingdom. Obviously, it was useless locking the front door if the back entrance and all the windows were left open. In other words, it was of little advantage to the revenue depriving the good people of Kent and Sussex of their direct supplies of liquor and baccy while these popular commodities could be imported duty free round the corner. Almost simultaneously, therefore, with the establishment of the blockade, active measures had been taken for suppressing the trade round the entire seaboard. For this purpose the old-established revenue cutter service—the only available organised force for the suppression of smuggling —was largely developed and utilised. A proportion of the men were detached to form boats' crews at the most notorious smuggling centres, and long after these boats' crews had become permanencies at the localities where they had been "detached" in the first instance, the men were still spoken of as belonging to the " boat," and were, in fact, always appointed to such and such " preventive boat."

From these detached boats' crews, which are still remembered by the proverbial " oldest inhabitant," we can trace through a series of evolutions, extending over half a century or more, the coastguard stations of modern times ; while, strictly speaking, the germ of the coastguard force must be sought for in the old revenue cutter service rather than in the hybrid force composing the " blockade."

The duties of the " boats' crews " at this particular time were, as implied by the title, exclusively naval. The men patrolled the coast in their boats* by night,

* By way of ensuring the proper performance of this duty, the "sitter," as the officer in charge of a preventive boat was somewhat ironically called in those days, was enjoined to take soundings at

or, if prevented from going afloat through stress of weather, the boat would be hauled up, the crew seeking refuge under a shelter composed of the boat's sails.

These detached "boats' crews," though undoubtedly a step in the right direction, were at best but a makeshift. The duty was imperfectly performed, partly from want of proper supervision, and partly from the nature of things. It was, of course, impossible for men thus situated to obtain information concerning the ways and means of the local smugglers, or to keep themselves *au courant* with their movements, though some ingenious ruses were occasionally resorted to by the more active officers with a view to acquiring this much-to be-desired knowledge. "When my father was in the *Lapwing* cutter," said an old pensioner to the writer, "all sorts of dodges used to be tried ; for instance, when they were stationed at Plymouth a boat would be sent ashore in Whitsand Bay, where the crew would haul her up and cover her over with seaweed, and then, after dressing themselves up in old clothes, and putting on a smock-frock, maybe, they would throw a bundle over their shoulder, and go away into the villages, where they would drop into the public-houses and listen to the talk. By this means they often managed to find out what the smugglers were about, and when cargoes were expected over. Then, as soon as it was dark, they would launch their boat and return to the cutter with the information they had picked up."

The next and most important step was the

certain stated times during the night, and to furnish a return of these periodically to the inspecting commander. Scandal has it that the process known as "fudging" was largely resorted to in the compilation of these returns by ingenious "sitters."

establishment of permanent boats' crews—"preventive boats," as they were called, and the appointment of responsible officers in command. The crews were now located on shore, in hired houses, or where, for various reasons, quarters were unobtainable—as was often the case in those days, owing to the very natural reluctance of the inhabitants to facilitate arrangements so entirely opposed to their notions of the eternal fitness of things*—the men were housed in old hulks, or "watch vessels."

And now we find the force designated in official documents as "The Preventive Water Guard," the duties still partaking largely of a naval character—rowing guard afloat by night, or patrolling the coast on shore when unable to launch the boat.

Before tracing out the subsequent stages of development, it may be as well, perhaps, to pause for a moment for the purpose of inquiring into the character and composition of the force at this stage of its history.

The officers appointed to the command of "boats" were, as in the case of the blockade, chiefly lieutenants of the Navy, of whom, as already observed, there was a plethora ; but in some instances what were called—for not very apparent reasons—"civilian officers," were selected from amongst the "deputation officers"—mates, gunners, etc., of the revenue cruisers—the individual holding this post being officially designated as "chief officer," regardless of his profession, real

---

* Polperro, in Cornwall, affords an illustration of this :—"Though active opposition was not politic, the people determined, one and all, to offer as much passive resistance as was safe. No one would let a coastguardman a house to live in at any price ; so the whole force was obliged to make a dwelling and guard-house of the hull of a vessel, which was moored to the old quay."—Couch's "History of Polperro."

rank, or status. The post was not a very glorious
one, perhaps, but there were always plenty of appli-
cants for it in the hard times which prevailed, and
if the pay was not exorbitant, the prize money, which
not infrequently accrued to a zealous and, perhaps,
lucky chief officer, was by no means the least of the
attractions of the post. There was plenty of hard
work certainly, and not a little fighting, for which,
however, no medals were granted, and in which little
glory was to be reaped.

With regard to the "crews," although the nucleus
was selected in the first instance from the revenue
cutter service, they were usually completed by the entry
of "'longshore" men. Whether by this means the most
desirable class of men was obtained seems a little
questionable. Old smugglers speak very contemp-
tuously of the preventive men of those days, but perhaps old smugglers are a little prejudiced. They
could scarcely be expected to recognise merit in a
preventive man. For all that, there would seem to
be a consensus of opinion that pretty nearly anyone
was taken—shoemakers, tailors, coopers, perhaps even
tinkers—anybody, in fact, who had interest with a
Member of Parliament, or friends in office to obtain
for them an appointment in the force.

Said an old coastguardman to the writer : " I can
mind, when a boy, many a time seeing the six-oared
galley at Polperro going off to board the cutters, the
men going floppity-flop with their oars, one after the
other, just like a lot of ploughboys."

CHAPTER II.

Salutary Precautions—Mixed Marriages Forbidden—Consolidation of the Revenue Forces—Riding Officers of the Customs—Employment of Dragoons—Aversion to the Work—Organisation and Duties of the Mounted Guard—Gradations of Rank in the Coastguard.

HAVING regard to the universal prevalence of smuggling, it may be safely averred that every man who joined the coastguard, even if he had never smuggled himself, most certainly had relatives engaged in the trade ; and as the strength of old associations is proverbial, no surprise will be felt at the elaborate precautions taken to prevent the possibility of collusion by severing all connection between men in the preventive service and their former associates. To this end it was enacted in the old regulations that "no individual can be appointed to any station within twenty miles of the place of his birth, or within twenty miles of the place at which he has resided for the six months previous to his appointment in the water guard." This regulation was extended subsequently to the place of residence of a man's wife. And again, "Any individual intermarrying with the family of a reputed or notorious smuggler, or lodging in his house, or contracting any improper intimacy with him, will be dismissed."*

* A case in point occurred in the Scilly Islands :—"Mr. Richard R——, chief officer of the Tresco station, has, since the last half-yearly report, married a woman belonging to St. Mary's Island, who may be a branch of a smuggler's family, or be connected with smugglers, of whom the island principally consists ; and, under the circumstances, I beg to suggest that he may be removed from the district." Let us hope that before taking this momentous step Mr. Richard R—— weighed well the comparative advantages of single blessedness in Tresco, or matrimonial joy in other lands.

A preventive man could not be too careful in the choice of his friends, "It was death in those days," old coastguardmen will tell you, "to be seen talking with a smuggler"—by which it is meant that it was ruin to all prospects of advancement in the force. That these precautions were by no means superfluous will be seen as this history proceeds.

The "preventive water guard" as well as the revenue cutter service were at this time under the "Lords Commissioners of his Majesty's Treasury," the executive command being vested in a "comptroller-general," who was a captain in the Royal Navy. In 1822 orders emanated from the Treasury department to the effect that "the whole of the forces for the prevention of smuggling, consisting of the revenue cruisers, preventive water guard, and riding officers, shall be consolidated, and be placed in like manner as the riding officers are at present, under the direction of the Board of Customs." It will be noticed that no reference is made to the "coast blockade," which was still in force, and undoubtedly a part of the "force for the prevention of smuggling," an omission which makes it clear that the officers and men employed on this service were only "detached," and still belonged to the Royal Navy.

Allusion was made just now to a branch of the preventive service which has not been mentioned before, namely, the riding officers. Some notice of their previous history is called for. The riding officers may be traced back for nearly a couple of centuries, and are therefore entitled to be regarded as the premier branch of the now consolidated force for the prevention of smuggling.

In an enactment passed in 1698, with a view to checking the export smuggling of wool along the south-east coast, we find provision made for the appointment of 299 riding officers at an annual cost of £20,000 ; and during the war which broke out subsequently between France and England the services of the riding officers were largely instrumental in checking clandestine communications with the enemy —a dishonourable vocation to which the smugglers betook themselves very largely in times of disturbance. From a report by Mr. Baker, supervisor of Customs for the counties of Kent and Sussex, dated December, 1703, we find the coast from the Isle of Sheppey in Kent to Emsworth in Hampshire, a stretch of about 200 miles, in charge of fifty riding officers, giving an average of one officer for every four miles of coast-line.

How utterly inadequate this force proved to suppress the illicit trade has been made abundantly clear. To compensate in some measure for the numerical inferiority of the preventive force proper, the practice of employing the mounted branch of the army was now largely resorted to. To quote from Mr. Baker's report, under date December, 1703, in which certain suggestions are submitted with the object of reducing the cost of the riding officers, he says :—" I further propose that the dragoons now quartered in Kent, and by her Majesty's order of 11th August last, to be detached into severall parts of the Marsh (Romney) to assist the officers, as from time to time I shall direct, may, if your Honours shall so please, be made useful in this service, pursuant to the Order in Councill by his late Majestie, bearing date the 23rd June, 1698, wherein it was ordered that for the encouragement of the said soldiers and the landlords of the houses that quarter them there (being an allowance of twopence per diem to each dragoon upon such service, and to

the officers in proportion) being revived. I can soe
dispose those soldiers that the nightly duty of the
officers shall not be interrupted, and everyone of them
shall always have one or more of them in the night
upon duty."*

The system of employing dragoons in conjunction
with the riding officers continued up to the time of
the "Consolidation Order," in 1822, at which particular period the riding officer might have been spoken
of as a man in authority with soldiers under him,
though whether the same ready obedience was
rendered to him by his subordinates, as we read of
in connection with a certain centurion of old, seems
extremely doubtful. There is ample evidence, indeed,
to show that the soldiers detested the work, were
hand and glove with the inhabitants of the places
where they were quartered, and nothing loth to do
a little smuggling on their own account when the
officer lay snug in bed.

From time immemorial, as indeed may easily be
supposed, considerable friction had taken place
between the military and the officers of the Customs,
and the formalities that had to be observed before
the assistance of the soldiers could be procured nulli-
fied to a great extent the advantages resulting from
their employment.

---

* A curious record of these days has come down to us in the shape
of a letter from an individual signing himself " Old Soldier," who, in
the course of some observations in which he deplores the deterioration
of a military spirit amongst the officers, says :—" I am sorry to say there
are some officers who never desire to make a campaign, except against
the smugglers, some who would be much better pleased to watch all
night for a seizure of tea and brandy than to march into trenches ; and
I do assure you they had much rather be commanded by a Custom
House officer than Prince Eugene or the Duke of Marlborough."—
Monthly Intelligence for 1737.

So far as the suppression of smuggling was concerned, this system had not been attended with
marked success. The riding officers by themselves were
easily overawed ; while,
as regards the military,
it was not a happy idea
this of setting dragoons
to catch smugglers —
rather, indeed, like setting
elephants to catch eels.
By the Treasury minute of
1822 the riding officers
were attached to the coastguard stations under the
orders of the chief officers,
the official designation
being altered at the same
time to that of " mounted
guard."

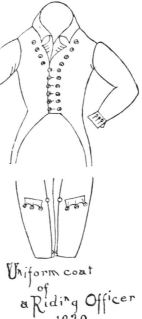

Uniform coat
of
a Riding Officer
1829

According to the regu-
lations of this date they
were " to be considered as
the movable force of the
district, and to be placed
at such stations as may
from time to time be deemed most beneficial to the
service."

Civilians were no longer eligible for this branch of
the service, appointments being confined to persons
"to be selected from cavalry regiments by the general
commanding-in-chief." *   The force was divided into

* How far the old " civilian " class of riding officers were adapted
to the rough and tumble work they were called on to perform, the
reader may judge from the following extract from the *Sussex Advertiser* of 1834 :—" Three riding officers of the Customs of the Arundel

three classes, viz., sergeants, corporals, and privates, while as regards their duties, to quote again from the regulations :—" The general and most important part of the duty of the mounted guard is, towards the close of the day and during the night, to examine carefully the by-roads, lanes, and in general every part of the neighbourhood of the station to which they are attached, for the purpose of discovering any preparations which may be making by the smugglers for effecting a landing, either by assembling carts or men, or in any other way . . . and in the event of a run being effected, pursuing the company, and endeavouring to intercept the carts in which they are conveying the goods. . . . All their movements in the night are to be conducted with the greatest secrecy, silence, and circumspection ; and it is expected that by their intelligence and vigilance they will be enabled to discover all the secret haunts of the working parties, become acquainted with the persons of those who reside in the immediate neighbourhood, and with the habits of life of that description of people in general who are suspected of being in any way concerned in illegal traffic . . . and thus render most important and valuable service in defeating the object of the smugglers."

This rather long digression may be thought superfluous ; but to enable the reader to understand the chapters which follow, it is essential that the duties of the several branches of the service should be clearly explained.

The practice of calling in the aid of the military, though but rarely resorted to after the establishment

district have been superannuated on full salaries. Their ages were eighty-four, eighty, and seventy-two respectively, and they had been fifty, fifty-four, and fifty-four years respectively in the service."

of the consolidated force, was still a recognised
custom, and was provided for under the regulations
" relative to the employment of dragoons in aid of
the revenue coastguard."

The coastguard having now assumed a definite
form and organisation, it may be as well at this point
to enumerate the several ranks of the service.   First,
there was the officer in charge of the station, known by
the title of " chief officer," next the " chief boatmen ";

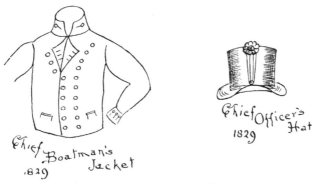

COASTGUARD UNIFORM, 1829.

while the rank and file, as it may be termed, consisted
of "commissioned boatmen" and " boatmen" ; and this
gradation, with the exception of the added rank of
" chief boatmen in charge," intermediate between
chief boatmen and chief officer, has remained un-
altered to the present day.

As time went on the custom of appointing
deserving chief boatmen to the post of chief officer
gradually came into vogue until the whole of the
stations round the coast were placed in charge of this
class of officer, and no lieutenant has held the post of
chief officer during the last thirty years.

J

CHAPTER III.

Tinkers and Tailors—Land Patrolling—Guard-rowing Afloat—Consequences of Neglect—Organisation and Duties—Revenue Cutter Service—Severity of Night Duty—Station Limits--Flying Detachments—A Novel Suggestion.

IT soon became evident to the authorities that the custom of entering "tinkers and tailors" was anything but conducive to the welfare or efficiency of the service; and accordingly, in 1829, we find regulations to the effect that "no person is to be admitted as a boatman in the coastguard service unless he is twenty and under thirty years of age, nor unless he has served six years at sea, or seven years' apprenticeship in fishing boats." In spite of this it was by no means unusual for 'longshore men to get admission under false pretences, and a friend at court could generally manage to overcome any little scruples concerning the qualifications of the applicant that might be entertained at headquarters.

The official designation of the force was now once more altered to "coastguard," a title which it has ever since retained, while all orders emanated henceforward from the "Coastguard Office, Custom House, London."

The duties, too, had become less naval in character, the land patrolling or coastguarding, as implied by the new title, rather than waterguarding, according to the old dispensation, having been found by far the most efficacious method of counteracting the operations of the smuggler. It must not, of course, be supposed that the duties of the force had been precisely assimilated round the entire seaboard, for obviously these were necessarily regulated by local conditions, such for instance as the nature of the coast, or the local smuggling customs. At some stations it was not only impracticable to row guard afloat, but highly undesirable, from the fact that by taking the crew away for this purpose the coast within station limits was left practically open and unprotected.

Guard-rowing afloat had one advantage, however, over the coast patrolling, in that after an offing had been gained, the course of the boat could be directed unperceived to any point on shore, whereas the movements of a land patrol were open to observation from the moment of a man leaving the watch-house till his arrival on the guards, and could be communicated to the smuggling boats off the coast by means of well-known signals. The matter was, therefore, left very much to the discretion of the chief officers, who, to quote the regulations, " were distinctly to understand that they were held responsible for any smuggling transactions which took place within the limits of their guards."

By way of still further impressing on the officers and men of the force the responsibilities attaching to them, the following order was issued about this time : " The Comptroller-general directs that officers and men be publicly informed that a list will in future be kept of every person serving at a station within which a run took place, and that no such officer or man will be considered eligible for promotion or entitled to any mark of indulgence or favour."

That this was no empty threat is evident from the fact that on a subsequent occasion we find all promotion in the Fowey division (Cornwall) stopped in consequence of several runs having taken place.

The old "preventive waterguard" having passed through a series of evolutions into a carefully organised and well-disciplined force, under the title of coastguard, a few words concerning its organisations and the duties pertaining to its several branches will make matters clear to the reader.

Briefly, then, at the time of which we speak (1830) a triple cordon had been established round the greater part of the United Kingdom, strong in some places, weak and attenuated in others, while some parts of the coast which, from their extreme isolation and inaccessibility seemed to offer no facilities to the illicit trader, were left practically unguarded. The protective cordon consisted first of the naval branch, or revenue cutters ; secondly of the coastguard, and lastly the mounted guard.

The revenue cutter service consisted of a fine fleet of over fifty vessels, comprising several splendid cutters of nearly 200 tons, with crews of from forty to fifty men, and commanded for the most part by lieutenants of the Navy. Taking the average of the crews at twenty-five, we have a floating force of nearly 1,300 officers and men engaged solely and entirely in the protection of the revenue.

The duties performed by this branch of the service were exceptionally arduous. The vessels cruised off the districts to which they were attached, for the purpose of intercepting smuggling vessels, and were seldom allowed in harbour except when driven in by stress of weather or for repairs.

The routine of duty in those days was somewhat as follows :—Towards dusk every day the vessels usually drew in towards land, and dropped their boats for the purpose of rowing guard along the coast during the night, picking them up again at daylight

next morning at some pre-arranged rendezvous. If
bad weather came on, the boats had to manage as
best they could—either to find the cruiser or run for
the nearest shelter. "Many a time I've been dropped
one side of the Isle of Wight in the evening and
picked up next morning on the other," said an old
cutter's man ; from which it may be gathered that
this "guard-rowing" in the winter months was no
sinecure. On the other hand there was always the
chance of falling in with a valuable prize.

Nor were the duties much lighter when the vessel
was in harbour, for the anchor was no sooner down
than orders would come off for the employment of
the boats during the ensuing night ; and even when
laid up for repairs the crews were given little opportunity for resting, being usually distributed amongst the
stations where smuggling was most rife, bunks being
fitted up in the watch-rooms for their accommodation.

It would be difficult to conceive of a finer school
of seamanship and pilotage, or of a sterner training, than was afforded by the old revenue cutter
service in its palmy days, and one cannot help
regretting that it has passed away, with all its historical associations and traditions. At the time,
indeed, of which we are treating, the service had
already come to be regarded as a mere accessory to
the coastguard, into which it was ultimately merged
just as the coastguard was itself afterwards absorbed
into the navy.

Passing on to the second line, or coastguard, we
have seen how, from mere tentative measures—detached "boats' crews"—the service blossomed forth
into a regular force with discipline and organisation,
and at this point a rather more detailed statement of
its character and functions will be acceptable.

For purposes of administration and discipline the several coastguard stations were divided off into "districts," each of which was under a commander of the Royal Navy, with the title of "inspecting commander," which officer was again directly responsible to the comptroller-general, who, with his "deputy comptroller-general"—a commander of the Royal Navy—was located at the Custom House in London. The various links in the chain of responsibility will now be clear.

As regards the duties of the coastguard, they were scarcely less irksome than those pertaining to the floating branch of the service. Speaking generally the peculiar nature of the work necessitated a complete inversion of the natural order of things. Thus, as the smuggler plied his vocation chiefly by night, so the coastguardman had to be most alert during the hours of darkness. His night, in fact, so far as his work was concerned, was turned into day, while the latter was chiefly given up to rest and refreshment.

"The work was terrible," old coastguardmen have often said to the writer. "Why, sir, in the winter months we had to be on our guards by dusk, which meant leaving home at four or half-past, and we never got back again till nearly eight next morning. The only 'nights in' we got was when our turn came round to be day watchman at the station—once in ten days or so ; and perhaps two nights before the full moon and two nights afterwards ; though, even then, we seldom got more than half nights off, and if smuggling boats were expected off the coast, of course all the crew had to be out. I've often been that done up that I could scarcely walk home, and many is the time I've gone down to the water and washed my face to keep my eyes open. Oh, it was

enough to kill a horse, I can tell you ; only a strong
man could stand the work ! "

Sixteen hours on the stretch through the winter
nights in snow, sleet, wind, and rain, without shelter
or protection of any kind, besides the chance of
being shot, tied down to the rocks, or pitched over
the cliff ! Coastguarding in those days was certainly no child's play. " You couldn't get men to
do the work now," my informants have often added,
the truth of which no one will be inclined to doubt ;
indeed, it required something more than the prospects of free quarters and regular pay to induce men
to do the work in those days. The particular form of
inducement that was held out to them will be seen in
due course.

It may be as well to explain with reference to the
" nights in," which the men calculated on before and
after full moon, that the smugglers only plied their
trade, as a rule, during the " darks "—as moonless
nights were styled—when, as a matter of course, their
movements were screened from observation ; hence,
unless information to the contrary was given, it was
taken for granted that no run would be attempted,
and one-half of the crew of the station were allowed
to rest during the light nights of the full moon.

The practice of weakening the guard during
stormy weather under the impression that smuggling
operations would be suspended, which crept in at
many stations, was studiously discouraged at headquarters, it being pointed out that many runs had
taken place in consequence of the relaxed vigilance
of the coastguard on these occasions, " the smugglers
caring nothing for the loss of their boats, so long as
they can run their goods."

With reference to the word " guard " which has

often been made use of, it may be as well to explain
that from a very early period—probably from the
first establishment of the blockade—the coast comprised within each station's limits had been divided
off into "guards" for patrolling purposes. The
number of guards into which a station was divided
depended on the strength of the crew, allowing one
man for each guard. The limits of the stations
varied very considerably, being usually regulated, in
the first instance at any rate, in accordance with the
smuggling facilities of the coast. How widely these
varied may be gathered from a comparison of the
several stations in the United Kingdom. Thus, while
in Kent and Sussex there are stations whose limits
scarcely exceeded a mile in extent, divided off into
fifteen or twenty guards, we find stations in other
parts of England comprising from eight to twenty
miles of coast, with crews of only eight or nine men
for patrolling purposes.

The wide extent of many of the stations, and the
impossibility of keeping a proper watch over the
coast in consequence thereof, led about this time, and
during subsequent years, as the necessity arose, to
the institution of what are officially styled "flying
detachments"—small look-out houses, where a couple
of men were detached for a week at a time from the
main station for patrolling the adjacent shore. In
coasting along the south-western portion of England,
especially the south coast of Devon and Cornwall, the
voyager will notice small white cottages perched on
extremely isolated and often almost inaccessible points,
the purport of which he might have some difficulty in
divining. These are the "flying detachments," each
of which has quite an interesting little smuggling
history of its own, and although the special circum-

stances which prompted their construction have disappeared with the lapse of time and change of habits of the coast population, these little houses still play a useful part in the coastguard economy of modern days.

It has been suggested, and the proposal is at least worth considering by an economical Government, that during the summer months, while the coastguard men are embarked for the manœuvres, these cottages might be made available at a moderate rent for honeymoon couples, where, free from the impertinent gaze of their fellow-mortals, and the cares of civilisation, surrounded by romantic, if not always beautiful, scenery, and undisturbed by the muffin bell, the tradesman's boy, or the postman's knock, they might dream away the golden days of early married life, the world forgetting, by the world forgot.

Such an excellent idea is, perhaps, too much in advance of the age to commend itself to the sense of the governing classes.

CHAPTER IV.

Routine of a Station—Dress and Equipment—Drill and Discipline—Possibility of Collusion—Sinking Goods—Creeping and Sweeping—Rewards for Seizures—Incentives to Duty—Corruption.

THE routine of a coastguard station was somewhat as follows :—At dusk every day the entire crew were assembled in the watch-house, fully equipped for their night's duty with arms, ammunition, and bluelight. Each man was then told off for the guard he was to take charge of, and, without holding further communication with any person, proceeded at once to his post.

The old regulations were most explicit and peremptory as to the importance of allowing no communications to take place between the men and their families, after having been detailed for the night's duty. They were equally explicit on the subject of permitting no man to have charge of the same guard two nights in succession. Experience had shown the necessity of these precautions against the possibility of collusion, and it required the utmost care and ingenuity to frustrate the unceasing efforts of the smugglers to discover the routine of duties at the several stations.

Not only was it permitted to no man to know the guard he was to occupy during the ensuing night, but at most stations it was the invariable custom to change the guards at least once during the night; while, to ensure the alertness of the patrols, each guard was visited twice every night at uncertain times and without notice by the chief officer of the station, and at rare intervals by the inspecting commander of the district.

Contrary to modern usage, the wearing of uniform was not obligatory on the men at night; indeed in many districts the practice was rather discouraged than otherwise as a means of avoiding observation, and thus throwing the smugglers off their guard.* One consequence of this was that the men often so encumbered themselves with wrappings as a protec-

---

* A case in point occurred in the Deal district (1832). The inspecting commander observing that, "having noticed the day look-out men at ——— station parading their posts in uniform, the first object is to have the day sentinels dressed as much as possible like the inhabitants, instead of placing them as *beacons* to warn the illicit traders, whom it is our duty to detect by disguise and every other means that can be devised."

tion from the dreadful weather to which they were exposed, that in the event of sudden attack they were unable to defend themselves properly, and were not infrequently overpowered and secured.

As regards arms, the patrols, when equipped for the night's duty, carried a brace of heavy pistols, a cutlass, several rounds of ammunition, and a blue-light for giving the alarm. The pistols were generally carried inside the breast of the great-coat. In some districts a musket and fixed bayonet was substituted for the cutlass, the bayonet being further secured by a lashing—details of this sort being regulated by the inspecting commanders to suit local circumstances.

Obviously, some knowledge of drill and the use of firearms was necessary for men who were liable at any moment to find themselves *vis-à-vis* with a gang of desperate smugglers ; but that the drill in those days was of an exceedingly primitive kind may be inferred from an official memorandum of so late a date as 1840, wherein we read that " it is presumed that the crews are now perfectly well trained in the use of firearms."

It seems to have been the custom at this time for an old soldier, possibly one of the mounted guard, to make a circuit of the divisions for the purpose of instructing men in the musket and cutlass drill, and funny stories are handed down of the methods by which this instruction was imparted to the crews.

In 1829 regulations of a most elaborate kind were issued with reference to the exercise of the crews on occasions of inspection, so as " to secure the uniform and creditable appearance of the whole force on inspections and all other occasions of parade, and to prevent that diversity of system which has hitherto

too much prevailed in different districts." The
musket drill was a tolerably simple affair, but the
cutlass exercise was so elaborate and complicated
that the coastguard intellect of the period must have
been sadly exercised to make head or tail of it.
Instead of being adapted to intellects of a humble
order, the drill consisted of no less than sixty-two
movements, the purport of which was, to use a
Dundrearian expression, what " no fellah could understand."

As regards the discipline of the " consolidated
force," though satisfactory in the main, there was a
tendency now and again to kick over the traces,
which was met by fines and dismissals. When,
indeed, it is stated that during the period between
August, 1825, and February, 1829—about three years
and a half—there were no less than 215 dismissals
from the force, we have pretty clear evidence of
the existence of a considerable element of rowdyism
in it. But as this phase of coastguard life is treated
at length in a subsequent chapter, it is needless to
go into the matter just now, beyond remarking on
what may seem the needless severity with which the
offence of patrols allowing themselves to be secured
by smugglers without offering a proper resistance was
invariably treated. Experience, however, had shown
the necessity for this. There was, indeed, no readier
means of evading the responsibilities of their post,
to say nothing of the personal risks involved in an
encounter with smugglers, than that of allowing
themselves to be seized and secured while a run was
being effected. To treat this offence with the
leniency which inexperience might have suggested
would have been simply placing a premium on collusion. What could have been easier than for a man

to have allowed himself to be secured—for a consideration, of course—and to have pleaded sudden
surprise in extenuation of his treachery? The fact,
therefore, of a coastguard man permitting himself to
be secured by smugglers without having made use of
his arms, or receiving any personal injury, or raising
any alarm, was regarded as *prima facie* evidence of
gross neglect, if not of absolute collusion, and was
punished accordingly.

It has been already explained how the duties of
the coastguard were for the most part conducted by
night, the day being generally given up to rest and refreshment ; * but although this was the rule, there were
exceptions, and probably of all their duties, not the
least harassing was that of "creeping " for sunken goods
off the coast. It must be explained that, as a result
of the increased efficiency and vigilance of the preventive service, and the greater difficulties experienced
in running goods, the smugglers now very generally
adopted the more cautious method of first sinking
them off the place where it was intended subsequently
to run them. In spite, however, of the secresy and
precautions exercised on these occasions, the fact of
a cargo having been sunk generally got to the ears of
the coastguard, who had now to use their utmost
endeavours to prevent the goods being run. To this
end, the boats belonging to the particular station
concerned were kept constantly afloat by day " creeping " and " sweeping " for the goods. Creeping consisted in dragging an iron grapnel, or " creep," as it
was called, along the bottom, so as to hook on to the

---

* It may be of interest to note that " libraries of books of an enter-
taining and moral tendency " were first supplied to coastguard stations
at the suggestion of a Mrs. Fry in 1833.

tubs ; while in sweeping, two boats were rowed along, parallel to each other, dragging the bight of a rope between them along the bottom. As these operations had to be persevered in as long as there was any reason to suppose the goods were down, a great deal

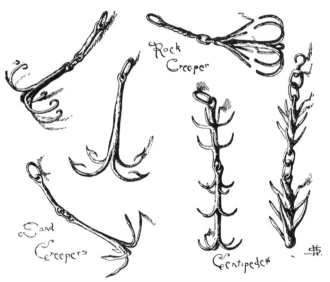

APPLIANCES USED FOR CREEPING UP SUNKEN GOODS.

of extra work was thus entailed on the crews. It must in fairness be stated, however, that in the event of the operations proving successful the reward amply recompensed the men for their labour.

When the harassing and arduous nature of the coastguard duties at this particular period are taken into consideration—not to mention the risks to life and limb which were constantly incurred—some surprise may be felt at men being found willing to sub-

mit to the hardships attaching to the service; and
certainly the bare prospect of wages would never of
itself have been found a sufficient inducement to enlistment. The service was not only hard but unpopular with the coast population. A higher incentive
was needed, and that was supplied on a lavish scale
in the shape of "rewards for seizures"—in plain
English, prize money. What this occasionally
amounted to may be dimly realised when we hear of
a thousand pounds having been distributed amongst
the officer and crew of a station for a single capture,
the smallest share, that of a boatman, amounting
to about £90.

The scale of rewards depended not only on the
value of goods seized, but on the number of smugglers
captured, in accordance with the regulations, wherein
it was laid down that "Every man employed in the
waterguard is to make it his first and most material
object to secure the person of the smuggler . . . .
and unless inspecting commanders certify that the
most active exertions were made to take the smugglers, no reward for or share of any seizure whatever
will be paid or allowed."

Briefly, a "full seizure" reward was granted only
in the event of the boat or vessel, as well as a fair
proportion of smugglers being captured, in addition
to the goods; only half being granted when the goods
alone were seized, unless, indeed, satisfactory reasons
were forthcoming to account for the escape of the
smugglers. As a still further incentive to exertion, a
reward of £20 was granted for every smuggler taken
and convicted. This was called "blood money" in
smuggling phraseology.

Seizure rewards were distributed in the following
fixed proportions :—

REVENUE CRUISERS.

Commander	...	...	...	...	100 Shares.
Chief mate	...	...	...	...	45 ,,
Second mate	...	...	...	...	35 ,,
Deputed mariners	...	...	...	20 ,,
Mariner	...	...	...	...	10 ,,
Boys	...	...	...	...	5 ,,

COASTGUARD STATIONS.

Chief officer	...	...	...	...	25 ,,
Chief boatman	...	..	...	10 ,,
Riding officer	...	...	...	...	10 ,,
Commissioned boatman	...	...	8 ,,
Boatman and extra men	...	...	6 ,,

It will be evident from what has been stated that inducements of a high order were extended to officers and men of all grades to exert themselves in the service of the Crown ; and yet it must be regretfully confessed that collusion with smugglers was by no means a rare offence at this particular period. The temptations were certainly very great, especially to poor men with large families, for the smugglers had immense sums of money at disposal, and were untiring in their efforts to corrupt the men. It was an easy matter for a coastguardman to connive at a smuggling transaction without exciting suspicion, and although conduct of this sort, if persevered in, was almost sure to leak out in time, the risk did not in every case deter men from " venturing."

CHAPTER V.

Sir James Graham's Minute—A New Departure—Withdrawal of the Blockade Men—Extension of the Coastguard—Summer Drills—Regularity of the Patrolling—Its Evil Consequences—When the Runs took Place.

WE have now arrived at a period in the history of the force which marks the first step in the direction of bringing it into closer association with the Royal Navy.* In the year 1831 negotiations were entered into between the Comptroller-general of Coastguard, the First Lord of the Admiralty, and the Lords of the Treasury, which led to results of high importance. The following extract from a Treasury minute of May 10th will show the direction in which the new departure tended : " Read letter from Sir Jas. Graham, dated March, 1831, enclosing letter from Comptroller-general of Coastguard, and submitting suggestions for improving the coastguard service in Great Britain

---

* In the "Navy List" for March, 1831, we find the following officers borne on the books of the guardships stationed in the Downs and at Newhaven, respectively, for blockade duties :—

Downs.
Talavera—74 ... 65 lieutenants, 15 assistant-surgeons.
Newhaven.
Hyperion—42 ... 65 lieutenants, 15 assistant-surgeons.

The "Navy List " for June, 1831, shows the following officers employed in the coastguard (the blockade having been abolished in April):—

STAFF IN LONDON.

1 Comptroller.   1 Inspector-General.   1 Deputy-Comptroller.
1 Deputy Inspector-General.

FOR INSPECTION OF DISTRICTS.

4 Captains.   43 Commanders.   10 Lieutenants.
282 Lieutenants employed as chief officers of stations.

K

and Ireland : 'My lords concur with the First Lord of the Admiralty in the expediency of remodelling the system of the coastguard service in Great Britain and Ireland, more especially as regards the appointments and promotion of officers and boatmen ; and in the opinion expressed by Sir Jas. Graham that in order to increase its efficiency it may be desirable to render it in all its branches essentially naval.'"

The changes thus shadowed forth were fraught with important results to the service, and took immediate effect in so far as the entry of men was concerned. From this time forward "instead of the nomination of the officers and boatmen of the coastguard of Scotland and Ireland and the boatmen in England resting with the Lords of the Treasury, the whole of such class was henceforth to be selected by the Lords of the Admiralty." And thus was a pretty piece of patronage transferred, with great advantage to the public service, from one department of state to the other.

The shoemaker and tailor element was by this means entirely eliminated, entries in the coastguard being confined to the crews of revenue cruisers and vessels of the royal navy ; every encouragement at the same time being offered to the sons of men serving in the coastguard to join the revenue cruisers.

The year 1831 was signalised by a still more important reform, namely, the break-up of the coast blockade,* and its supersession by the now well-

---

* *Apropos* of this, the *Sussex Advertiser*, under date March 21st, 1831, makes the following observations:—"The coast blockade, it is understood, will be abolished in April . . The measure is the reverse of calculated to excite regret in this part of Sussex." And again, under date April 4th, 1831, " the coastguard establishment under the regulations of the customs has commenced its duties within the last

matured coastguard force, which simply stepped into
the quarters of its predecessors as these were
gradually withdrawn, without causing any break in
the system of guard which had been so carefully

COASTGUARD SENTRY, 1831.

built up. The officers who had been in command of
stations under the blockade were, as a rule, permitted
to retain their posts, the only change of importance
being the appointment of inspecting commanders
over the districts, so as to assimilate the system with
that already in vogue in other parts of the kingdom.

fortnight, and on Thursday twelve of the horse-police* arrived as
Hastings for the performance of the interior duty for the prevention of
smuggling. They are rather well-looking men, and accoutred in a
manner calculated for the service.

* The new mounted guard."

K 2

Beyond the transference of the right of appointment of men and officers to the Admiralty department, and the consolidation of the whole prevention force, both afloat and ashore, under one head, every preventive station on shore and every revenue cruiser afloat still flew the Customs flag, and continued, so far as administration was concerned, as a branch of the Customs department. Smuggling, indeed, was far too rife round the coast of the United Kingdom to admit of any relaxation of vigilance for purposes other than those for which the force had been especially instituted, and for that reason nothing special seems to have been attempted in the way of drill for many years subsequently. It was not till 1840 that instructions were given for the crews of coastguard stations "to be drilled in common formations to enable them to move in bodies without confusion."

The custom of utilising the coastguard in aid of the civil power, for the preservation of order in times of social disturbance which had been resorted to on more than one occasion of late, notably the Chartist riots, had doubtless suggested the propriety of an order such as the one above named. To give effect to it the crews of adjoining stations were frequently assembled during the summer months at some convenient rendezvous for purposes of drill, the services of the mounted guard being usually called into requisition for instructional purposes on these occasions. Although the activity of the smugglers had by this time considerably abated, the withdrawal of the men from their stations, even during the day-time, was not altogether devoid of risk, and the authorities so far recognised this as to enjoin on the officers of stations the importance of maintaining secresy regarding the time and place of assembly for drill. The short nights of the summer months enabled these drills to be gone through without unduly harassing the men, or breaking into their much-needed repose ; but with the return of long nights the drills had, of course, to be suspended, the whole energies of the crews being required for the prevention of smuggling.

There is a tendency in most professions, but especially in the various branches of the Government service, to crystallise into a system whereof each part is complete and well-ordered. Such a tendency soon manifested itself in the coastguard, and herein lurked a danger, for, unfortunately, the very method and regularity which is so generally admired not infrequently constitutes a source of weakness. A secret code may be elaborated with marvellous skill and ingenuity ; but if the key is discovered, the system is at the mercy of the discoverer. Thus it mattered little how elaborate was the system of coastguard patrolling, if the smuggler once succeeded in mastering it, for, as a matter of course, he could then break through it at pleasure. The coastguardman, excellent fellow as he proved himself, was only human, and, like most people, he was fond of regular hours—for going to bed, for getting up, and for patrolling. The consequence was that a system of patrolling and conference, which seemed perfect to the superficial observer, and as well calculated as any humanly devised system could be to defy the efforts of an enterprising foe, was constantly being set at nought and rendered of no avail.

The failure was brought about in this wise. The smuggler was a keen, vigilant fellow, ever on the alert to discover the weak points in the coastguard defence, with his soul in his work, and grudging neither time nor money in the attainment of his object. He well knew that if the "master-key" to coastguard routine was once obtained, he could snap his fingers at the patrols, and to this end would often spend a week watching every movement of the patrols from the time of their leaving the watch-room till their return home the follow-ing morning, and venturing no-thing till he had mastered the entire routine.

Donkey or Rump-stool

Now we all know that "rou-tine," or in other words, "custom," is dear to the heart of man, and an excellent thing custom is in its way ; but Bacon, who is generally accounted to have been a shrewd fellow in his way, and certainly knew a thing or two, tells us that "custom doth make dotards of us all." Therefore, to obviate the disastrous effects of custom on the coastguard, it became neces-sary again and again to attack the routine of the stations, to destroy the regularity so dear to the hearts of the men, and thus to thwart the machinations of the foe. Thus, so far back as 1829, we meet with the following general order:—"The patrolling in some districts having become so regular and uniform, the smugglers take advantage of it, and particularly of the way the coast is left unguarded immediately after daylight." And from this time forward the order books of the stations teem with injunctions to the crews to be on their guard against the ever-varying tactics of the smugglers. It was one long story of plot and counterplot, each side trying to outwit the other—with what success on either side will be seen as our inquiry proceeds.

It may be as well to explain that the coastguard patrols were always withdrawn from their guards at daylight, the look-out duties being then taken over by the day-watchman, who, from some prominent position near the station, could observe the approach of any vessel to the coast. The smugglers, being well aware of this custom, frequently timed their run immediately after the withdrawal of the patrols, who, by way of saving time, were often in the habit of closing into the station before it was really light enough for the day-watchman to see what was going on along the coast.

Smuggling operations on a large scale were seldom attempted in the day-time, but on one occasion on the Sussex coast the smugglers, reckoning on the absence of the crew of a station one Sunday morning at church, attempted a run of goods under the very shadow of the station. But whether owing to the remissness of the men at their devotional exercises, or for some other reason, the smugglers were caught *in flagrante delicto*, and the goods seized.

Following the custom that obtained under the blockade, the coastguard patrols on the coast of Kent and Sussex were all within hail of each other at night, and yet, by either force or stratagem, the smugglers were constantly breaking through the chain of defence. Recognising the impossibility of men remaining on their feet the whole night, the patrols in many districts were permitted to provide themselves with one-legged stools, called "rump-

stools," or "donkeys." By sticking this into the
loose shingle at a slight inclination, the men's own
legs with the leg of the stool formed a sort of tripod
for the body to rest on, any inclination of the body
from the upright position caused by sleep at once
bringing the carefully-balanced structure to the
ground.

CHAPTER VI.

A Reserve for the Fleet—Conditions of Entry—Dual Capacity of the Force
—First Steps in Gun Drill—Value of the Force—A Revival of Smuggling
—Commander Sparshott—Abolition of the Custom House Flag—
Absorption into the Navy.

THE idea of utilising the coastguard as a reserve for
the fleet in time of war is by no means of modern
origin. It was, indeed, but natural that, as smuggling
became suppressed, some attempt should be made to
render the large force of men engaged in protecting
the revenue available for purposes of national defence
in emergency, and it is interesting to watch the steps
by which this idea was gradually put into practical
shape.

To give effect to this policy some alteration in the
conditions of entry into the coastguard became necessary, and accordingly in 1845 instructions were issued
that "no seaman is to be appointed in future to the
coastguard who will not enter into a written agreement binding himself to serve on board any of her
Majesty's ships, in the event of his services being
required ; but he is to be given to understand that he
will not be called upon to serve unless in cases of
emergency."

The administration of the force was henceforward

based on a full and clear recognition of the dual capacity it had now assumed, viz., first, as a preventive service ; secondly, as a reserve for the fleet in war time ; and just as its functions in the former capacity receded in importance, so the force acquired increased value as a reserve, and measures having for their object an increase of its efficiency in a naval sense were now being constantly introduced.

In the same year, 1845, we have the first proposal to utilise the crews of coastguard stations for the defence of the coast. This curious and little known memorandum is dated May 2nd, 1845, and after pointing out the desirability under certain conditions of placing guns of large calibre on prominent points of the coast, " not so much for the protection of landing places, as in expectation that by their extensive range with shot or shell they may deter the enemies' steam vessels from approaching the coast, and afford protection to the coasting trade," it is added that " regard must also be had to the situation of the coastguard stations, and on the force of each, as on them will depend the working of the gun, though it is probable that in the first instance the same, together with the ammunition, will be placed in charge of a seaman gunner from the *Excellent.*" No steps were taken to give effect to this proposal, and nothing was attempted in the way of gun-drill till three years later, 1848, when, as a preliminary measure, orders were given for one man " young, and likely to receive instruction," to be sent from certain stations to the nearest naval port for the purpose of being " instructed in the great gun exercise." But the Comptroller-general having expressed a wish that the whole of the coastguardmen should be taught the drill with as little delay as possible, the crews were sent up in relays for a week at the time, until the whole force, including the crews of revenue cutters— with the exception of men over fifty years of age, had received instruction.

The zeal and intelligence evinced by the men on this occasion elicited both from the Comptroller-general and the Admiralty letters of warm commendation. Mention is made at this particular period for the first time of the "gunnery department of the coastguard," under Commander Jernyngham, R.N.

The following allusion to a somewhat novel addition to the armament of coastguard stations shows how thoroughly the gun-drill had become a part of coastguard training. Referring to the progress made in this branch of instruction a general order of this date observes that "the ingenuity displayed in fitting the wooden guns now supplied to the respective stations will be taken advantage of as a means of perfecting the officers and men in the drill, and perfecting them for a satisfactory inspection by the Comptroller-general."

The wooden guns have long disappeared from the economy of coastguard stations, but here and there the tradition of their existence still survives, and traces may even be seen in the shape of a "half-port" in a watch-room window, or perhaps a training tackle bolt in the floor. The gun-drill having become a recognised part of a coastguardman's training, the crews of stations were now sent up once a year to the nearest naval port, battery, or man-of-war, for the purpose of keeping them proficient, while small drill-books were supplied to the stations to enable the crews to refresh their knowledge of the subject, and on all occasions of inspection the men were put through so much of the drill as could be achieved with the limited appliances available.

At this stage of the force's history it may not be amiss to quote the opinion entertained regarding its value to the nation by an officer whose position afforded the best opportunities of judging. In a valedictory address issued by the Comptroller-general, under date February 11th, 1850, the following passages occur :—

" I believe that her Majesty has not a more respectable body of officers and men in her dominions. . . . I must always recollect with peculiar satisfaction the patriotic readiness with which the sudden call for service in Ireland was met, as well as the invariable zeal and cheerful intelligence displayed throughout those districts in which the great gun exercise has been established.

" Should the time of trial come, I am convinced that her Majesty may securely rely upon the loyal efforts of the coastguard to aid in any operations, offensive and defensive, which shall be undertaken for the protection of the country. — HOUSTON STEWART."

About this time there seems to have been a partial revival of smuggling, but whether owing to relaxed vigilance on the part of the coastguard, or to an impression amongst the smugglers that the occasional withdrawal of the men for drill purposes offered facilities for prosecuting their trade cannot now be decided. The fact, however, remains, and drew forth the following remarks from the Comptroller-general, dated July 18th, 1850 :—

" It is with much regret I call the attention of the officers and men of the coastguard, ashore and afloat, to the fact that the contraband trade has greatly increased, and that the smugglers appear determined to carry on their illicit practices with increased vigour during the ensuing winter."

This was the last flicker up of smuggling before its final suppression, for although the trade was carried on in a quiet, unobtrusive way for many years after with varying success, the old methods had long been extinct, and a run of goods in the old style was only a curious matter of history; comparatively little activity or daring was brought to the task, and, so far as this history is concerned, "smuggling days" may be said to have come to an end.

Singularly enough, this particular time was marked by the death of Commander Sparshott, the Deputy Comptroller-general, who, from his long and intimate connection with the force might in truth have been styled the Father of the Coastguard. Having been associated with it almost from its inception, he possessed a wider and more detailed knowledge of this branch of the public service than any living person, and his death at this particular period of its history was a singular coincidence.

The following allusion to this event occurs in a general order, dated November 13th, 1851 :—

" The Board of Customs and Comptroller-general of the Coastguard desire to record their sense of the loss which the coastguard service has sustained in the death of Commander Samuel Sparshott, R.N., which took place on the 10th inst., at ten a.m., and whose long experience and zealous attention to the duties of his office as Deputy Comptroller-general of the Coastguard during a period of nearly twenty-five years the Board of Customs and Comptroller-general have fully appreciated."

The subsequent history of the coastguard is of

little interest to the general reader, from a smuggling standpoint, and may be told in a very few words.

When the Crimean war broke out, and found the country totally unprepared for a struggle with a colossal power like Russia, the value of the coastguard as a naval reserve was clearly shown, and every available man was drafted to the fleet, the vacancies thus created being filled up with "extra men" * and old pensioners. With the return of peace the absorption of the force into the navy was very shortly accomplished.

Early in 1857 the Custom House ensign, which had been the distinguishing badge of the service since its inception, was discontinued afloat and on shore, and the naval flags and signal code brought into use.

Closely following on this came the final measure, on the lines originally shadowed forth in the Treasury minute of 1831 ; and the extinction of the old coastguard service, with all its traditions, historical associations, and smuggling reminiscences, was rendered complete. In May, 1857, the districts were placed under the orders of captains of the royal navy—district-captains, as they are now called—the vessels of which they were in command being stationed at suitable points round the coasts of the United Kingdom.

From this time forward the coastguard became not only essentially naval, but so far as its administration was concerned, a mere offshoot from the navy itself. For its history during recent years the reader

---

* It was an old-established custom to engage civilians for temporary service at stations, in the place of men incapacitated by sickness, or other cause ; and such men were officially termed " extra men." It was not an uncommon thing for these "casuals" to do a little smuggling *sub rosa* when not protecting the revenue !

must be referred to those grand monuments of official industry—the blue-books and literature of a kindred nature, wherein, if he be blessed with an average amount of health and the prospect of longevity, and brings sufficient application to the task, he will find every detail connected with the service set down with astonishing precision, "even to the last button on the gaiter."

One word before concluding the chapter. The question is often asked by thoughtless people : "What is the good of keeping up the coastguard when there is no smuggling?" Now, without pausing to demonstrate the fallacy involved here, we would reply by asking another question: "What is the good of keeping up a fleet and army when the country is not at war?" *Si vis pacem para bellum* applies with just as much force to the question of maintaining a preventive force for the protection of the revenue, as to the maintenance of a fleet and army, for, while it is doubtful if any nation would instantly seize the opportunity for attacking us while our claws were clipped, there are plenty of unscrupulous people whom only the fear of detection now restrains from defrauding the revenue on a gigantic scale, and who but for the existence of the coastguard would instantly commence operations.

Part IV.

BLACK SHEEP.

*A PEEP BEHIND THE SCENES IN
THE COASTGUARD.*

CHAPTER I.

Black Sheep in the Coastguard—Nature of Offences—Drunkenness—Conduct of Cutter's Men—Spiling Casks—A Regular Old Smuggler—Collusion—A Coastguard Smuggler—Mistaken Vocations—The Looe Case.

IN a force comprising some 4,000 men and officers it was only natural that there should be a proportion of black sheep, and the large number of dismissals that took place during the early years of its history shows that the composition of the force was not all that could be desired from a disciplinary point of view. A brief notice of the offences which figured most prominently at this particular time will enable the reader to realise the peculiar temptations to which the members of the force were exposed, and by this means to form a truer conception of smuggling days than would otherwise be the case.

From careful inquiry it seems that during the period, August, 1825 to February, 1829, there were no less than 215 dismissals from the coastguard for various offences, the most common being—first, drunkenness; second, "mutinous and most outrageous conduct." Of this large number, however, it is only fair to state that by far the greater proportion were from the revenue cutters, for mutinous conduct and for desertion. As regards the first of these offences there can be no doubt that the temptations to drink were exceedingly strong; indeed, with so much cheap liquor about it was hardly to be expected that temperance principles should be in the ascendant. It was a practice, subsequently prohibited, though winked at, whenever a seizure was made to reserve one or two—usually two, possibly three—tubs for the refreshment of the crew; in the words of a quaint official order of those days "to afford cheerfulness and buoyancy of spirits."

The evil consequences of such a practice were not long in manifesting themselves, and in one instance, at least, a very graphic picture of this particular phase of coastguard life has been preserved as a lesson and a warning. Thus it is recorded that in 1827 the chief officer of the Langston Harbour Station was dismissed for allowing a flagon of spirits to be broached by his crew which led to the death of an "extra man" from excessive drinking, and then ordering the flagon to be taken to his own residence.

But if half of what the writer has heard be true, the drinking afloat was worse than on shore. The revenue cruisers were constantly employed in conveying seized spirits to the custom houses, and the crews seldom allowed a crop to pass through their hands without exacting toll, the *modus operandi* being as follows:—A tub having been deftly abstracted from the crop would be taken below, one of the hoops knocked back, a small hole bored, and a gallon run off; a "spile" would then be forced into the hole, the hoop knocked up into place again, and the tub returned. Watching the opportunity, the same operations would be repeated, and so on, until perhaps half a dozen gallons had been run off.*

Not content, however, with these minor depredations, which did little harm to the revenue, we find the crews on two occasions concerned in extensive smuggling transactions on their own account. Thus, in 1825, the entire crew of the *Rose*, revenue cruiser, was dismissed for attempting to "run" a large quantity of tobacco. And again in 1832, the *Nimble's* crew were dismissed for being concerned in the smuggling of a quantity of spirits at Exmouth. The temptation was no doubt great, for the vessels were constantly running across to the Channel Islands, whence a considerable contraband trade was still carried on with the English coast.

Said an old man to the writer :—" The *Fox* was nothing but a regular old smuggler. I know that, for my daughter married the mate, and the kitchen of the house where they lived was hung all over with loaves of sugar, and lots of other things which were contraband in those days, that he brought across from the Channel Islands."

After all, we must not judge these jolly mariners too harshly on account of their bibulous tendencies, for the duties of a preventive man in those days were such as no free and enlightened Briton would voluntarily undertake at the present time for double the pay, and it would have been thought poor fun handling tubs all day without getting ever a sup.†

---

* That these depredations were not the result of "want" is evident when it is stated that the daily spirit ration of each cutter's man was one gill of rum.

† One of the most flagrant cases of "reversion" was that of the first preventive boats' crew stationed at Gorran Haven, in Cornwall, who, let us hope unknown to the "sitter," finding a difficulty possibly

L

Collusion, in one form or another, was a contingency which the authorities had ever to guard against. Isolated as were the crews of coastguard stations in many parts of the kingdom, there was an ever-present temptation to the men, if not actually to connive, to wink at the practices of the surrounding population—practices in which it is well to remember they had themselves most probably at one time engaged, and with which they possibly still inwardly sympathised. To ensure probity amongst the various ranks of the preventive service under such conditions was not always an easy task, and if a weak brother succumbed to temptations now and again, the fact will cause no surprise to the student of human nature. Indeed, considering the unpopularity of the service amongst the masses and the strong temptations that were held out, the wonder is that a far greater number of defections are not recorded than is actually the case.

During the period when the coasts of Kent and Sussex were guarded by the blockade men, collusion was notoriously rife, and it is a curious fact that after the coastguard was substituted, the worst cases of the same nature occurred on this portion of the seaboard. Thus, the very year in which the blockade was removed several runs took place in the Deal district, and collusion being suspected, two of the mounted guard, two chief boatmen, and two boatmen of the coastguard were dismissed (1831).

A flagrant case of bribery occurred the following year in the same district, which is thus referred to (October 10th, 1832) :—"A big landing of goods is

in obtaining good liquor in this remote spot, or for lack of excitement, "ventured" a cargo of spirits on their own account, were "bowled out," and promptly cashiered.

discovered to have taken place at Hope Point, Kings-
down station, on the guard of Henry Cogen, who
deserted. On inquiry it is found that the chief officer
was in the habit of telling the men overnight their
guards for the following morning, hence the smugglers with their usual cunning would not have trusted
so valuable a cargo to chance, had they not, owing to
this improper practice, known where and when to
find this corrupt character." And again, the year
after, a boatman of the Walmer station in the same
district is dismissed for receiving a bribe of £20 from
a smuggler, and arranging for the landing of goods
on his guard.

That the practice of corrupting the men was still
largely and successfully resorted to in this district for
some time after the above cases were discovered, is
shown by instructions issued to the officers of stations
directing them to "try and discover a bribed man
amongst their crews, which can with ease be effected"
—the order goes on to say, "by looking to the mode of
living of the men, and by ascertaining if the men off
watch are really in their beds, as a case lately came
to knowledge where a bribed character (a boatman in
the Deal district) actually assisted the smugglers in
working a cargo of fifty tubs upon the guard of one
of his messmates after he had been relieved from
day-watch, and, of course, supposed to be in bed, for
which he received a bribe of £10, and returned to
his quarters ready for midnight relief." *

In some instances even officers in charge of stations

---

* *Apropos* of this, the following order from the Brighton district
(1831) is worthy of note :—" There being reason to fear that an attempt
will be made to corrupt our men through the medium of females, it is
my direction that patrols hold no communication with any person,
either male or female."

so far forgot their allegiance as to connive at the very practices they were employed to suppress. At Lulworth, in Dorsetshire, for example (1827), the chief officer, Lieutenant B——, R.N., was dismissed under very suspicious circumstances, viz., allowing a run to take place with every appearance of connivance on his part ; for not reporting the run, and denying that such landing had taken place ; for not attempting to secure the goods after they had been landed ; for having withdrawn a patrol from the place where the run occurred, and sending him to another guard ; and for having been frequently at the house of, and in company with, a reputed smuggler.

The service was certainly to be congratulated on having parted with Lieutenant B——, who would seem to have mistaken his vocation. This affair had a sad sequel, for the officer who succeeded Lieutenant B—— at Lulworth so exasperated the smugglers by the activity with which he interfered with their illicit practices, that they brutally murdered him and threw his body over a cliff.

A somewhat similar case is that of Lieutenant P——, R.N., chief officer at Paignton, in Devon, who was dismissed for releasing two smugglers who were taken escorting a cart containing contraband goods ; for prevailing on his crew to sign a false seizure report; and for concealing the fact that any men were present when a seizure was made of a cart, two horses, and forty-six tubs of spirits.

In Norfolk, at about the same time, Lieutenant J——, R.N., was dismissed for continuing an intimacy with a notorious smuggler, after having been repeatedly cautioned by his inspecting commander.

But perhaps the most singular case of this description occurred at Looe, in Cornwall, from which station during a very short space of time no less than three chief officers in succession were dismissed under circumstances which pointed in the most direct manner to collusion.

The only other case of note in which an officer was concerned is that of Lieutenant Samuel B——, R.N., in charge of a station in Ireland, who was dismissed for drawing his sword on the Rev. J. C—— and another gentleman, and thrusting it through the waistcoat of the latter, and for grossly insulting a respectable farmer.

CHAPTER II.

Negligence of Patrols—Precautions Against Surprise—Assault on a Patrol at Sandgate—Running with the Hare and Hunting with the Hounds — Smuggler Recruits — Improvements in Discipline — Comptroller-General's Opinion of the Coastguard.

AN offence, at one time rather frequent, and which was visited with a severity that to the uninitiated might seem uncalled for, was that of patrols allowing themselves to be secured by smugglers without offering a proper resistance. It must be borne in mind, however, that the men were provided with firearms for the express purpose of defending themselves against sudden attacks, and the very fact of being surprised and overpowered argued a want of vigilance in the first place, and of courage in the second. There was always a strong temptation to succumb to superior numbers, instead of showing the bold front which was often quite sufficient to check the attack of smugglers until assistance arrived, and therefore, unless the clearest evidence was forthcoming of the men having used their arms in self-defence, and offered a proper resistance, they were almost invariably punished by dismissal.

The fact is collusion was apt to assume so many sinister disguises, that it would never have done to admit the plea of a surprise as a valid excuse for a run. There was nothing easier for a corrupt man than to allow himself to be surprised, secured, and his arms taken from him while a run of goods was accomplished—in consideration of favours received of course—and this became so frequent at one period that the authorities determined to put a stop to it by the exercise of a severity which, but for a knowledge of the facts above stated, might seem unwarrantable. Thus, in 1822, we find the chief officer and riding officer of Cromer station, in Norfolk, dismissed for allowing themselves to be secured by smugglers, and although in this particular instance it is difficult to believe that corrupt motives were at work, it would never have done to pass by lightly over such a want of vigilance or courage as was here implied.

There were cases, of course, when the utmost vigilance on the part of the patrols was of no avail against the machinations of the foe who was as cunning as he was unscrupulous in the use of means to his end, and every allowance was made for the men under these conditions. Thus, in the Folkestone district (1836), information was given to the coast-guard of an intended run to be carried out as follows :—" Four men of desperate character are hired to secure two adjoining patrols—two to each, and if they succeed, the boat is to come in immediately, if they fail the run is to be forced "

In the blockade days the smugglers usually

gained their ends by bribing the sentries, but with the establishment of the coastguard the difficulties connected with the arrangements for a run of goods increased every year, and the importance of securing the patrols as a preliminary to a smuggling transaction on a large scale became more important as time went on. This was, of course, well known to the authorities, and on certain portions of the Kent coast the patrols were specially cautioned to be on their guard against surprise. In the Deal district, for instance, the inspecting commander enjoined on all chief officers " to caution the men before going on duty against surprise, by not allowing anyone to approach their guard till satisfied it is their officer, as I am persuaded the smugglers will attempt to seize them at their posts by assuming a false character. Chief officers are also to be properly armed and on their guard when passing through plantations, turning corners, or near cliff edges, as I am informed on the very best authority that each company of smugglers will be accompanied by a number of 'batmen,' whose first and grand object will be to secure the officer " (November, 1831).

That cautions of this nature were by no means superfluous is shown by an occurrence in the Folkestone district so late as the year 1842, when on the night of the 2nd October a patrol was seized by smugglers at Sandgate, and had his arms taken from him. The way this was effected was by whistling to the man, who, on going to see what it was, found himself tripped up by five men who held him down and tried to stop his mouth or choke him. His cries gave the alarm, and the smugglers ran off, taking his arms with them.

A curious case of running with the hare and

hunting with the hounds is that of James Rowatt, boatman, and a native of Polperro, who was dismissed in the year 1827 for having purchased a boat intended to be employed in smuggling.

In 1831 a mariner of the *Tartar*, revenue cruiser, is dismissed for making known the means taken to disguise the vessel when in chase of a smuggler.

A curious case was that of a boatman who had contracted Oriental notions on the subject of matrimony, or, to quote from the official version of his offence, "for having two wives, and families by each." Though why, having taken unto himself a second wife, it should have been regarded as specially sinful having "families by each" passeth understanding.

In many instances the men who were dismissed from the coastguard service went over to the opposite camp and became expert and active smugglers, deriving no small advantage, doubtless, from their knowledge of coastguard routine. Thus, two boys belonging to the *Rose*, revenue cruiser, natives of Cawsand in Cornwall, who were dismissed in 1826, took to smuggling, and eventually became some of the most notorious smugglers in the place.

The same may be said of Richard S——, at one time gunner of the *Nimble*, revenue cruiser—whose crew, it will be remembered, were dismissed for being concerned in a smuggling transaction at Exmouth (1832). Also of Philip L——, at one time a boy in the *Fox*, revenue cruiser.

The *Mary*, of Cawsand, a well-known smuggling craft, was owned and commanded by John F——, formerly chief boatman in the coastguard, dismissed from his station in the Isle of Wight for refusing to proceed with his crew to assist in preserving the public peace on the occasion of a riot (1830). His smuggling career was brief, however, for he was lost in the vessel on her first trip

All the above belonged to Cawsand. Of others may be mentioned Thomas H——, at one time in the *Repulse*, revenue cruiser, and afterwards in the *Daniel and William*, one of the most notorious smuggling vessels on the south coast. Also George P——, native of Gorran Haven, Cornwall, dismissed from the *Fox* on suspicion of being concerned in a run of goods which took place at Gorran Haven while he was at home on leave, and who afterwards took to smuggling.

Then we find a vessel engaged in smuggling on the coast of Galway with Anthony M——, late commander of the *Nepean*, revenue cruiser, on board as pilot, and the names of many other men occur from time to time in the same connection, only one of whom need be mentioned here, viz., Richard K——*, a native of Yealm, in Devonshire, who, after serving for a number of years in the coastguard, turned smuggler, and for some twenty years gave more trouble to the men of the preventive service than any other smuggler on the coast. He eventually became a shipbroker at Plymouth, in which capacity he was able to indulge his tastes for illicit trading with more profit and less risk than before, and achieved a more enduring reputation as the " smuggler broker " than he ever could have attained in his original capacity as guardian of the revenue.

It would be easy, of course, to prolong the list of offences, but enough has been said to give the reader an idea of the peculiar temptations to which the force was exposed, and those to which the men most readily

* A brother of this enterprising trader rose to the rank of admiral in the Royal Navy.

succumbed ; and if the dismissals were more numerous at one time than might be expected in a branch of the public service to which high responsibilities were attached, there can be no doubt that as time went on and the bonds of discipline were drawn tighter, a vast improvement was to be noticed in the general tone and conduct of the force, an improvement which it may be observed did not pass unnoticed by those whose position enabled them to realise the full significance of this change.

Of the several officers charged with the administration of this department of the public service, there was no one whose opinion is entitled to more respect than the Comptroller-general, who, from a connection with the force extending over a long course of years, commencing almost from its first inception, must have acquired a pretty clear insight into its working, as well as of the merits of the officers and men composing it. In resigning his office on promotion in January, 1842, Admiral Bowles issued a valedictory address to the force, which will form a fitting conclusion to this chapter :—

" *Coastguard Office,*

"*January 5th,* 1842.

" The Comptroller-general cannot resign the office he has so long held, and which the zeal, obedience, and good conduct of the officers and men under his orders have enabled him to fill with so much pride and pleasure, without recording his most sincere acknowledgments to those by whose cordial co-operation, subordination, and fidelity, the revenue has been protected, the danger and losses by shipwreck so materially diminished, and the public tranquillity often preserved on emergency, when no other armed force could be procured in aid of the civil power.

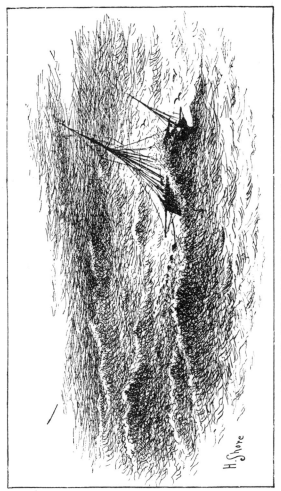

A CAWSAND SMUGGLING BOAT RIDING BY HER TUBS IN A GALE.

"The Comptroller-general is fully aware of the exemplary manner in which those various services have been performed.   He has, he trusts, always endeavoured to do justice to the exertions, and to reward the merits of those who have distinguished themselves in the execution of such arduous and laborious duties, and it is with the most heartfelt satisfaction that he has assured his successor of the full confidence with which he may rely on the fidelity, discipline, and steadiness of the whole force about to be placed under his orders, to which he him-self now bids farewell with the sincerest wishes for their future credit and welfare, and with the firmest confidence that the coastguard will preserve unim-paired the high character it has acquired and main-tained.   WILLIAM BOWLES."

Part V.

THE SMUGGLER:

HIS CHARACTERISTICS AND METHODS.

CHAPTER I.

The Halcyon Days of Smuggling—An Unwelcome Change—Opposition of the Masses—Nature of a Smuggling Transaction—Qualifications of a Smuggler—A Fine School of Seamanship—Advantages of a Direct Run—Method of Sinking a Cargo.

IN the old free-trade days the smuggler was regarded, if not as the most respectable, certainly as one of the most useful members of society, and we have seen with what a delightful simplicity of method he plied his vocation. It was, in fact, a mere question of industry and numbers. But with the establishment of the blockade, together with the introduction of an efficient preventive service, a wholly new range of conditions was developed, and the smuggler observed with sorrow that the jolly times he had hitherto enjoyed were drawing to a close, and that he must either adapt himself to the altered circumstances of the trade, or seek pastures new. Being a practical man, however, he experienced little difficulty in accommodating himself to the times, and noting that science, cunning, and resource were now the chief elements of success, he threw himself heart and soul into the business, and during the next twenty years displayed an amount of skill, daring, and ingenuity which might well serve as an example to toilers in more prosaic fields.

That the smugglers and their allies should regard the new-fangled notions that were being promulgated by the authorities with contempt and aversion was, of course, only natural ; and that they bitterly resented the efforts of the executive to interfere with their calling we can well understand.   But, unfortunately, they gave expression to these feelings in a form which we must all condemn, and which, indeed, could never be tolerated in a country aspiring to the title of civilised.   The armed conflicts which had taken place from time to time under the old *régime* between the free-traders and the king's officers were at first renewed with almost greater frequency than of old, while a spirit of lawlessness and violent antagonism to authority was displayed along a con-siderable portion of the southern coast which it is difficult now to realise.

It is always a troublesome task trying to inculcate sound ideas on the subject of " duty " amongst people who view all attempts to enforce a law which they dislike as an act of coercion.   The idea of there being any reasonableness in the payment of taxes on such necessaries of life as liquor and baccy was quite beyond the comprehension of the simple folk of old ; and it was only after some twenty years of conflict that they became unwilling converts to the new doctrine.

We have seen what manner of man the smuggler of free-trade days was ; it now remains to give some account of his representative of more recent times, and his ways of doing business.

Smuggling methods were, of course, infinitely varied, depending, as we shall see, upon a great variety of circumstances, as, for instance, the nature of the coast, the distance to the opposite shore, the positions of the preventive stations, and strength of the crews. Speaking generally, there were three distinct operations to be provided for in a smuggling transaction— first, bringing over the goods ; second, landing them ; third, running them in-

MⒹE *of* Carrying TvBS

land, the primary and principal object being to elude, or, if neces-sary, to break through the triple line of de-fence which encircled the coast, and to con-vey the goods with the utmost possible despatch to safe *depôts* pending their distribu-tion.

The *personnel* en-gaged in these opera-tions may be divided into three classes— first, the freighter, or principal ; second, the boatmen, or agents employed for bringing over the goods ; third, the tub-carriers, or porters, or land smugglers as they were called in old times, whose duty it was to clear the boats and convey the goods inland.

Of the three, the second was by far the nobler calling—if, indeed, such a term be permissible with reference to smuggling—involving endurance, presence of mind, pluck, ready resource, besides being attended with great risk, and often terrible hardship, the winter as we have seen, being the favourite time of year for plying the trade ; in short, to be a successful sea-

smuggler, it was necessary to display the best characteristics of British seamen ; and that the smuggling
trade was a matchless school of seamanship, and
produced a matchless class of seamen, we have
abundant evidence. "Almost every man was the
beau idéal of a British sailor," says the historian of
Guernsey in describing the smugglers who visited
this great *entrepôt* during the early years of the
century : "active, daring, and prodigal of their
dangerous gains, they forgot, in the pleasures of the
day, the risks of the morrow." *

The three lines of defence which had to be eluded
or overcome in a smuggling transaction consisted, as
previously explained, of the revenue cutters afloat,
and the coastguard and mounted guard on shore.
Of these, the coastguard was the one from which the
gravest danger was to be apprehended. The vigilance
of the men was so keen, and the chain of patrols so
complete, that it was useless now attempting a run
without first ascertaining, by careful observation, the
weak points in the defence, and making every preparation beforehand.

In many respects the smugglers, being the attacking party, enjoyed great advantages over the defence,
not only from their superior ingenuity and cunning,
but especially by reason of their power of massing

---

* Another Guernsey man, recording his youthful experiences, bears
the following high tribute to the attributes of the smugglers :—" There
was a class of vessels which, when a boy, were my admiration, and I
could never cease gazing at them—I mean the cutters and luggers ;
. . . and the smugglers with their athletic crews, who looked and
lived like gentlemen. How many happy hours they have made me
pass by merely looking at them. That hardy race is gone by, and is,
it would seem, extinct . . Smuggling, with all its faults, had its
advantages too, as it created and kept up a bold and active race of seamen."—Tupper's " History of Guernsey " (1840).

their forces on a given point, without notice, on a long attenuated line of coastguard patrols, and of choosing their own time of attack.

Besides all this, the smugglers possessed a surprising knowledge of the duties and routine of the coastguard service, acquired partly by observation, but often by means of " perverts " from the coastguard camp. As a matter of fact, the ranks of the smugglers were constantly receiving accessions from their opponents—men discharged for bad conduct, as well as others, attracted, perhaps, by the large profits that still, in their opinion, counterbalanced the attendant risks. It is well known that some of the most successful smugglers had served first in the coastguard; while, on the other hand, the smugglers contributed several valuable recruits to the ranks of the coastguard.

If it was feasible, the smugglers greatly preferred making one job of the business; though, of course, this could only be managed when the distance to be traversed by the boats was short, so that the time of their arrival on the coast could be depended on with some certainty, and the carriers be assembled, ready to act on the moment. A direct run of this sort was a common occurrence in Kent, and in many parts of Sussex, while farther west, and north, it was rather the exception than the rule, although the length of the guards compensated, in some measure, for the difficulties experienced in calculating the time of a boat's arrival.

Where it was too risky to attempt a direct landing, the business would be managed as follows :—On the arrival of the smuggling boat off the coast, the goods would be sunk to the bottom, on well-defined bearings, the task of picking them up afterwards, and

M

"working" them—*i.e.*, landing them—being entrusted to local men, who, from their intimate knowledge of the coastguard routine, were best fitted for this important and extremely hazardous duty.

Method of Slinging Tubs

The tub-sling consisted of a piece of small left-handed rope (French), secured round each end of the tub, so as to leave two ends, or "tails," of equal length. If the cargo was sunk, one only of these tails would be used for fastening the tub to the sinking-rope, so that if, as was usually the case, this tail was cut off in the hurry of "working' the crop, there would still be one left. The tub-carrier would then be able to sling his pair of tubs by taking the tail from each tub over the shoulder and securing it to the other tub, as shown in the drawing on page 191.

Along the Kent and Sussex shore, where direct runs were in high favour, the goods were either brought across in smuggling galleys—very fast boats especially built for this purpose, rowing ten and twelve oars, and making the passage in a few hours— or in "tub-boats," mere shells, run up of cheap materials, roughly put together, and of little value. These boats were towed across by French luggers, dropped within a convenient distance of the appointed spot, and then rowed on shore. Being worth little, they were often broken up after a run ; or, if surprised, abandoned. It was, indeed, an axiom with the preventive men "that the smugglers wholly disregard the loss of their boats, provided they can run their goods."

In sinking a cargo the *modus operandi* was as follows :—The tubs, which it must be premised were always supplied by the merchants abroad ready fitted with rope slings, were secured, at intervals of a few feet, along a stout rope called the "sinking rope," or "drift line ;" between each tub a stone, sufficiently large to sink the tub, was attached to the same rope, the whole being hung round the vessel outside by slight fastenings from the gunwale, with stouter ones at bow and stern, ready to be cut away and slipped at a moment's notice. To reduce the risk as much as possible, the preparations for sinking were usually completed before the smuggling boat approached the coast, so that in case of alarm the cargo could be instantly slipped.* And here it may be as well to explain that a smuggling boat usually timed its departure from the foreign port so as to sight the British coast just before dusk, veiling its movements from the coastguard watchman by mixing with fishing boats, or "dousing" its sails till darkness set in ; and then, with all the stealth and power of seeing in

---

* In the event of meeting a contrary gale which threatened to compromise the safety of the boat, it was the custom with the more expert West country smugglers to "lighten ship" by putting all the tubs out in a long string, and to ride by them until the weather moderated. (*See* sketch, page 187.)

M 2

the dark which is associated with the cat, the boat would stand in as close as she dare.   A suitable spot

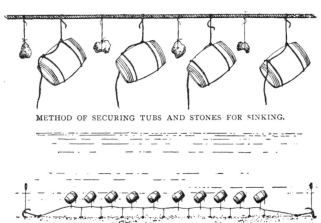

METHOD OF SECURING TUBS AND STONES FOR SINKING.

A CROP SUNK.

having been selected, down went the helm, the boat shot up into the wind, and watching for the moment when her "way" was lost, word would be passed to "cut away," careful cross-bearings of prominent points of land being simultaneously taken, and as soon as "all clear" was given, the boat's head would be "payed" off, and an offing made as soon as possible.

CHAPTER II.

Anchoring a Crop of Tubs—"Stinkibus"—Working the Goods—Smuggling Dodges—Precautions Before a Run—How a Run was Effected—The Informer—Overpowering the Patrols—Forcing the Runs—Fighting Gangs–Concealments for Run Goods.

To ensure a "crop of goods" from drifting from its bearings an anchor was secured to one end of the drift line ; and if the position was exposed, or the goods likely to be long under water, they were further secured by an anchor at the other end of the line.

A crop sunk in deep water, provided it was secured in a workmanlike manner, would lie for several weeks without damage ; but as goods were sometimes put down hurriedly in bad situations tubs were often " chafed " off the sinking rope, and by drifting about, or washing ashore, betrayed the presence of the crop to the ever-watchful coastguard.

As a rule the contents of the tubs suffered no deterioration from submersion but occasionally—depending, it is said, on the nature of the bottom—after very long submersion the spirits turned bad, and a crop of this sort was known amongst coastguardmen in the West of England as "stinkibus," from the offensive smell given off. The feelings of the men on hauling in a crop of " stinkibus," after creeping for several consecutive days, can be more easily imagined than described !

The next thing to be arranged for after sinking a crop was "working" it, an operation entrusted, as already stated, to local smugglers. It was a delicate and risky business, requiring nerve, resource, and experience, and depending, in regard to the methods employed, to a great extent on local conditions. For instance, if sunk off the open coast, where no fishing operations could be used as a cloak to the illicit proceedings, the entire crop would be worked and run in one operation. In this case, the men entrusted with the job would start off soon after dark, in one or more boats, using every artifice to disguise their movements and intentions, and usually, if there was reason to suppose that their departure had been noticed, rowing for some distance in a contrary direction

to that of the goods. Then, when an offing had
been gained, the boat would be turned and rowed as
quickly as possible to the real spot. The cross-
bearings having been fixed, "creepers" would be
dropped and dragged backwards and forwards along
the bottom until "brought up" by the goods. In
some instances, if, for example, the goods had drifted
from their position and could not be hooked, "sweeping" was resorted to, a process already described in
connection with the coastguard.

The goods having been hooked, they were
promptly hauled up, cut from the drift line, and
stowed in the boat, the sinking line and anchors being
saved if possible, although, often enough, in the
hurry and excitement of the moment, these had to be
sacrificed to the safety of the men and goods; for it
was ten to one if the coastguard boat was not afloat,
and at the slightest sound it was a case of "cut and
run" and devil take the hindmost. Indeed, there were
few operations which more frequently afforded a
practical illustration of the truth of the old adage
that "there is many a slip," etc.

The next thing was to run the goods, an operation
which will be described in due course.

On many parts of the coast the sunken goods could
be worked with more deliberation and less risk. In
places where crabbing was largely followed, for instance, goods were sunk by choice on the crabbing
grounds, and while the other boats were working their
pots the smugglers would take the opportunity of
pulling up the end of the sinking line—probably
buoyed in this case in the same way as the crab-pots
were—cutting off three or four tubs, and stowing them
snugly underneath the pots in the bottom of the
boat, row quietly on shore, and, watching the oppor-

tunity, run the tubs in broad daylight. In other places, again, where seaweed cutting was practised on the rocks and islands off the coast, tubs would often be run on shore under a load of weed. There was, in fact, no limit to the number of dodges in vogue, and it would only weary the reader to enumerate the various channels through which the patrons of the trade drew their supplies of the good old cognac, which they loved, not always wisely, but too well.

In the various operations of smuggling there was no more dangerous or exciting an event than a run of goods on a large scale. It was at this particular stage of the proceedings that the smugglers incurred the greatest risk of coming into collision with the coastguard, and not only of losing their goods but of forfeiting their liberty, for a time at least. To ensure a successful run it was necessary to fix on a spot, where, judging from a careful observation of the patrols, there was least likelihood of discovery. The time for the landing was another matter of the highest importance. Before deciding on these points it was a common practice with the smugglers to set a watch for several consecutive days and nights on the movements of the coastguard patrols, who would be "shadowed" from the time they left the station till their return next morning, special attention being paid to the line of route they followed, going out and coming in, the place and time of conference with the patrols of flank stations, and the usual hour at which the patrols were withdrawn and the coast left in charge of the day watchman.

A careful study of the above data usually disclosed certain important facts, showing a degree of regularity in the movements of the coastguardmen which, however admirable from a disciplinary point of

view, offered facilities for running a cargo which the
expert smuggler was not slow to avail himself of.

The time and place having been decided on, the
next thing to be considered was the collection of a
sufficiency of porters or tub-carriers, of whom any
number could be got together in those days without

AN OLD TUB-CARRIER.

the slightest difficulty, consisting for the most part of
agricultural labourers and artisans, attracted by the
prospect of earning half-a-crown or five shillings for
the night's work.   These men would be warned off
the day before that on which the run was intended,
with full directions where to rendezvous ; and shortly
before the appointed hour they would flock in from
all directions, remaining quiet and well out of observation some little distance behind the guards—a barn,
cottage, or farm-building affording them shelter until

the critical moment arrived. It was impossible, of course, in every case to guarantee the arrival of the tub-boat at the precise hour named, but the time usually selected for a run was in the early part of the night, to avoid keeping a large body of men hanging about with nothing to do for any length of time. Long waiting not only made them restless and noisy, but, as a matter of course, increased the risk of discovery.

Everything being ready, the man in charge of the party would be all eyes and ears, so to speak, to detect not only the approach of the boat but the presence of the patrols. At length a dark object looms dimly through the gloom, the word is passed along to the carriers to be ready, and almost before the boat's keel grates on the beach, the party surround her, seize and sling the tubs, every man a pair, and make off with all despatch inland. The whole affair is over in from three to five minutes, and all that remains the following morning to inform the coastguard of what has occurred are some pieces of "sling-stuff" and the tracks of the men's feet across the sand. The retreat of the smuggling party inland was not, as may be supposed, always a very orderly procceding, and on a dark night, over broken ground, the carriers had tough work getting along with their tubs. It was customary, on reaching what was considered safe distance inland, to call a halt, when a flagon, or small cask of spirits— which always found a place in a run cargo—would be broached and passed around. It was on these occasions, that by the indiscreet libations of the younger hands, and the resultant exaltation of spirits, the whereabouts of the party would sometimes be revealed to the coastguard, and mischief ensued. " Eh ! dear me," said an old smuggler to the writer, " I've seen some pretty 'rigs' along o' they tub-carriers at times, I can tell ye." And he would recount with a merry chuckle the extraordinary scenes of drunkenness that often took place after a run of goods in the old style.

A "run" was a risky thing at the best, and the apprehensions of the smugglers were often increased by the dread lest the informer had been plying his insidious trade, in which case all the craft and vigilance displayed would be of no avail. Old smugglers invariably declare that the informer was a product of later times, but there was always a pretty crop of doublefaced scoundrels about in every age ready to sell their souls for a share of "information money," and the informer was a factor that could never be safely omitted from the smuggler's calculations.

It was quite possible, in the natural order of things, that a patrol might light on the scene at an unfortunate moment, and throw matters into confusion, and it was on occasions such as this that the nerve and resource of the older hands stood the venturers in good stead, and often staved off a disaster. For, as a rule, the tub-carriers—country bumpkins mostly, with a fine regard for their own skins—would cut and run at the first whisper of alarm, "lightening ship" without the least hesitation, and leaving their freight as a prize to the foe, and thus, of course, forfeiting their night's wage. The older men who had been out before would try and save one at least of their tubs, and even show fight rather than relinquish their freight or be taken.

As an encouragement to the men to hold on to their tubs when attacked, the venturers were ac-

customed to pay ten shillings for every tub saved on
these occasions.

If the coast was too well guarded to admit of a
run being accomplished without discovery, it was a
common practice as a preliminary measure to seize
and overpower the patrols on the guard selected for
the attempt, especially along the Kent and Sussex
shore. In some instances the smugglers, rather than
run the risk themselves, would hire desperate characters for the job, and these ruffians, creeping up
behind the patrols on a stormy night, would watch
their opportunity, and while the men were chatting
or having a quiet pipe, dash at them and have them
down and their arms removed before ever they could
raise an alarm. The boat would then be signalled in,
and the run accomplished.

A " forced run " was a run effected in spite of the
coastguard, and was of common occurrence along the
south-east coast during the first quarter of the
present century. It was, in fact, the rule, whenever a
large and valuable cargo was at stake. The arrangements for forcing a run were necessarily more
elaborate and extensive than in other cases, the
essential difference being in the employment of an
armed party, or " fighting gang," as it was called, for
the protection of the " tub-carriers," in the event of
attack. The weapons carried on these occasions were
swingles—instruments like a flail—" bats " (the local
term for long ash bludgeons), and firearms, and many
very serious affrays took place between these
" gangs " and the revenue forces. The practice of
forcing the runs continued as late as the year 1833,
at which time one of the most desperate encounters
that ever disgraced the southern counties was continued through the greater part of a November night,

and resulted in the death of four of the smuggling party, their complete defeat, and the loss of nearly all their goods.*

Far inland, out of harm's way, horses and carts would usually be in waiting to relieve the carriers of their tubs, and to carry them off to the smuggling depôts, which, in those days, abounded in all the maritime counties. But just as it is never safe to halloo before you are out of the wood, so the smugglers could never reckon on the goods being safe because the coastguard patrols had been evaded, bearing in mind that it was the special duty of the mounted guard "to examine carefully the by-roads, lanes, etc., for the purpose of discovering any preparations that might be made by the smugglers for effecting a landing by assembling carts or men. . . and, in the event of a run being effected, pursuing the company and endeavouring to intercept the carts in which they are conveying the goods."

Remembering, therefore, that "the best laid schemes o' mice and men gang aft agley," the smugglers, with a view to minimising the risks of capture, were in the habit of excavating "private places" or

---

* Some curious details concerning smuggling in Sussex are furnished in a report by Mr. Majendie on "the disturbed districts of East Sussex" to her Majesty's commissioners, "as to the administration and operations of the Poor Law" (1833), from which the following extracts are made :—"The smugglers are divided into two classes, the carriers or bearers who receive from five shillings per night and upwards, according to the number of tubs they secure, and the "batmen," so called from the provincial term of bat for a bludgeon they use, who consider themselves of a superior class. They go out in disguise, frequently with their faces blackened, and now with firearms ; they confine their services to the protection of others, and are paid twenty shillings or more per night, *and many, perhaps most of them, are, at the same time, in receipt of parish relief.*"

concealments, in the shape of caves and underground cellars in secluded places on the coast as well as inland, where the goods could be deposited pending favourable opportunities for conveying them to their destinations. In some parts of England the coast may almost be said to be honeycombed, figuratively speaking, with these " cave dwellings" of other days, and, notwithstanding the obliteration of many by the action of water and other causes, several are still pointed out by the old men who knew their uses, while others, known only to those who excavated them, remain undiscovered, the secret of their whereabouts having died with their owners.

Besides these concealments, there was scarcely a house along the coast, or a farmhouse, or inn within easy distance, but had its cellar or " private place," or " hide " as these receptacles were called, and the ingenuity displayed in their construction was certainly very wonderful. So admirably were they contrived in many instances, that on change of ownership their very existence has been unsuspected, until the subsidence of a beam, or alterations in the house have laid open cavities which doubtless held many a good tub of brandy in their time.

CHAPTER III.

Modern Developments—Collecting a Freight—The Cnannel Passage— Duties of a Spotsman—Rafting a Cargo—Smuggling Signals—Honour among Smugglers—Profits of the Trade—The Sea Smuggler—Land Smugglers—Sea Rovers and Smugglers.

A FEW words concerning the method of procedure in a smuggling transaction and the vocation will have been made clear to the reader from beginning to end.

In the days of free-trade the business was chiefly conducted by smuggling companies on a grand scale, like any other commercial transaction, and a vast amount of capital was embarked in the business. Under the new conditions, however, the trade, though enormous in the aggregate, had perforce drifted into more numerous and smaller channels, and was conducted chiefly by individuals, who, as agents, made arrangements for the disposal of the funds entrusted to them by their patrons in the manner that seemed most suitable. These agents were the principals in smuggling transactions, and were usually called "freighters," from the fact that they collected the freight-money, and chartered the vessels to bring over the goods.

The procedure was somewhat as follows :—The freighter having collected enough money for a cargo, proceeded to engage a vessel, and having arranged this matter would embark and set off without delay for the port selected for the purchase of the spirits. Before leaving, however, he would arrange with his confederates the various details connected with the intended run—time, place, etc.—usually naming one or more alternative places in the event of being " put off" from that decided on in the first instance. As there were no telegraphs or steamers in those days, by means of which alterations of plan could be rapidly communicated to the parties concerned, there was necessarily a considerable element of chance in the matter, the uncertainty increasing with the distance to be traversed from the opposite coast.

To calculate the time of a vessel's arrival required, therefore, very nice judgment, depending as it did on a variety of causes beyond the control of man, such

as direction and strength of wind, set of tide, etc. ;
but old smugglers could generally tell pretty nearly
when to expect the vessel, and during the afternoon
preceding the run would be anxiously scanning the
horizon for the well-known craft. We are speaking
now of cases in which the distance to be traversed
was considerable, and the size of boat large.

The movements of the smuggling boat, and preparations usually made on board before approaching

The sinking stones were always bent on, and kept on deck till just before
slipping.

the coast, have been already described. The running
of a cargo direct from the vessel or boat involved far
greater risks, and therefore required greater care and
preparation. In this case the boat, under cover of
darkness—the least suggestion of a moon being fatal
to the chances of success—would stand in as near to
the spot as safety would admit, the utmost vigilance
being necessary to detect any symptoms of danger, or
the slightest signal from the party on shore, whose
duty it was to watch all the approaches to the landing

place, and instantly flash off a warning to the boat in case of alarm. These signals consisted of a fire lighted on a prominent point inland, a " flink " with a flint and steel, which on a dark night was easily discernible by the practised eye of a smuggler quite a mile from the shore, and a flash from a dark lantern, or peculiarly-constructed telescopic lantern, which, while throwing a bright light seaward, concealed the rays from observers on either side.

The smuggler who acted as pilot on these occasions, guiding the vessel in with cat-like acuteness of vision to the appointed spot, was known in smuggling parlance as " spotsman," and the skill and intelligence displayed by these men was little short of miraculous. The services of the "spotsman" were only required when the cargo was about to be run on a coast which was strange to the master of the vessel, the freighter often acting as his own " spotsman."

On arrival at a suitable distance from the shore— the coast being clear for the run—the sinking stones would be hastily cut off from the sinking rope, a punt or small boat would dash in with the end of a rope the other end of which would be secured to the string of tubs, and on reaching the beach the end of the line would be seized by the tub-carriers, and the tubs " rafted " ashore—as the operation of floating them in was called.

As regards signals, it may be remarked that as making signals of any sort—even "whooping " to boats off the coast at night—was an indictable offence, according to the "smuggling laws," the utmost circumspection was necessary to avoid detection.

Just picture the feelings of a free and independent elector of Great Britain at the present day, who, when taking his walks abroad on a fine night, and happening

to strike a match wherewith to light his pipe, is suddenly pounced on by a couple of burly coastguardmen
and marched off to the nearest station! And yet
such was the fate that awaited anyone who in the old
smuggling days was unguarded enough to make what
might be interpreted into a smuggling signal. There
will be more to say on this subject hereafter.

The goods having been landed, it was the object
of those on board the smuggling boat to get away
from the scene of operations as soon as possible ; the
crew in the meantime busying themselves in removing
every trace of their late cargo. The importance that
was attached to a piece of French bread, a bit of left-
handed rope, or a piece of "sling-stuff" in a boat,
must seem incomprehensible to the uninitiated ; but
it was by close attention to these details that success
in the smuggler's vocation was best ensured, and the
suspicions of the preventive men disarmed. The
smallest thing in those days was enough to supply a
clue to the business in which a boat had been engaged,
leading to arrest, with detention and all its vexatious
delays and anxieties, and for that reason the expert
smuggler would set to work, immediately after a run,
in removing everything likely to excite suspicion concerning the illicit nature of his proceedings.

The saying that "there is honour amongst thieves"
was curiously illustrated in the dealings of the smugglers, their staunchness towards each other being certainly very remarkable, especially when the slender
nature of the tie which bound them together is considered. True, the informer, like the poor, is always
with us, a smuggler might complain, but when we
bear in mind the large number of men necessarily
engaged in a smuggling transaction, it was very much
to their credit that so few cases have been recorded of

N

treachery on the part of accomplices. And even when a humble tub-carrier was captured and sent to " quod," there is no instance on record—so far, at least. as the writer is aware of—in which this individual was known to have " rounded " on his employers.

To what extent the smugglers ultimately profited by their vocation can now only be matter of speculation.   Certainly, some of the " principals " made large sums—for a time, at least ; but so far as the writer's inquiries have extended, the case of a smuggler who permanently and materially benefited himself by the illicit trade was certainly exceptional. As a rule, it was all the other way, and many curious instances might be cited in proof of this statement.

After all, smuggling was only a species of gambling, with the additional risk of imprisonment, or five years in a man-of-war, and, like every other sort of gambling. without doubt exercised a most demoralising influence on all concerned in it. An immense amount of capital was embarked in the trade, and an equally large number of people were by its means afforded a precarious sort of employment. Besides which, it offered a field for adventurous spirits, attracted no less by the large profits than the spice of danger involved, and, so far as the sea smugglers were concerned, developed a magnificent class of seamen.   There was a fascination about smuggling, too, which possessed an irresistible attraction to a large class—not of ne'er-do-wells alone, but of individuals who, with no lack of ability, had an unconquerable aversion to steady employment of any sort.   The very ingenuity which these people brought to their tasks shows that, but for the unfortunate bent of their genius, they possessed qualities which ought to have ensured success in more honourable walks of life, in proof of which may be

cited the fact that many of these men who, through
some occult means, had been brought to see the error
of their ways, and had entered the coastguard service,
rose subsequently to posts of honour and responsibility.*

The "smuggler bold" was a product of the times,
and though a desperate fellow enough when driven to
bay, fighting was not his vocation ; it was rather an
accident of it. For the rest, he was a man of like
passions with ourselves, and if not the heroic creature
fervid imaginations are apt to depict, it would be
wrong to infer that he was the bloodthirsty ruffian
which some people are fond of picturing him.

Of the land smuggler, in distinction from the class
we have been describing, little can be said that is
favourable. Following too closely in the footsteps of
his predecessors of the last century, his proceedings
were not such as to provoke the slightest enthusiasm
in the breasts of right-minded Englishmen ; rather,
indeed, by his reckless disregard for the lives of others,

---

* Of smugglers of the " pre-scientific period " who rose into promi-
nence, the gallant Thurot (*Anglicè*, O'Farrell), an Irish commodore
in the French service, whose name was a terror to the mercantile fleet
of this kingdom, is worthy of notice. He had been stationed in his
early days in the Isle of Man in the service of a Welsh smuggler, and
it was while thus engaged that he acquired the intimate knowledge
of the British coast that proved so useful to him in after years. By
a curious coincidence the action between his fleet and that under Captain
Elliot, in which he met defeat and death, occurred off the Isle of Man
(1760). His end is thus noticed by the author of "Lands and their
Owners in Galloway":—"Amongst the bodies that drifted to land
after the action was that of M. Thurot, dressed in uniform and sewed
up in a silk velvet carpet. His body, which was fully identified, was
found on the Monreith property, and was interred in the old kirk-yard
of Kirkmaiden, Sir Wm. Maxwell acting as chief mourner. Unfortunately the spot where the remains of the brave Thurot were laid
cannot now be traced. He is stated to have been only twenty-seven
years of age."

N 2

his readiness to shed blood and commit acts of base ruffianism in pursuit of his ends—the total absence, indeed, of anything approaching to chivalry in his conduct or character, his adventures merely excite a feeling of abhorrence, and every peace-loving citizen must rejoice at the suppression of a trade which afforded scope for his villainies.*

In a curious old document, which has drifted down through some fourteen centuries, a Roman official of high rank has drawn a picture for us of the sea rovers who haunted the coasts of Britain during the fifth century, as they appeared to his contemporaries, which, with but slight alteration, might be accepted as an accurate portrait of the contrabandists of later days.

Addressing a friend, who, as an officer in the Imperial service had recently embarked in one of the vessels of the Channel fleet that was employed in looking after the pirate boats of the Saxons, this Roman provincial writes :—

* In the Report on the "Disturbed Districts of Sussex," previously quoted, the following noteworthy observations occur :— "Since the establishment of the preventive service smuggling is much diminished. This diminution has had the effect of increasing the poor rate, or, as was expressed by an overseer, who is supposed to have had formerly a very accurate acquaintance with the business, 'the putting down of smuggling is the ruin of the coast.' The labourers of Bexhill and of the villages proceeding eastward towards Kent used to have plenty of work in the summer, and had no difficulty in finding employment in smuggling during the winter. . . . Large capitals have been invested in the business, particularly at Bexhill. Many of the small farmers, if they do not participate, certainly connive at these practices ; those who do not directly profit by smuggling consider that it is advantageous as finding employment for many who otherwise would be thrown on their parishes " (1833). The reader will note how little the habits and ideas of the Sussex people had altered with regard to smuggling during the hundred years intervening since the Hawkhurst gang roamed unmolested through the county.

"I have to warn you to be more than ever on your guard in this warfare. Your foe is of all foes the most active. He attacks unexpectedly; if you expect him he makes his escape; he despises those who wish to block his path; he overthrows those who are off their guard, while for himself he never fails to escape when he is forced to fly. And more than this, to these men a shipwreck is a school of seamanship rather than a matter of dread. They know the dangers of the deep like men who are every day in combat with them. For since a storm throws those whom they wish to surprise off their guard, while it hinders their own coming onset from being seen from afar, they gladly risk themselves in the midst of wrecks and surf-beaten rocks in the hope of making profit out of the very tempest." (Letter from Sidonius Apollinaris, quoted in Green's "Making of England.")

Part VI.
PAINS AND PENALTIES;
A SKETCH OF THE
"*LAWS FOR THE PREVENTION OF SMUGGLING.*"

CHAPTER I.

Primitive Systems of Free Trade Days—A Barbarous Sentence—Laws for the Prevention of Smuggling—Shipping Regulations—Harassing Enactments—Armed Smugglers—Disguises Prohibited—Dangers of Loitering—Rewards for Informers.

WHETHER the somewhat promiscuous hanging indulged in by our forefathers was the most efficacious method of inducing smugglers to recognise the errors of their ways and to seek more honourable callings seems a little doubtful, in view of certain facts which have come down to us. Thus, many criminals on the eve of their execution for highway robbery and other questionable proceedings declared themselves to be outlawed smugglers, who had been driven to commit these crimes as a means of livelihood, in consequence of every other channel of industry being closed to them.

But if the more enlightened sense of the present generation is inclined to blame the punitive systems of the past, it is just as well to remember that the country was in a very different state to what it is now, and that if our progenitors displayed a shocking readiness to "string up" their erring brothers for what may seem comparatively venial offences, the criminal classes, and the smugglers especially, showed an equal readiness to take life where their own safety was concerned.

Still, we must admit that hanging was just a wee bit overdone, more especially in regard to the crime of smuggling. Writing in 1752—the halcyon days of free-trade—Horace Walpole remarks :—" It is shocking to think what a shambles this country is grown ! Seventeen were executed this morning." * Certainly smuggling never languished for lack of martyrs to the cause. So late as the end of last century we are told of one of the crew of a smuggling vessel who was sentenced to be hanged and "to be afterwards anatomised" for the wilful murder of a boatswain in the service of the Customs, who was shot while endeavouring to board the vessel. By what means this sentence was carried out we are not informed, as, happily, no details of this sensational punishment have been preserved for the benefit of the morbidly curious.

A glance at the "Laws for the Prevention of Smuggling" of the year 1816—the commencement of the period with which we are especially concerned —will give us some idea of the punitive measures deemed necessary for coping with the contraband trade at that particular time.

It will be impossible, of course, to give more than the briefest *résumé* here, and for that reason, as well

* Horace Walpole to Mann, March 23rd, 1752.

It is further interesting to note that at this time fashionable ladies belonging to the set denominated "smart," for lack of the excitement nowadays supplied by divorce court proceedings, and society "cases," were wont to visit these criminals in gaol, and hear them recount their experiences.

as to avoid the charge of tediousness, the chief points only will be touched on.

To strike effectually at a traffic of the nature of smuggling in an insular kingdom it was obviously necessary to exercise a strict supervision over the various craft that offered special facilities for the conduct of the trade ; and to that end regulations of the most intricate character were compiled with regard to construction, tonnage, rig, equipment, number of crew, and the thousand and one things involved in the successful conduct of a maritime trade ; while the penalties attaching to infringements of the smallest of these matters were such as the modern Briton would deem intolerable.

As the reader would probably resent being inflicted with verbatim extracts from these regulations, which, being compiled in a species of legal jargon distinct from the vulgar tongue, are somewhat difficult of comprehension, the more salient points will be explained in language understanded of the people.

First, then, it was enacted that any boat built to row with more than four oars, found upon land or water within the counties of Middlesex, Surrey, Kent, or Sussex, or in the river Thames, or within the limits of the ports of London, Sandwich, or Ipswich, or any other boat rowing with more than six oars, found either upon land or water, in any other port, or within two leagues of the coast of Great Britain, " shall be forfeited with the tackle and furniture, and every person using or rowing in such boat shall forfeit £40."

And any boat rowing with more than six oars, found hovering, or within four leagues of that part of the coast which is between the North Foreland and Beachy Head, or within eight leagues of any other part of the coast, "shall be forfeited."

Certain boats were exempted from these laws, as, for instance, those belonging to merchant ships of a certain tonnage, and such as held special licences from the Admiralty or the Customs. But the regulations were framed with a view to the fast-pulling smuggling galleys that ran across to the French coast, and were the source of endless worry to the preventive men.

Rules of a precise nature were laid down also with regard to the equipment of sailing craft; thus, it was enacted that any cutter, lugger, shallop, wherry, sloop, smack, or yawl, having a bowsprit which shall exceed in length more than two-thirds of the length of such craft found within 100 leagues of the coasts of Great Britain or Ireland, shall be forfeited. Even the "steave," or inclination of the bowsprit, together with its method of fitment and securings were subject to rule; while the size and lead of the jib-stay were regulated to a nicety.

These details, unimportant as they may seem to most of us, were so intimately connected with the sailing qualities of a vessel where speed was a consideration, that every effort was made by the authorities to handicap every species of craft that might be tempted to elude the vigilance of the revenue cruisers. And, just for this reason, it was further enacted that any vessel of over 50 tons burthen rigged as a lugger, was liable to forfeiture.

Equally stringent were the regulations affecting the method of construction, proportions, thickness of planking, dimensions and positions of the timbers, and their distance apart, non-compliance with which entailed forfeiture and other penalties.

The number of crew was regulated in accordance with tonnage, any excess over the proper complement being regarded as *prima facie* evidence of an intention to engage in illicit proceedings, and entailing severe penalties.

Restrictions such as those enumerated above, when considered from a modern standpoint, may seem harassing and arbitrary, and the indignant clamour which an attempt to enforce them at the present day would call forth can be more easily imagined than described. Probably they were regarded as equally obnoxious by the free-and-easy traders of old.

The law struck at everything concerned in a smuggling transaction ; thus, all vessels and boats, and all horses and carriages, made use of in the landing or removal of contraband goods, were declared forfeit to the Crown ; and these, after due legal condemnation, were sold, and the proceeds, after deduction for legal expenses, were distributed, in certain fixed proportions, amongst the seizing officers as prize money.

The regulations under the head of " Smugglers " give us a curious insight into the ways of the time. Thus, if any persons to the number of three or more, armed with firearms or other offensive weapons, " shall be assembled in order to assist in the rescuing of any goods, they shall, on being lawfully convicted, be adjudged guilty of felony, and shall suffer death."

Again, persons more than five in company, who shall forcibly hinder or resist any officer of the Customs or Excise in seizing any run goods, shall, on being convicted, be adjudged guilty of felony, and be transported as felons to his Majesty's colonies or plantations in America for a term of five years.

For the same offence, committed with firearms, or

other weapons, or for dangerously wounding any
officer, "such person shall be adjudged guilty of
felony, and shall suffer death as in cases of felony,
without benefit of clergy."

In the event of the offender not being apprehended within six months, the Rape, Lath, or
Hundred, where the offence was committed, was to
make satisfaction, not exceeding £40, for the damages
by wounding, and to pay to the executors, or ad-
ministrators, for each person killed, £100, to be levied
upon the inhabitants by a proportionate tax.

The wearing of disguises or masks while engaged
in a smuggling transaction was regarded as a particularly heinous offence, if the penalty attaching
thereto may be accepted as a criterion. Thus, if any
person "shall have his face blacked, or shall wear any
mask or other disguise when passing with prohibited
goods, and be convicted, he shall be adjudged guilty
of felony, and shall suffer death," to which the
following curious note is appended—"That wearing
any disguise is to be deemed felony *with* benefit of
clergy."

The mere fact of loitering near the coast was
sufficient in those days to bring a person, however
innocent his intentions, within the law's grasp. Thus,
"any person loitering within five miles of the sea-coast
or any navigable river, with intent, as is suspected,
to assist in running goods, is to be brought before a
justice ; and if unable to give a satisfactory account
of his calling or employment, shall be committed to
the House of Correction, to be whipped and kept to
hard labour for any time not exceeding one month.
And if any person shall desire time for making it
clear that he was not concerned in any fraudulent
practices, the justice may commit him to gaol until

he shall make proof to the satisfaction of the justice."

In connection with the above, it was decreed that the informer was to receive 20s. for every person so arrested.

CHAPTER II.

The Navy as a Reformatory for Smugglers—Bravery of Smugglers in Action—Prison *versus* Men-of-War—Smuggling Signals—Fate of Smuggling Boats—Prohibited Imports.

THE army and navy being regarded by an enlightened administration at this particular period as fit receptacles for social rubbish of all sorts, they were largely used as reformatories for the smuggling classes. Thus— "Every person found assisting in unshipping any goods may be arrested, and, if convicted, is to be committed to hard labour in the House of Correction for any term not exceeding three years, nor less than one year ; " but, the regulations add, " If any person so convicted is approved of as fit to serve his Majesty, the justices may adjudge him to serve as a soldier or sailor for a term of five years."

The same penalty attached to persons found on board any vessel or boat liable to seizure.

Apropos of the above, the following curious document—which the writer chanced on—concerning the transfer of a smuggler to the naval service is not without interest :—

12th *February*, 1807.

" Gentlemen,—

" I beg leave to inform you that James Harris the person detained by me on board the *Diana*,

smuggling cutter, in the act of running her cargo
of contraband goods, has been since released by the
magistrates, on his making his election to enter as a
seaman in his Majesty's navy.　I herewith enclose a
certificate of his being received into H.M. naval
service from Lieut. Ellary of the impress service,
and beg you will crave of the Honorable Board the
reward allowed me under the Act.

" I am, etc.,

" JOHN CARTER,

" Commander."

[Enclosure.]

Poole Rendezvous,

5th February, 1807.

" Received from Mr. John Strong, Esquire, Mayor
of Poole :—James Harris, belonging to the *Diana*
smuggling cutter, captured by the *Seagull,* Jno.
Carter, Commander.

" ROBERT ELLARY,

" Lieutenant."

In consequence of the above law there were few
ships in H.M. fleet but had a proportion of smugglers
on board, many of whom, through the influence of
their captains—who usually proved sympathetic
gaolers—adopted the profession, and, by their seamanlike qualities marked themselves out for advancement to petty-officer's ratings.　Others, again,
taking unkindly to the restraint and discipline of
a man-of-war prison—leave of absence to visit the
shore being often withheld by their captains, who
were personably responsible to Government for the
safe keeping of smugglers during the term of their
conviction—usually availed themselves of the first
opportunity of desertion.

Lord Exmouth's ship at the battle of Algiers had several smugglers on board; and, according to the statement of a friend of one of these men, the captain called the smugglers on deck after the action and complimented them greatly on the way they had fought.

A curious confirmation of this story comes from another quarter. An old man, who during his early years took a very prominent part in smuggling, and suffered martyrdom, in the shape of a term of enforced idleness in Bodmin gaol at Government expense, told the writer that on one occasion Lord Exmouth visited the gaol—the governor being a personal friend or relative—and on being informed that a party of fine active young fellows were smugglers, Lord Exmouth told them he was sorry to see them there, as he had several smugglers in his ship at Algiers, and they were some of the best men he had on board.

That the smugglers greatly preferred being sent to prison instead of to a man-of-war is not surprising, when it is stated that they were not always made to work in gaol, and were very tenderly dealt with by the prison officials, who, like everyone else, had a "soft side" to their natures for smugglers. But the chief reason for this preference was explained to the writer by an old smuggler; namely, that after conviction, the friends and sympathisers of the delinquent immediately set in motion all the interest they could bring to bear on the Government, with a view to obtaining a remission of the sentence; and unless the smuggler was an old offender, they almost always succeeded in getting him out of prison before the expiration of his term; while in the case of a man sent afloat, the chances were extremely remote of his

gaining his liberty before the expiration of the term
of service, especially as the ship he was in was probably on a distant station. The evil consequences
arising from the practice of making H.M. ships receptacles for criminals and law-breakers having been
at length brought home to the authorities, smugglers
were henceforth sent to prison, and the naval service
knew them no more.

The explanation of this change, vouchsafed by
an old naval pensioner to the writer, has at least the
merit of originality. He said he believed the reason
why smugglers were no longer sent into the navy was
because they got on too well—that in some ships the
captains gave nearly all the ratings to smugglers. If
not strictly accurate, this was paying a high com-
pliment to the smugglers, and fully bears out what
has been stated elsewhere regarding their seamanlike
qualities.

Of the various regulations for the prevention of
smuggling, there are none so curiously suggestive of
other days as those relating to the making of signals
to boats and vessels off the coast.

The reader is probably aware of this custom, so
common in old days, and which usually took the form
of fires lit on prominent points inland, by which the
smuggling vessel was warned off the coast, and the
vigilance of the revenue officers rendered of no avail.
The success of a smuggling transaction depended, in
fact, to a great extent, on the efficient working of
these signals, and for this reason signalling was made
an indictable offence. Thus, it was enacted, that if
any person after sunset and before sunrise between
the 21st September and 1st April, or after the hour
of eight in the evening and before six in the morning
between the last day of March and 22nd September,

shall make, or assist in making any light, fire, flash, or
blaze, or any signal by smoke, or by rocket, fireworks
flags, firing of guns, or other firearms, or any other
contrivance, within six miles of the coast, for the
purpose of giving signal to any person on board any
smuggling vessel or boat, the offender, on conviction,
shall either forfeit £100, or be committed to prison
and kept to hard labour for a term not exceeding one
year.

So much for the smugglers.

Of the smuggling boats, suffice it to say, that on
condemnation they were sawn through in three
places. In some instances, however, if suitable for
revenue purposes, they were taken into the service, and
owing to their good sailing qualities often proved
valuable acquisitions.

Of the various articles comprising the stock-in-
trade of the contrabandist spirits and tobacco figured
the most largely, not only because they were in the
greatest demand, but because large profits were to be
derived from a successful " venture." The only other
article approaching to these in importance, from an
economic point of view, was salt, which, strange to
say, was dutiable during the first quarter of the
century. Smuggling in salt was extensively carried
on by old women, who obtained their supplies from
the fish-curing establishments, and secreting it in
ways familiar to the feminine mind, carried it about
the country for sale. Many were committed to gaol
for this offence.

The variety of articles on which an impecunious
Government laid its hand for the benefit of the Exchequer was almost infinite. The difficulty, indeed,
was to find anything which was permitted to pass
the wistful gaze of the exciseman or revenue officer

without payment of toll. Under these circumstances it
may not be without interest to enumerate the articles
which a free born Briton was forbidden to import or
use *under any conditions whatever*. The list is taken
from the "table of goods wholly prohibited to be
imported or to be worn, or to be used in Great
Britain."

> Gold or silver brocade.
> Cocoanut shells, or husks without their nuts.
> Foreign embroidery.
> Manufactures of gold, or silver, or metal.
> Ribbons, laces, and girdles.
> Chocolate, or cocoa paste.
> Calicoes, printed or dyed in Persia, China, or East Indies.
> Gloves, or mits of silk or leather.
> Foreign needlework.
> Silks (wrought).
> (All the above to be forfeited, and the importers fined.)

Judged from a modern standpoint, the "laws for
the prevention of smuggling" of 1816 seemed to
have been specially designed by some misdirected
genius for the express purpose of harassing his
fellow-creatures, and one can only marvel at the
much-enduring patience of a generation which put up
with it all. In these days, when Governments are
only tolerated on the condition of making things
pleasant all round, and the promise of large con-
cessions to popular clamour, it would be interesting
to note the effect of any attempt to enforce measures
involving the liberty of the subject to the extent
which was possible in the early years of the present
century.

The question arises how far these laws were
effective in securing the end for which they were
designed. This can only be satisfactorily answered
by a reference to the criminal statistics of this particular period.

O

But to judge by certain facts which have drifted to
the surface, it must be admitted that the pains and
penalties enumerated in the smuggling laws signally
failed in their object : nor is the reason hard to
divine.   To quote a writer in the *Edinburgh Review*
(Vol. xxxvi.)—" To create by means of high duties an
overwhelming temptation to indulge in crimes, and
then to punish men for indulging in it, is a proceeding
wholly and completely subversive of every principle
of justice.   It revolts the natural feelings of the
people, and teaches them to feel an interest in the
worst characters, to espouse their cause, and to avenge
their wrongs."

Part VII.

CURIOSITIES OF SMUGGLING

CHAPTER I.

Good Liquor Pays Toll—A Wool-gathering Expedition—The Troubles of a Riding Officer—The Tyneham Smugglers—H. M.'s Donkeys—Dog Watches—A Smuggler's Letter—The *Bold Venture* of Looe.

IN pursuance of the object with which this work is designed—to place before the reader a true and faithful picture of smuggling days—the writer now proposes to select from the mass of driftwood which has floated down on the waves of time such specimens as may best serve to illustrate the subject, and give life and reality to other days.

Here, for example, is a quaint fragment from Poole, in Dorsetshire, showing the capacity for stowing away good liquor in a short time that distinguished the men of Dorset in old days :—

" Poole, 26th September, 1806.

" By the enclosed report respecting some prize wine and brandy brought coastwise to this port in the *Dove,* Samuel Baker, master, from Weymouth, your Honors will perceive that there are twenty-eight gallons of brandy and ten gallons of wine short of the quantity shipped at Weymouth.

" From the number of pegs driven into the casks in different places, and the particular circumstances of the seizure made by the surveyor, its being

O 2

delivered to him by the owner and supercargo, as part of the cargo before mentioned, and embezzled by the crew, we have recommended the surveyor to report the whole of the matter to us.

"We are, etc."

The *Dove* would scarcely maintain the reputation of being a " dry " ship at sea after this !

We hear a great deal about the grievances of the farming interest at the present day. What would the British farmer think of the following :—

"*Poole*, 15*th October*, 1806.

"We most respectfully transmit an account of the seizure of a quantity of wool, etc., by Mr. N. Florence, riding officer at this port, for the prosecution of which we humbly pray your Honor's directions.

" Pursuant to your Honor's general order of 28th January, 1796, we beg permission to report that the wool is worth about £250, the waggon £20, and the horses £48, making together £318.

"We are, etc."

"17*th October*.

"The wool appears to us to be forfeited under the 11th Sec. of Wool Act, for being found removing within five miles of the sea coast without a permit, or a certificate of such wool having been previously entered at the Custom House, and the waggon and horses for being used in removing the same.

"We are, etc."

Worthy Mr. Florence had been "wool-gathering" to some purpose. That he was an active officer of the revenue we shall see in due course, though whether his lot had fallen in pleasant places is a matter that must be left to the judgment of the reader. Certainly he had to fish in very troubled waters sometimes, and did not always land his catch with the same agreeable facility that attended his wool-gathering expedition. Take the following for instance :—

" Wareham, 17th October, 1806.

"Gentlemen,—I think it my duty to inform you in order that you may represent to the Honorable Board that a troop of the 14th Regiment of Light Dragoons is stationed at Wareham Barracks. I have called on the commanding officer to know if he could assist me with a party of men and horses if there should be occasion for them to help to take the smugglers. He informed me that it will be necessary for him to have an order from the War Office before he can assist me. I have been informed that a good deal of smuggling has taken place this winter, and the smugglers have got so daring and impudent, that they will not give up any quantity of goods except an officer has got a military assistance with him. It will be of great use to the service if the Honorable Board will be pleased to get an order obtained from the War Office for their assistance.

"I am, etc.,
"NATHANIEL FLORENCE."

And again on the 17th November, 1806—

" Gentlemen,—

"I beg to represent to you in order for you to acquaint the Honble. Board that smuggling has rapidly increased in this fortnight past. I have been informed that the smugglers have landed a great quantity of goods which they kept concealed in caves, and sell it out to country people that come for it twice and sometimes thrice a week. About eight or ten of them come together in defiance to any officer. I have applied to the commanding officer of the 14th Reg^t Light Dragoons at the Wareham Barracks for assistance to help me take them. The officer informed me that he cannot assist me with a party without orders from the War Office or General. Your application to the Honble. Board to get the soldiers to assist me will be of very great use to the service.—I am, etc.,

"NATHANIEL FLORENCE."

Evidently this worthy officer had gone to the wrong shop in search of sympathy with his efforts to check the flow of good old cognac. There were no laurels to be won by the gallant 14th Light Dragoons in the pursuit of Dorset smugglers, who doubtless kept these dashing troopers well supplied with liquor and baccy, duty free. Meanwhile the riding officer and his defiant free-traders were left to arrange matters as best they could while this question of military assistance was being "considered" at headquarters. Not till February 4th, 1807, was an answer vouchsafed. And then, oh pity the sorrows of a poor riding officer! It was to "call upon the officer to state whether in the cases alluded to by him in his report, when the aid of the military was withheld, whether he had any direct information either of the place where the goods had been laid up, or where they would be met with, etc. etc." Three months nearly of weary waiting, and then! Well it was a far cry in those days from Wareham to the War Office, so Mr. Florence has to suppress his feelings and sit down and collect his thoughts, with the following result :—

"*6th February*, 1807.

"Gentlemen,—

"In answer to the Honble. Board's query I most respectfully report that in the instance alluded to I had an information of goods intended to be run in Tyneham parish by a gang of smugglers on horseback, who had made a common practice for some time of carrying goods from Tyneham across the country, but in such large gangs that it was impossible for me to do anything without military assistance. I have never applied for military assistance without having a direct information, or some great probability of making a seizure. And this assertion, I trust, will appear reasonable, when it is considered that the taking out of the military is always attended with an expense, *the soldiers expecting to be treated by the officer of Customs;* besides, the officers of the Customs, I presume, by taking out the military without a probability of making a seizure, would not only harass the soldiers but unnecessarily harass themselves.

"Humbly submitted,

"NATHANIEL FLORENCE."

This was certainly a clincher, but what effect it produced in the circumlocution offices of the year 1807 we can only dimly surmise, the curtain dropping at this point as suddenly as it rose, leaving us in the dark so far as concerns the future of the Tyneham smugglers and worthy Mr. Florence.

Foreign silks were contraband in old times, as above mentioned, and many were the ingenious contrivances for evading the vigilance of the Customs, but the following strikes one as an altogether novel method of importation :—Under date November, 1822, it is reported that three Russian frigates are taking in large quantities of French silks, laces, and other contraband goods at Copenhagen for the purpose of landing them in England.

Here is something that concerns the farming interest :—June, 1824. " It having come to the knowledge of the authorities that a man called Calvert, an Englishman, intends exporting a large quantity of Leicester sheep to France, and the same being illegal, instructions are given to the preventive officers to prevent it."

One of the most momentous questions that ever engaged the attention of a great department of State is briefly touched on in the following extract. It must be premised, by way of explanation, that at some of the coastguard stations on the coast of Kent donkeys were provided by a generous country for the purpose of conveying water and stores. Here is an extract from a general order in the Folkestone district :—" January, 1839. The board have expressed disapprobation at the amount hitherto charged for forage for donkeys in this district, adding that in their opinion the purchase of *beans* is *wholly unnecessary*, and also that too many oats have been given."

Why the poor cuddies should be debarred from the mild dissipations of the " bean-feast " passeth human understanding. Evidently the board was not in sympathy with these hard-working servants of the Crown. A chief officer in the Deal district having been detected by his inspecting commander going his night rounds " athwart " a Government jackass, is brought severely to book by his said superior officer.

Once more, in the year 1847, the jackass question crops up again, showing that the smallest

details are not beneath the notice of really great
minds.

"June 15th. The board having ordered the disposal of the donkey at 27 Tower, I have to direct,
in the first place, that the one now at that station be
exchanged for one at Lydd station, as complaints of
the latter have been made to me of his being of
vicious habits. As soon as this exchange takes place
the commanding boatman at 27 Tower will sell the
Lydd donkey at Dymchurch by public auction."

It was a common practice in smuggling days for
the coastguard patrols to take dogs with them on
night duty, not only for companionship, but to give
warning of the approach of smugglers, and thus
minimise the risk of being overpowered unawares.
The practice had its drawbacks, as we shall see.
Thus, we find in November, 1835, an order from the
inspecting officer of the Folkestone district calling
attention to the excessive number of dogs at the stations—" But as I conceive the dogs are certainly of
use on the beach during the night with the patrols,
I have no objection to their being kennelled near
the station during the day."

The objections to the system of "dog watches"
are shown in an order in the Weymouth district, dated
January, 1841:—"Having frequently found on visiting
the guards, either by land or water, that my approach
has generally been noticed by the dogs the men are
in the habit of taking with them, long before I could
see the patrol, I wish to draw the attention of the
officers to this point—as it would be quite sufficient
warning to a smuggling boat to put off—and to
desire that unless they think it may be beneficial in
particular places, to order the men to discontinue
the practice of taking dogs with them."

Here is an interesting little relic from other days under the heading "Dismissals from the Revenue Service, September, 1839":—

Thomas Galway, mariner, of the *Greyhound*, age 23.

Offence.	Place of Nativity.
Absconded, taking with him two hammocks and the boatswain's watch.	Near Waterloo (in which battle his father was slain); his parents were Scotch.

Quite a touching little bit of family history. Born one might almost say on the field of battle. Sad that the virtues of acquisitiveness should have taken a wrong turn. Truly Galway *père* was spared some sorrow!

The following is in quite another vein. A smuggler's letter, to wit—anonymous—from near Plymouth:—

"*St. Germain's Point, July 27th,* 1843.

"Dear Friend,—

"I hope you will excuse the freedom I take in addressing you with these few lines, but it is a great respect which I have for you which cause me to do it. I feel confident that you will not take it amiss. Dear friend, I have lived in and near a very great smuggling village this last twenty years, but never in my life had I reason to notice so much intimacy between an officer of the preventive station and some of the head smugglers of this parish as I have at this time with your officer, Mr. —— I mean. I have written this to you, and not to you alone, but to the whole of the boat's crew that are with you, that you might beware of yourselves, for this is and certainly will be carried, and many things which not only prove a loss to you but a very great injury.

"Likewise, and it is likely it will all be through the intimacy that is carried on with those I have mentioned. This, I trust, in love, hoping these few lines will save you from great trouble. I beg to remain a very great friend of yours, " ———— "

" The above is a true copy of a letter received by Peter Smith, boatman, of this station.

" ————, Chief Officer."

As the services of Mr. Peter Smith, boatman, were required elsewhere shortly after, there would seem to have been something irregular about his " dear friend's " solicitude for the purity of the revenue service.

Here is an interesting item from the same neighbourhood, February, 1835 :—" Cornelius Roose and John Coast, who sailed in the *Bold Venture* on the 5th instant, returned to Looe on the 7th, and are drinking and carousing on the money that was gathered for a freight. The parties are most enraged at it." We can well believe it, and although the law will not give them satisfaction, no doubt the " parties " will have their pound of flesh out of Messrs. Cornelius and John when they get a chance.

In July, 1844, a general order was issued to the coastguard on the subject of "certain men in the service of the revenue in Ireland having joined an association for the repeal of the Union of Great Britain and Ireland."

CHAPTER II.

Sympathisers on the Bench—A Deserter—Friends in Office—Gossiping Coastguardmen—Sunday Smugglers—James Ellory and His Plan—A Stout Man from Portloe—Coastguardmen and Wreckers.

THE difficulty of getting a conviction in the case of smuggling, in old days, was a very real one, owing,

no doubt, to the numerous sympathisers to be found
on the magisterial bench; consequently, we meet
with several orders, issued from to time, dealing with
the method to be pursued in bringing smugglers for
trial, as, for instance, "When more than one smuggler
is detained for the same offence, the parties are to be
proceeded against singly, so that in the event of an
acquittal on account of objection, the information
against the remaining parties may be amended"
(July, 1833).*   And again the same year: "A case
having occurred in which, out of five smugglers
brought before the Dorsetshire magistrates, the most
notorious of the party, who was tried first, escaped
conviction owing to some technical flaw in the proceedings, it is ordered that in future the first one to
be tried should be one whose conviction is of the
least consequence."   The magisterial mind was
doubtless hard to convince on these matters in old
times, and had a lynx eye for technical flaws.   It
was hard to send one's best friend to prison!

Here is something that concerns a poor smuggler
who has managed to give the authorities the slip.
"July, 1834.   It is ascertained that the man who was
at Mevagissey lately in the *Mary Ann* smuggling
boat, of Cawsand, and called himself Chas. Chapple,
is young Jno. D——, who was taken in the *Susannah*
and convicted for five years, and went out in H.M.S.
Conway to Havannah, where he deserted.   If caught he

---

* *Apropos* of this may be mentioned an old order, to the effect that
when in chase of a smuggling boat, in the event of tubs being thrown
overboard to lighten ship, a "mark-buoy" is to be thrown as near
to the tubs as possible before continuing the chase.   This order had its
origin in several cases of miscarriage of justice, in consequence of the
coastguard being unable to swear to the tubs produced in court as
having formed part of the cargo thrown over by the smuggling boat
they had chased.

is to be sent to the flag-ship at Devonport as a deserter." From which it may be inferred that John junior prefers the uncertain profits of the *Mary Ann* to the hard work and small pay of a man-of-war. Everyone to his hobby!

That the smugglers had friends in office goes without saying. In 1831 we find an order calling attention to the fact that "smugglers are in the habit of gaining information contained in confidential memos.," and by this means frustrating the good intentions of the preventive men. Officers are therefore enjoined to keep an eye on their lock-up places. Open pigeon-holing won't do with so many inquisitive people about.

Foiled in this respect, we find the wary smuggler trying it on by other means. " 1834 : Several persons, in the interests of the Cawsand and other smugglers, are using every means in their power to find out the movements of the coastguard in the Fowey district, both afloat and ashore, and that one of their plans is to endeavour to draw the men into conversation. The officers and men are cautioned to be on their guard accordingly." The Scriptural injunction about bridling that unruly member, the tongue, must be attended to in future. Indeed, there is no knowing in these exciting times what damage the revenue might suffer through a gossiping coastguardman —or his wife.

Whether the coastguard were able to spare time for church-going in those days seems a little open to doubt, in view of what was expected of them ; but from the frequency with which runs were attempted on Sunday, it seems that the smugglers expected some relaxation of vigilance on this day, and in November, 1839, it is recorded that " the smugglers at

Kingston, Littlehampton, made a daring attempt to run goods at noon on Sunday, under the impression that the crew would be at rest," from which we infer that the crew were found, on the contrary, very much on the alert. "The better the day, the better the deed," was the smuggler's motto.

In November, 1848, a correspondent, writing from Guernsey, says that "he overheard a conversation between a smuggler from Plymouth and a Frenchman, in which the former described a new plan of working goods successfully, by learning the extent of guards when the men met to confer. The smuggler then keeps watch on the place of conference to see when the men part, one to go east and the other west, thereby throwing the guards open, and then by making a flash with a congreve match the boat comes in without fear." The "novelty," however, only lay in the unguarded way in which the plan was communicated so that it was overheard by an interested listener. It had been practised with vast success by the leading "chevaliers d'industrie" for many a year past, and was, in fact, the only plan by which goods could be run with any prospect of success on a well-guarded coast.

The practice of hiding a vessel's name, and of using a *nom de plume* when taking in contraband cargoes in foreign ports, has already been alluded to. The reason is obvious, namely, to put spies or Government agents who might be on the spot off the scent, and thus prevent news of their movements reaching the coastguard stationed where they proposed running goods. There were always gossiping folk about, and oftentimes on arrival at the pre-arranged spot the spotsman found to his disgust and indignation that news of his intentions had travelled "on the wings of the wind" in advance, and that the coastguard were very much on the alert. For this reason it was the great object of the experienced smuggler to get in his goods and be off before the informer or the Government agent could despatch their news across Channel. Various and ingenious were the means employed to effect this object. But it was reserved for a very celebrated Cornish smuggler —to wit, Jas. Ellory, of Probus—to elaborate a method of doing business which, if it had been carried out in the same spirit in which it had been devised, would have successfully foiled all attempts to forestall his movements. Unfortunately, however—or fortunately for the sake of the honest trader—there was generally a weak link in the smuggler's chain, and he, above all men, was constantly, to his mortification, experiencing the truth of the old adage that there's many a slip 'twixt the cup and the lip. Jas. Ellory's method, according to "information," was as follows :—

"1834. January 30th.—A person named Jas. Ellory, of Probus, has made arrangements with a spirit merchant and with the shipbrokers at Brest for carrying on the smuggling trade to the coast of Cornwall in such a manner as to prevent any information. It is managed as follows :—He writes to the broker to advise the day of his sailing from England and the port he is coming to. On his arrival an express is sent to Brest, the tubs of brandy are carted to the outport, the broker goes there, enters and clears the vessel (always under a false name) ; she sails, and Ellory is on the English coast before any others at Brest, except the shipbrokers and spirit merchant, are aware that he has been in France. This person has recently stated that he has succeeded in safely landing his cargo, and has desired another to be kept in readiness, as he would appear in a few days, and has added that 36 hours after his arrival on the coast he would go to Brest and have the cargo taken to the coast. On the last occasion he took 10 tubs of crystal (cut glass) with him, and has ordered more for the next."

Poor James, little dreamt he that his pretty system had been "blown on" almost before it had been tried! The last mention of this smuggler occurs in April, 1837, to the effect that "Ellory, of Probus, has come to reside at Liskeard to carry on smuggling more to the eastward, having been very unsuccessful on the S.W. coast of Cornwall." And here the curtain drops on Ellory and his "plan." We may at least indulge the hope that, like many another smuggler, he discovered through bitter experience that after all honesty is the best policy.

Here is a curious entry having reference to an old ally of our friend Mr. Ellory, of Probus :—

"Plymouth, February 4th, 1851.—A stout man belonging to Portloe came across in the Jersey packet yesterday, in a devil of a hurry to get ashore. He has gone west as fast as coach can take him.* I am informed that he is on business"—of a pressing nature, evidently. Look out for runs.

The duties pertaining to the coastguard when first established, and for many subsequent years, were solely and entirely for the prevention of smuggling. The protection of the fisheries, and the multifarious duties that belong to the force at the present time are of comparatively recent origin, having been

---

* Cornishmen who are "in the know" will have no difficulty in recognising from the above description a notorious smuggler-butcher belonging to Grampound, who was in the habit of landing his cargoes about Portloe.

tacked on from time to time as the necessity arose. Now, one of the most important of these duties is the prevention of plunder on occasion of shipwreck, as well as the protection of life and property. That this was not regarded as coastguard duty in old times, is evident from the fact that in the year 1826 a chief boatman in Ireland was dismissed for "not preventing his crew from plundering a wreck;" and it was not till 1837 that we find any active step taken to place the question of "wrecking" *en évidence*. In September of that year it is recorded that, in consequence of evidence given before a commission in London, to the effect that "considerable plunder and disgraceful outrages take place frequently on the occurrence of wrecks along some parts of the coast," the coastguard are directed to furnish information on the subject.

CHAPTER III.

Methods of Smuggling Silk—Ingenuity of the Tea Smugglers—Hollow Masts and Yards - Tobacco Smuggling—Artful Dodges—Stinking Fish—False Bottoms—A Pandora's Box.

To the student of smuggling days few things are more curious than the ingenuity brought to bear on the various contrivances for eluding the vigilance of the preventive men; and one cannot help thinking that the amount of time, labour, and thought, which many of these devices must have cost their authors, might have been more advantageously bestowed on some legitimate line of business.

A brief description of some of the most noted

P

smuggling contrivances will place the reader in a better position for realising the amount of vigilance that was required in those days for detecting the machinations of the contrabandist. Tobacco and spirits were the chief staples of the trade, but from time to time we meet with interesting accounts of devices for the smuggling of tea, silk, and other articles, which are worth a passing notice.

So far back as 1821 the following ingenious system of smuggling silk goods inside hams was discovered,

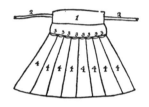

1 *Collar*   2 *Tiers*
3 *Mouths of Pockets*   4 *Pockets of Tea*

METHODS OF SMUGGLING TEA.—I.

viz.: the meat and bones of hams were scooped out very clean, except at the knuckle and the extremity of the thick end. The skin was then lined with calico, the silk packed very tight and hard in paper, covered over with oiled silk, and deposited within; the interstices between the packages being stuffed with rags to plump it up, the orifice then very neatly closed, and the whole rubbed with dirt and sawdust so as effectually to conceal the aperture.

During the year 1831 an extensive system of smuggling tea was discovered to be carried on from Havre de Grâce, the cargoes being generally run in the Thames, at the back of the Isle of Wight, and on the Hampshire coast. The tea was packed in cases made to fit between the timbers of vessels, so as to resemble the flooring.

A few years later, in 1833, another method was discovered by means of which tea and dry goods were often brought into the country, viz., inside of a cape, or suspended from the shoulders under a great-

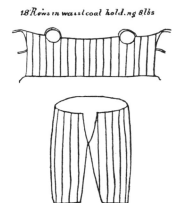

18 Rows in waistcoat holding 8lbs

Drawers stuffed with 10 lbs of Tea

METHODS OF SMUGGLING TEA.—II.

coat, or under petticoat-trousers, such as were used by fishermen and pilots (*See* opposite page).

And again, in 1834, we find another method, which is said to have come into frequent use in consequence of certain alterations about this time in the law affecting the tea trade. (*See* drawing.)

A year later, 1835, a curious device was discovered to be in use amongst the Deal boatmen,

P 2

concealed under their tarpaulin jackets and trousers. (*See* drawing).

Of various contrivances for smuggling dry goods the following are worth noticing :—

In 1820 three boats were seized on the coast of

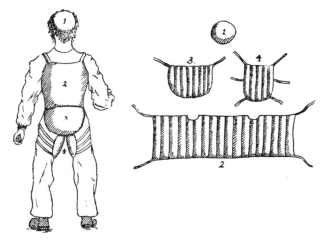

METHODS OF SMUGGLING TEA. — III.

1, Cotton bag to fit crown of hat ; 2, Cotton stays or waistcoat ; 3, Bustle for lower part of back ; 4, Thigh pieces. N.B.—The whole contained 30 lbs of tea.

Kent with contraband goods concealed inside spare masts and outriggers, which were hollowed out from head to foot, and the ends neatly plugged up and painted. Another boat was discovered with goods concealed inside iron ballast, cast hollow for the purpose ; while yet another endeavoured to smuggle inside large ballast stones, hollowed out on the underside.

The year following a boat was seized at Dover with a hollow keel and hollow yards, made of tin and painted to resemble wood, and containing spirits. And about the same time several small casks of spirits were discovered cased with cement and chalk, and seaweed fastened thereon, having every appearance of being chalk stones, in which state they had been sunk amongst rocks, to be afterwards picked up and smuggled on shore.

The year following another boat was seized with a hollow mast, inside of which was a tin tube, and so constructed as to be concealed from observation when the mast was stepped ; while a Deal boat was discovered with silk goods packed in bales to represent ballast bags.

In 1837 the following novel mode of smuggling was discovered to have been very successfully practised in rivers, harbours, and roadsteads, by vessels from abroad :—A cask, apparently empty, was substituted for a buoy, slung, fresh tarred, and fixed to the buoy rope. This was filled with light and valuable goods, and when the anchor was down opportunity was taken to remove the buoy by persons on the look-out.

Sundry and curious were the means adopted for smuggling tobacco. So far back as 1820 we hear of it concealed inside ships' hawsers. The tobacco was first made up into a rope of two strands, and then a hawser of three strands was laid over it, so that the deception could not be detected without either cutting or unlaying the hawser.

Two years later there was reported to be on sale at Flushing, for the purpose of smuggling into England, tobacco made up into ropes, varying in size from " tyers," for sails, up to hawsers, and which, upon being slightly washed with rum, had every appearance of being hempen rope.

In 1842 some tobacco was seized at Portsmouth which had been cut into the shape of a man's shoe. And a large quantity was discovered to have been

brought over from Jersey concealed in casks of bones. (*See* drawing.)

That our friends north of the Tweed were not behindhand in the smuggling art is evident from the following methods, discovered to have been practised on the west coast of Scotland. The tobacco was laid up so as to resemble a piece of old junk,

METHOD OF SMUGGLING TOBACCO.

an eye was perhaps spliced in the end, and after being "parcelled" and partially "served," was stowed amongst the old rope, and on the vessel's arrival in dock was landed without suspicion. About the same time (1844) a seizure was made on board a vessel of several cases containing tobacco, made of strong oak plank, one inch thick, measuring two feet long by fourteen inches square, having the appearance, when placed amongst a raft of timbers, of a log end. The manufactured tobacco was so tightly pressed in as to require chisel and hammer to separate it from the wood. Some years later a still more ingenious method was hit on, viz., inside blocks, the sheaves of which were discovered to be made of tobacco.

The concealment of large consignments of contraband goods underneath other descriptions of cargo, such as fruit, lime, coal, and dung, was, of course, a common occurrence, but the following device is worth mentioning as having the merit of originality. In 1837 a vessel was reported to be taking in tubs of spirits at Dunkirk, with the intention of covering them with sprats, and delaying her arrival in England until they stunk so much that she would not be thoroughly examined!

But the most successful contrivances for smuggling, by reason of the difficulty experienced in detecting them, were by means of false bottoms, or ingeniously contrived concealments inside the vessel itself.

Of the former description, the following are most worthy of notice :—

The first recorded case is that of the *Levant*, cutter, of Chichester, in 1820, which was discovered to have brought over a large quantity of contraband goods inside a double bottom, the outer one being made of strong timbers, copper-fastened, leaving an intervening space of about two feet. The next is that of the *Strawberry*, of Deal, in the year following, with this difference, however, that the false bottom was built inside, thus : two leaden cases were fixed on the timbers the entire length of the hold, one on each side of the keelson, and " ceiled " over, the usual ceiling having the ballast placed over it. These cases opened one on each side of the hold by taking out a plank of the ordinary ceiling.

At the same time the *Flower of Rye*, smack, was seized with a false bow, holding from forty to fifty half-ankers of spirits. The entrance to this conceal-ment was discovered on the port side of the false bow, where a small piece, which could be removed, was fastened by two screws, the heads of which were concealed by wooden plugs, imitating trenails. That this system of smuggling was well thought of amongst the craft is evident from the fact that the *Mary*, of Plymouth, the *Plough*, of Hastings, and the *Provi-dence*, of Rye, were discovered to have similar con-cealments.

The next case is that of the smack *Asp*, in 1824, which must have been something like a conjurer's cabinet, so full was she of concealments, the ingenuity of which would have done no discredit to the proprietors of any " Home of Mystery." They must have been designed by a past master of the art, and a brief description of the vessel will be of interest :—

1. A false bottom extended as far aft as the ballast bulkhead, entrance to which was by means of two scuttles, one on each side of her false keelson, secured by screws so neatly fitted as to render them scarcely perceptible.

2. There were also concealments on each side of her cabin bed-places, so contrived as to deceive any person who might judge from boring holes through the lining and then trying the intervening space between this and the supposed side of the ship. That such had actually been the case was evident from several old gimlet marks through the lining. What had been mistaken for her side was only an intermediate planking, the actual concealment being between that and the vessel's side.

3. A false bow constructed on similar principles to this had been already detected on board the same vessel. To get at the concealment described above (No. 2), it was necessary first of all to remove the bedding, so as to come fairly at the lining, when two small pieces of wood, about an inch square, appeared, let in to the plank. These being removed with the point of a knife, small circular pieces of cork were visible, which, on being taken out, exposed to view the heads of bed-screws, which, on being unscrewed, allowed two boards, the whole length of the bed-places, to be taken up, and discovered the concealment.

Two years later, 1826, the smacks *Fox* and
Lively Lass, of Portsmouth, were discovered to have a
quantity of kegs concealed under their bottom in a
temporary casing, extending from about two feet below the water-line to the keel, and which could not be

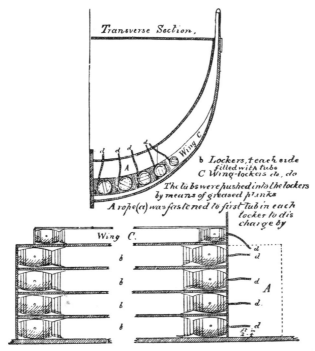

CONCEALMENT ON BOARD THE *RAMBLER*.

detected until the vessels were laid on shore, as there
was no communication between the concealments and
the interior of the vessels. The facility with which
this arrangement could be fitted on to a vessel, and
stripped off again afterwards, soon brought it into

favour; and we hear of it again in connection with
the *Love*, of Fowey, which vessel brought over seventy
tubs concealed in this manner, the planking having

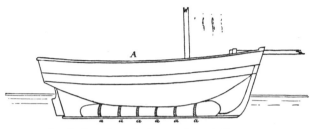

A   Section of vessel, showing false bottom on

a   Six timbers on each side, fastened to the keel, and bilge, 1 ft. above keel

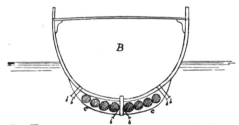

B   Transverse section, showing false bottom
(with tubs in position)

b   nails through false timbers

c   sheathing of ½ inch planking nailed to each timber, finely edged
above, forward and aft; the tubs being built in and stowed fore -
and -aft in the chambers

N B   The bottom was built on the ground in Barfleur, in two tides

CONCEALMENT ON BOARD THE *CHARLES AND HANNAH*.

been fitted to her at Roscoff.   And again in the
Daniel and William, of Portsmouth.

In 1834 we **find the smack** *Rambler*, of Jersey,
seized in Langston harbour with 141 casks of spirits
concealed in a false bottom of peculiar construction,

(full particulars of which are shown on page 249); and in the same year the *Charles and Hannah*, of Portsmouth, was taken with a large number of casks of spirits in a concealment of somewhat similar nature to that of the *Rambler*, as will be seen from the drawing on the opposite page.

CHAPTER IV.

A French Chasse-Marée—The *Black Rover* of Sandwich—A Capacious Hold—The *Good Intent* of London—Cowes Pilot Cutters—The *Speedwell* of Colchester—Successful Runs at Poole—A Clever Discovery.

DOUBLE bottoms were excellent provisions in their way, but obviously the circumstances under which the vessel was employed were not always such as to admit of this system being successfully applied, while the discovery of it in so many cases would incline the more sagacious to regard it as in great measure " played out," so to say. Hence from the earliest times we find the ingenuity of the smuggler applied in a variety of other ways to baffle the scrutiny of the " rummaging " officer.

Here, for example, in 1821, we find a smack seized which, on examination, was discovered to have a large " trunk " underneath the ballast, divided into four compartments, each fifteen feet long. One end of the trunk was fixed against the cabin bulkhead, and extended the entire length of the hold, opening at the fore part of the hold, close to the keelson, by means of two pieces of the bulkhead unshipping.

And the following year, on a French chasse-marée being broken up at Dartmouth, it was discovered to have false beams fitted in the after-part, which were hollow and capable of containing a quantity of dry

goods. These beams were arranged in a most ingenious manner, being dovetailed at one end, and,
by removing small wedges, neatly fitted, the beams

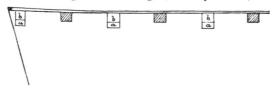

a. pieces of the upper clamp fitted under the false
   beams, which when taken out enable them to fall
b hollow beams
c the bolts in the knees fitted against the false beams
   only penetrate the knees, to make the deception greater

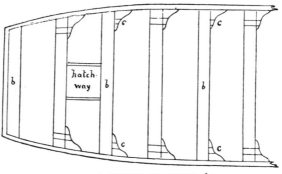

A FRENCH CHASSE-MARÉE.

fell, and could again be replaced, as shown in the
drawing.

Next we find the *Black Rover*, of Sandwich, seized
for having a concealment containing spirits, discovered
as follows :—On taking up the "foot-layings" one of

the timbers was found not to be fitting as usual, and
on pricking through this with a knife, a small scuttle
hatch was discovered that took up on both sides of
the boat.   On lifting this a concealment was disclosed, containing tin cases holding several gallons
of spirits.   A concealment similar to this was also
discovered in the smack *Isis*, of Rye, which was fitted
with another capable of holding a large number of
casks, as follows :—The entrance to it was effected by
taking down part of the bulkhead, and discovery was
guarded against by the erection of a false stem inside, from which the false lining was spread so as to
make a complete bow, distinct from the original one.

A concealment of a totally different nature on a
very large scale was discovered in 1824 on board the
brig *Sprightly*, of London.   It was capable of holding
from 400 to 500 tubs, and was thus arranged :—Two
shifting boards in the forecastle opened into the fore-
peak on to the coals ; and down on the starboard
side in a bulkhead abaft the foremast were three
shifting boards which admitted to a cavity in the
mainhold, six feet long, and the breadth of the ship.

A charming contrivance was discovered on board
the smack *Good Intent*, of London, which, in addition
to the same highly ingenious concealments as those
already described in the case of the *Asp*, had a false
stanchion abaft the fore-scuttle, through which a
leaden pipe was carried—after being brought up
through the keelson and garboard strakes, and through
the deck abaft.   By this means a rope attached to a
raft of tubs could be introduced, the tubs then hauled
up, and thus confined directly under the bottom.
Covering the top of the pipe and flush with the
deck was a square piece of wood, tarred over, and
scarcely perceptible.

A boat was seized at Folkestone in 1828 with a concealment running from the stern to the transom, and from the keel up to the under-part of the thwarts. The entrance was by means of four scuttles, very neatly and ingeniously fitted with nails fore and aft through the timbers, to secure them from moving, one on each side of the keelson, about a foot before

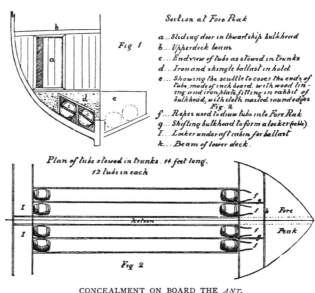

Section at Fore Peak

Fig 1

a ... Sliding door in thwartship bulkhead
b ... Upperdeck beam
c ... Endview of tubs as stowed in trunks
d ... Iron and shingle ballast in hold
e ... Showing the scuttle to cover the ends of
      tubs, made of inch board, with wood lin-
      ing and iron plate fitting in rabbit of
      bulkhead, with cloth nailed round edges
      Fig. 2
f ... Ropes used to draw tubs into Fore Peak
g ... Shifting bulkhead to form a locker (table)
I ... Locker under aft cabin for ballast
k ... Beam of lower deck.

Plan of tubs stowed in trunks. 14 feet long.
12 tubs in each

Keelson

Fore
Peak

Fig 2

CONCEALMENT ON BOARD THE *ANT*.

the stern-sheets, and one on each side of the keelson, under the fore-thwart.

Another boat was taken at Shoreham with half-ankers of spirits lashed fore and aft along her bottom on each side of the keel, and fastened by small lines passing through the garboard strake, and made fast under the ballast. This could only be discovered by "sweeping" under the boat's bottom.

A Portsmouth boat, the *Captain*, was discovered
(1832) to have a "half-deck" made double, the intervening space being capable of holding a quantity of
gloves and silk goods.

The next case of interest was that of the *Ant*, a
Cowes pilot vessel, which was seized in 1835 with
a conccalment containing forty-seven half-ankers of
spirits, description of which is given in the drawing on the opposite page.

In the same year, the sloop *Emulation*, of Cowes, was
captured by the *Adder*, revenue cruiser, with 108 tubs
and 56 flagons of spirits and some tea in a concealment which is described in the accompanying sketch.

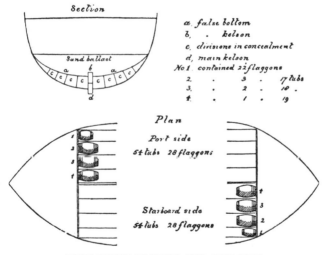

CONCEALMENT ON BOARD THE *EMULATION*.

The vessel had been "rummaged" and her ballast
"spitted" by a boat's crew from the *Adder* the day
previous, without discovering her false bottom, and
she would most probably have succeeded in running

her cargo, had not her subsequent proceedings excited suspicion and led to further examination. From a number of similar seizures made at this time it seems that this mode of smuggling had become very general, and in vessels least open to suspicion.

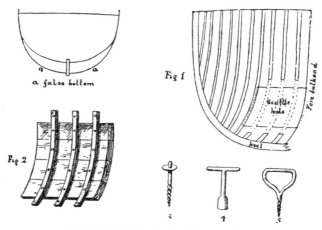

CONCEALMENT ON BOARD THE *SPEEDWELL*.

Fig. 2.—The scuttle, which is cut out of the original planking and has three shifting timbers over it, is secured, so as to appear fixed, by means of screws at the points marked **O**. The black dots denote short or false trenails; the screw-heads are counter-sunk into the timbers, and covered with cork to represent trenails. The scuttle is concealed forward by passing a short distance under a fixed timber (as shown by dotted line in Fig. 1), and aft, in the same way under the fore-bulkhead, and when the shifting timbers are unscrewed from the planking and the scuttle, the latter admits of being moved aft to liberate the fore end, when it can be lifted by the hand-screw (No. 5) and inserted into one of the screw-holes of No. 3.

No. 4.—Key fitting the head of No. 3, for the purpose of unscrewing the timbers.

Note.—Nos. 3, 4, and 5 were given up by the smugglers after the concealment was discovered and the seizure made.

An ingenious method of getting rid of a cargo in the event of chase was discovered at this time in a fishing-smack, by means of sinking the tubs through a hole made by taking out three planks from the bottom of her well.

During this year another smack, the *Speedwell*, of Colchester, was seized at Littlehampton with a concealment containing 133 casks of spirits of various sizes, concealed in four divisions on each side, extending fore and aft the run, and were stowed by means of a scuttle (Fig. 2) on each side of the fore-peak, as shown in Fig. 1, page 256, to which the reader must be referred.

These concealments were not always discovered before it was too late to prevent their contents from being run, as we find in January of this year the chief officer of the Poole station (Dorsetshire) dismissed for allowing a vessel to proceed up Poole harbour without examining her, although informed that she had a false bottom, whereby a considerable run of goods took place. And again, in July, the *Mary Ann*, of Poole, entered the harbour, supposed to be laden with coal, but with 800 tubs of spirits on board, 600 of which she succeeded in " running " before any discovery was made.

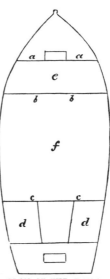

PLAN OF THE *TAM-O-SHANTER*.

a, Fore-bulkhead ; *b*, False bulkhead ; *c*, After-bulkhead ; *d*, Tubs stowed under Cabins ; *e*, Concealment with tubs ; *f*, Cargo of Coal.

Next year the *Tam-o'-Shanter*, 72 tons, of Plymouth, was seized at Padstow with a concealment containing a large number of tubs, as shown in the above plan ; and in 1837, the French schooner *Auguste*

Q

and schooner *Good Intent*, of Newport, were captured with concealments, as shown in the drawing.

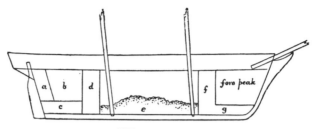

THE *GOOD INTENT.*

a, Sail and Store-room ; *b,* Concealment behind bed-place on port side, containing 26 kegs ; *c,* Space under cabin deck, containing coal and 26 kegs ; *d,* Space between after-bulkhead and a false one, containing 138 kegs ; *e,* Limestone ballast in hold ; *f,* Space between fore-bulkhead and a false one, containing 148 kegs ; *g,* 21 kegs under fore-peak. *Note.*—The false bulkheads had been freshly coal-tarred, the smell from which completely overpowered that from the spirits.

Two years later (1839) another description of concealment was discovered in the schooner *Maria Victoria*, taken at St. Mawes, Cornwall.

About this time a method of smuggling in tin cases became common. The first was a Deal fishing boat, fitted with tin cases, sixteen in number, between the timbers, from the one under the afterpart of the fore-thwart to that under the after-thwart, the depth of the cases being about a quarter of an inch less than the thickness of the timbers, and extending the distance the bottom boards usually run. These cases contained about eight gallons of spirits. The other was that of a vessel in which a large quantity of tobacco was smuggled by means of tin cases sunk to the bottom of the water-tank, and with a line attached, which was fastened to a small buoy.

Next we come to a concealment discovered in

1852 by the *Mermaid*, revenue cruiser, on board the wherry *Hold On*, of Ryde, sketch of which is annexed.

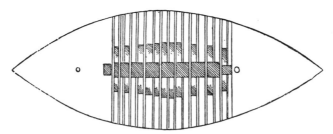

The shaded portion represents the tin cases of spirits, 32 in number, fitted between the timbers

Sectional view

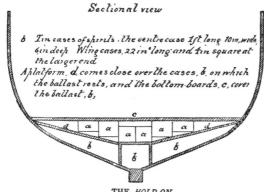

b   Tin cases of spirits, the centre case 1ft. long 10in, wide, 6in deep   Wing cases, 22 in. long and 4in square at the larger end
A platform, d comes close over the cases, b, on which the ballast rests, and the bottom-boards, c, cover the ballast, b,

THE *HOLD ON.*

And, in the same year, the fishing smack *Elizabeth*, of Lynn, was captured by the *Defence*, revenue cruiser, with concealments capable of containing 200 gallons of spirits in bulk.   (*See* plan next page.)

In March, 1838, a concealment was discovered in the *Mary Ann*, fishing boat, of Rye.   It was so constructed, that no "sweep-rope" would touch it, nor could it be discovered whilst the vessel was afloat, or lying on soft mud ; it could be ripped off in a few

moments. The drawing on the opposite page is somewhat exaggerated, the better to show the concealment.

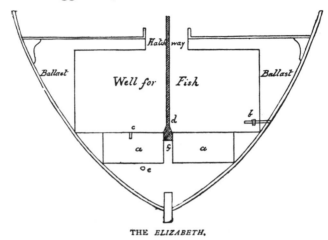

THE *ELIZABETH.*

a, Concealment 9 feet long, 10 inches deep, 6 feet broad, lined with lead,
and capable of holding 200 gallons of spirits in bulk; *b*, Lock to let
water into well; *d*, Plug to fit in pipe *f*, and confine water in well; *c*,
Hole to start spirits into concealment, secured by a pipe; *e*, Cock
under the cabin store to draw off spirits from the concealment; *f*,
Cock and pipe leading from well through concealment to let out water.
N.B.—This contrivance was not discovered till the water had been let
off from the well, when the cock *b* and plug *c* were observed.

Very ingenious was the concealment discovered
on board the French ship *St. Antoine*, at Shoreham
(April, 1823). The upper part of the cabin was fitted
with two cupboards with shelves to take down, the
back of which might be supposed to be the lining of
the transom ; on taking this up, the timbers appeared,
and the planks, on close inspection, were found to
overlap each other, and the timbers made to act as
fastenings. By striking the lower end of the false
timbers on one side it moved round on a bolt, and
one plank with the timber was made to shift on each

side of the false stern-post, and formed a stern frame
within.   The other, below the cupboards down to the
run of the vessel, was on the same principle—the entrance to which was gained by taking down the seats
and lockers in the cabin, when a false post appeared

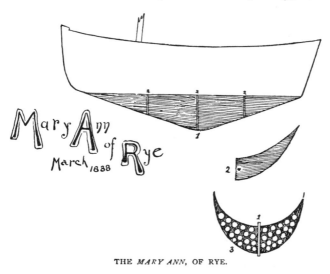

THE *MARY ANN*, OF RYE.

1, False keel, 12 in. deep ; 2, Pieces of 2 in. plank, three on each side,
   secured at right angles to the keel to keep the tubs in position, and to
   which the covering was nailed ; 3, Section of concealment which was
   covered in with ¾ in. elm plank, closely fitted but not water-tight.

to be fastened with a forelock and ring ; by unfasten-
ing the same, the false stern-post and middle plank
might be taken down.

   At Sandwich, the *Albion*, of London, was seized
(1822), with the following concealments :—First, a
false bow, access to which was obtained through the
bed cabin, the entrance being secured by screws
covered with false trenails ; second, a complete false
stern frame, entrance being gained through a small

locker on the port and starboard sides of an *apparent* stern-post fastened by false trenails, and on removing the timbers a scuttle-board, 16 inches × 12, took out.

Few concealments were more cleverly contrived to deceive the ever-suspicious Customs searcher than those fitted on board the brig *Badajoz*, of London, taken at Kilrush, Ireland (1822). In reality, she might have been described as two vessels, one within the other, about eighteen inches apart at the bottom, and closing together at a point under the beams. The bows between the two vessels were rather fuller and extended to the deck. Within, the vessel was as substantial and complete as on the outside, being framed and trenailed, and with scantlings of timber, keelson, bilge, ceiling, and every appearance inside indicating the perfect vessel in every respect ; but the contrivance to admit goods into the concealment was the most ingenious possible—small trap scuttles being at each end of the false keelson just before and abaft the ballast, lined and framed the same as any other part of the vessel, and two scantlings of the ceiling boards covered the traps and a broken joint, and were fastened in the centre by screw-bolts, the heads of which were hid by corks representing trenails, and the planks were secured by false trenails, for deception.

The vigilant officer of the Customs who detected this fraud thus describes the way in which it was discovered :—" It was at the head of one of these planks I made the first attempt at discovery, and so confident were the crew of the vessel, that one of them handed a marline-spike and gave every assistance to explore the particular place, trusting that nothing would start the screws ; and I am sure the heads of the planks were left without being nailed, that the minds of the persons searching might be the sooner satisfied, for so it was with persons that accompanied me. After prizing up the heads of the planks about an inch or two, the timbers and perfect vessel, as it were, showed themselves, and what was near satisfying my own mind, was natural decay in the side of one of the planks, which I found afterwards to be also intended for deception. Three times did we come and leave this place, satisfied that all was

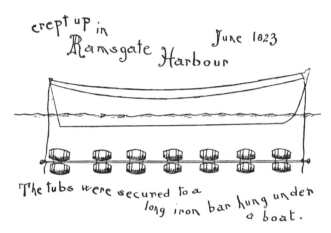

crept up in Ramsgate Harbour June 1823

The tubs were secured to a long iron bar hung under a boat.

correct there, until, wearied from searching, I made the last effort at the same place, and succeeded in forcing one of the planks out of its berth. My suspicions were immediately aroused by the dryness and huskiness of the lower planks and screws, never having seen even a copper-bottomed vessel that did not show an oozing of some kind through the outside plank. I therefore persevered and got the next plank forced out of its place, and the screw-holes shortly led to a trap scuttle and the concealments. In the sides of the forecastle berths were openings exactly on the same principle as that described, but it was not till after the concealment was emptied that the other traps were discovered from the inside, so completely concealed were the whole, which a person knowing the secret would have unravelled in a minute or two. There was no boy on board, for fear he should disclose the secret."

CHAPTER V.

Rafting—A Curious Light-buoy—Extraordinary Ingenuity of the Langston Harbour Smugglers—A Novel Boat—Deceptions Practised by Smugglers—The *Daniel and William*—A Complete Disguise—Smuggling at Woolwich—The Liverpool Lighter—The *Rival*, of Chichester.

BUT by far the greatest ingenuity was brought to bear on the system of smuggling known as rafting, which in some notable instances was carried to such perfection that it may well be dignified by the name of " science." This system was used for the purpose of floating cargoes, by means of the natural current, up tidal harbours and estuaries at night, and the most famous of those which came under the observation of the preventive men are well worth describing. "There is a tide which, taken at the flood, leads on to fortune," might well have been adopted as the motto of the successful smuggler in this particular line of trade.

The first recorded case was in 1826, when a raft consisting of forty-one tubs was seized, with a curiously contrived light-buoy attached to it. This buoy was so constructed with a false bottom and double lamp, that it would not be illuminated until such portion of the candle as the smugglers might think sufficient to last the time necessary for floating the tubs to the intended spot, was consumed in the upper part. The tubs were all attached to a warp, and the buoy, which being very small and painted white, could not be seen at any distance, was lashed on the top of them. They floated with the buoy darkened until they had got some distance beyond the coastguard station, when, the candle having burnt down in one of the sockets, illuminated the lamp beneath.

At the same time (November, 1826) another very curious smuggling contrivance was thus described :—
" The boat containing tubs approaches the coast near enough to be still beyond the observation of the coastguard ; some flints are then fastened to the half-ankers (which are lashed together and put overboard) of sufficient weight to keep them just under the surface of the water, and the end of a line, which is wound on a reel under the boat's bottom, is fastened to the tubs, so that when the boat pulls in upon the flood-tide, the twine runs off the reel. The smugglers then watch their opportunity, and haul in the line with the tubs attached. The reel is capable of holding about 1,200 fathoms (600 yards) of twine."

The next case was at Langston Harbour, Hants, in March, 1829, when a seizure was made of a raft of tubs drifting in with the flood-tide having a curiously-constructed lantern—on somewhat the same principle as that already described, affixed to a piece of board measuring $3\frac{1}{2}$ feet × $1\frac{1}{2}$ feet, with four holes, and lashed upon the top of the raft. There were two candles burning in the lantern at the time, but no light was visible, the lantern being so contrived that after the candles had been completely burnt down, they would instantly communicate to two lamps of oil in the lower part, which were intended to show the smugglers in waiting an excellent light from six small panes of glass, two in front, and one on each side.

Nothing further of interest is mentioned till July, 1833, when the following contrivance was dis-

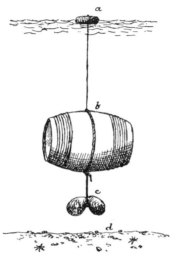

A CLEVER CONTRIVANCE.

covered :—" Each tub, with a bag of ballast, *c*, attached, is suspended by a line from a piece of cork, *a*, which floats on the surface. The tubs thus arranged are set floating with the flood-tide at the mouth of a river, or creek, and are carried by the current to a point where persons are on the look-out for them."

The same year we find the Langston smugglers busy again with a new contrivance of equal ingenuity to the last, which, however, did not succeed in escaping the lynx-eyed vigilance of the coastguard. The method was as follows :—The tubs, sixty-three in number, were firmly lashed together in a form resembling a pile of shot. To the slings of each tub was seized a plate of cast-iron, 14 inches long, 2¾ inches broad, and ¾ inch thick, weighing from 7½ to 8 lbs., cast for the purpose, with a stop-shoulder at each end for the seizing. The tops of the tubs were all painted white. The raft drew, and grounded in seven feet of water, and only three of the tubs were ever visible

on the surface. Two small grapnels were fast to the
tubs for the purpose of bringing them up—it is
supposed, when the tide had carried them to the
intended spot, and where, no doubt, a sweep-line was
ready to stop them. (*See* drawing.)

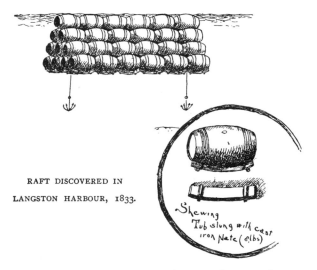

RAFT DISCOVERED IN
LANGSTON HARBOUR, 1833.

Shewing
Tub slung with cast
iron plate (?lbs)

But perhaps the most curious and masterly contrivance that ever emanated from the fertile brains of
the Langston Harbour smugglers was that discovered by the coastguard of the Langston station in
August, 1835, which will be better understood by a
reference to the drawing on the next page.

The next case recorded is in 1838, at Poole,
Dorset, where a system very similar to that already
described was discovered, viz., a cast-iron plate of the
length of a half-anker, corresponding in shape with
the curve of the bilge, and evidently made for the
purpose, was secured to each tub. The plate, which
weighed 7 lbs., was just sufficient to sink a half-anker

below the surface. The tubs thus arranged were drifted
by the tide up the harbour, and afterwards landed.

The last mention of this method of smuggling
occurs in 1845, when a raft of 38 tubs was found

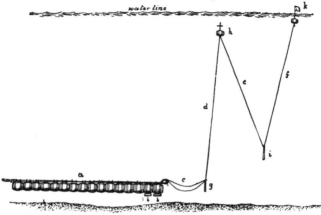

RAFT DISCOVERED IN LANGSTON HARBOUR, 1835.

a, Showing the tubs (19) at the bottom in ten fathoms of water, fastened
with small line to a piece of 2-inch shroud hawser; *b*, Pieces of cast-
iron, each weighing 8 lbs., fastened to the slings of the tubs to sink
them; *c*, 17 fathoms of ½ inch double line; *d*, 63 fathoms of ½ inch
single line; *e*, 45 fathoms of double twine, very strong; *f*, 55 fathoms
of single twine, *g*, Hand-lead of 7 lbs. ; *h*, Floating mark under
water ; *i*, Iron weight of 1½ lbs. ; *k*, Floating mark with a small blue
flag, the upper part of the staff just showing above water when in the
eddy tide, but not showing when in the strength of the tide.

Note.—The quantity of the line and the weights appeared to have been
calculated with great nicety, so as to run the marks *h* and *k* under water
when in the strength of the tides in the part of the harbour always guarded
near the entrance, and when arrived in the eddies, or the slack water at
the upper part of the harbour, they would rise to the surface.

floating near the Nab Light, off Portsmouth by the
Cameleon, revenue cruiser. The tubs were ballasted
with cast-iron plates, exactly similar to those just
described, and had evidently been drifted out to sea
instead of to their intended destination, showing once
more how " the best laid schemes," etc.

Though not exactly *apropos* to the subject of rafting, a peculiarly-constructed flat-bottomed boat which was driven on shore during a gale at Bognor in 1837 is worth noticing. From its curious design it was supposed to have been entirely calculated for towing under the surface of the water so as to escape detection on entering harbours. The sides being composed simply of three wide deal planks without

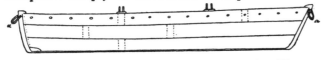

Sides made of three deal planks length .16ft breadth .4ft
a a grummets   depth . 2ft 2in

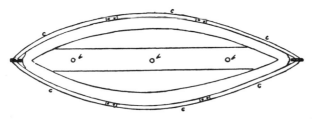

Bottom made of three deal planks   b.b.b. large holes . c. 24in decl.

Section

No thwarts, but ash timbers secured with common French nails.
N.B the holes in the gunwale were used for lacing a net across, when the tubs were in the boat; the net being made of line, the size of tub-slings.
CURIOUS BOAT FOUND AT BOGNOR.

thwarts, were easily broken up and disposed of after landing the goods. (*See* drawing.)

Besides the various systems of concealments already described, sundry devices were resorted to for disguising the identity of the vessels employed, or suspected of being employed in the contraband trade. For instance, painting and numbering to resemble pilot cutters was of frequent occurrence. In 1829 we find the smuggling lugger *Maria* discovered to have on board a pendant marked with the Crown and R. Y. C., similar to what was flown by vessels of the Royal Yacht Club, which one of the crew admitted was for use if required. Feigned names were often adopted on the visits of the vessels to foreign ports for the purpose of getting contraband cargoes, so that information of their movements could not be obtained from correspondents on the spot.

Another device was that of having two complete sets of sails of different cut and colour. For instance, the sloop *Daniel and William*, 30 tons, of Portsmouth —a most notorious smuggling craft, whose operations were usually conducted on the coast of Cornwall— used always to be seen with white sails, but had a tanned set on board, which she occasionally set for disguise when on a smuggling trip. Her gaff topsail had a square head, but she would sometimes set a jib for a gaff top-sail, and when on smuggling trips would set one one day and the other the next.

The most complete system of disguise was that adopted by the *Sarah Jacobe*, a Dutch smuggling cutter, of 70 tons, captured in October, 1843, off Ardglass, in Ireland, by the *Chance*, revenue cruiser. She was supplied with spars, crosstrees, stump topmast, and all fittings to turn her into a cutter, sloop, dandy, or trawler, at will in a few moments. She was also provided with shifting quarterpieces to ship and unship for disguise. The name of the vessel was on a shifting board to fasten on with staples and toggles, and the white streak, which was still wet, had evidently been painted on her at sea.

The crew of the *Chance*,* revenue cutter, must have blessed their good luck when they dropped on to the *Sarah Jacobe* of smuggling fame. Lucky chance!

Reference has already been made in the course of this history to the smuggling by the East India ships. A curious case occurred at Woolwich in 1816, on which occasion advantage was taken of condemned Government stores for the purpose of introducing contraband goods of immense value. In one packet alone, marked " Returned Congreve rockets," were goods value £7,000 for one man. " In the mortars were laces, gloves, cambrics, etc.; in the tumbrils were claret, champagne, etc. Many people had long supplied themselves and friends with wines in this way, and their wives with finery." This was the only vessel which had been detected, but the trade had long and successfully been carried on to a great extent. The secret was discovered by a carpenter on the voyage home in securing the packages. He informed the Custom House on arrival, but ten days elapsed before any inspection took place, and then much had been landed. The informer got about £1,000 reward. In 1817 a large lighter was fitted out at Liverpool on the model of a foreign merchantman, with false keel, decks, sides, masts, sails, and rigging, complete in all respects, to outward appearance. She was entered out at the Custom House for a foreign country, with a valuable cargo of goods, on which there was the largest drawback—the whole duties being returned. She sailed into the Irish Channel, where a metamorphosis took place ; her false sides

---

* This vessel was captured as a smuggling cutter on the coast of Scotland in October, 1827, and, like several others, was taken into the revenue service.

were knocked in, her masts struck, and with the
appearance of an ordinary Liverpool lighter she sailed
again up to Runcorn, where her cargo was landed,
and despatched by various routes and conveyances to
agents in London.   The ruse was discovered by
pure accident, a lighterman saying, on the quay at
Liverpool, that pepper and other Colonial produce
was being landed at Runcorn, and that he should like
a job of that sort.   Inquiry having shown that no
lighters had left Liverpool, the fraud was detected,
and several seizures of the goods were made in

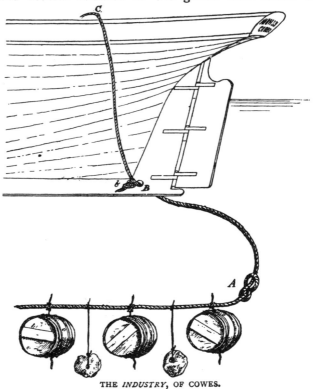

THE *INDUSTRY*, OF COWES.

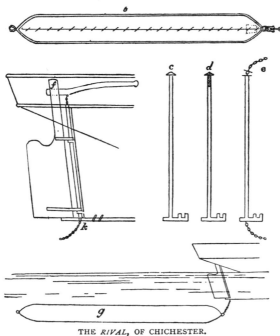

THE *RIVAL,* OF CHICHESTER.

b, Shows the line of tubs (thirteen) contained inside two cloths of No. 1 canvas, fifteen feet long, turned in, wrapped round and with lacing holes worked all round, and blacked over. Flat bars and small pieces of iron were placed inside for ballast about 56lbs altogether—and one end contained a half-hundred weight, with the ring outwards, and a shackle to secure the chain to ; *c,* The proper pintle bolt to secure the rudder, of solid iron, nine feet long, and resting in the socket of the iron shoe, on the keel of the vessel ; *d,* The false pintle, hollow, one inch diameter, with a stopper on the head to represent the proper one, *c ; e,* The same with stopper *out,* chain rove, and a small iron pin, through a top link, ready to let slip ; *f,* The rudder with false pintle and chain rove, resting on socket of the shoe, which has a hole the size of the bore of the pipe, so that when the vessel is on shore it could never be discovered ; *g,* The tubs, when towing, about two or three feet under water ; *k,* Iron shoe.

N.B.—In the drawing the rudder is made to stand off from the stern-post, so as to show the bolt better. There is a notch in the under part of the tiller, to allow the top links of the chain to be turned into the rudder-head, and that it may be used as a " compressor," when the pin is withdrawn in time of danger.

R

London.   The parties concerned were believed to
have carried this on for some time.

In 1832 the day watchman at Number Two Tower,
Dungeness, observed a feather floating at some little
distance from the shore, and, noticing that it remained
stationary, his suspicions were aroused.   He accordingly stripped and swam out to it, and found the feather
fixed to a small piece of cork, to which some twine
was attached, and on hauling on it he soon got hold
of a piece of three-quarter inch rope, by means of
which he drew on shore thirty-two tubs of spirits.

Of various ingenious contrivances for towing into
harbour tubs of spirits, without exciting the suspicions
of the coastguard, that discovered on board the smack
Industry, of Cowes, by the *Rose*, revenue cutter, in
December, 1827, is worthy of notice.   A reference to
the drawing (p. 272)—which shows the stern of the
vessel and the mode of attaching the tubs—will make
the contrivance clear to the reader.   The tubs and their
sinking stones were fastened to the hawser, commencing at the knot A, the length from which to the
securing part at *b* was about ten fathoms.   Supposing,
then, the raft of tubs to be lowered into the water,
and that danger is apprehended—and providing time
would allow—the smugglers on board would then
have to haul up the hawser by the small lead line, C,
fastened to the securing knot at *b*; then by cutting
off the securing knot they would discharge their
illegal cargo, as the hawser would then readily slide
away through the hole in the stern-post at B.

A contrivance, somewhat similar in principle to
the above, though differing in the details, was found
on board the *Rival*, taken in Chichester Harbour,
October, 1850, which will be better understood by an
examination of the drawing on page 273.

CHAPTER VI.

An Old Lydd Smuggler—English Gold and French Armaments—Smugglers in War-time—Johnson, the Hampshire Smuggler—Harry Paulet and Lord Hawke—Napoleon's Patronage of Smuggling—Clandestine Intercourse with France—Injurious Effects of Smuggling.

"WHEN I joined the Folkestone Division in 1831," said an old coastguard pensioner to the writer, "there was a very old man living at Lydd who often told me how he smuggled gold over to France during the war. He would run across in one of the smuggling galleys, taking a quantity of guineas with him—you see, he could get twenty-five or thirty shillings for each English guinea over there. I've heard him say he was employed by the R———s. When he was over in France he would get information about the French fleet, and on his way back call alongside the English men-of-war to let them know what he'd heard over there." *

When first this was told to the writer, he thought that his informant's memory must be at fault, or that very possibly he had confused matters ; but the following passage from Barry O'Meara's " Napoleon at St. Helena " throws quite a new light on the matter :—

"Explaining how he raised money for carrying on his wars, Napoleon said, ' I did not receive money

---

* From further inquiries it seems that this old man—who was seventy years of age when he imparted this information, and a fisherman by trade—was master of a 12-oared galley during the war, and usually crossed from either Dover or Folkestone to Calais. Having a pass from both English and French he was never stopped by the men-of-war of either nation. "He often told me," added my informant, "that guineas were so plentiful with the smugglers in those days that they used to play pitch and toss with them."

R 2

direct from Spain.   I got bills upon Vera Cruz, which
certain agents sent by circuitous routes, by Amster-
dam, Hamburg, and other places, to London, as I
had no direct communication.   The bills were dis-
counted by merchants in London, to whom ten per
cent., and sometimes a premium, was paid as their
reward.   Bills were then given by them upon different
bankers in Europe for the greatest part of the
amount, and the remainder in gold, which last was
brought over to France by the smugglers.   Even for the
equipping my last expedition after my return from
Elba a great part of the money was raised in
London.' "

The smugglers of the south coast of England
played a far more important part in our several wars
with France than is generally known, and the adventurous careers of some of the most famous of these
men—could the details only be rescued from the
oblivion into which most of them have fallen—would
form a volume of thrilling interest.

Johnson, the Hampshire smuggler, was one of the
most remarkable of these men.   He flourished in the
very early years of the present century, and contemporary papers are full of his exploits.   Though a
smuggler, he proved staur.ch enough when the honour
of his country was at stake.   Thus, on one occasion,
when offered a large reward by Napoleon if he would
pilot a French fleet to the English coast, he replied,
" I am a smuggler, but a true lover of my country,
and no traitor."   He was then imprisoned at Flushing,
but escaped ; and offering his services to the Government, was appointed to the *Fox*, revenue cutter, where,
from his wide knowledge of smuggling he proved of
great use, and he served the Government so well that
when at Plymouth he scarcely dared venture out of

the ship. He was in several engagements with French privateers, and during the Walcheren expedition performed a daring and brilliant feat, swimming with a rope to the ramparts and causing a terrible explosion of an infernal machine.

As an instance of the fertility of invention displayed by smugglers, the submarine boats contrived by Johnson are worthy of mention. The author of the article on "Submarine Warfare" in Whitaker's Almanack (1890) observes:—"The remarkable invention of the celebrated smuggler, Johnson, had for its object the carrying off the ex-Emperor Napoleon from St. Helena to the United States, and had it succeeded the history of Europe would have been changed. The boat was 100 feet long, with masts and sails that could be doused and stowed away handily when diving became necessary. Johnson was to have been rewarded munificently after the exile's escape, besides receiving £40,000 on the day when his boat was ready for sea. The death of Napoleon, however, put an end to the scheme."

In one of the early volumes of the "Annual Register" there is mention of another famous Hampshire smuggler, Harry Paulet, who made his escape from a French vessel with a bag of despatches he saw hanging up in the cabin. On another occasion, when bringing over a cargo of brandy, he sighted the French fleet, and, preferring patriotism to his cargo, sailed direct to Lord Hawke in a neighbouring bay with the news. Lord Hawke vowed to hang him if his information proved false, or to make his fortune if it was true. The result was Lord Hawke's victory, and Harry Paulet in consequence lived and died a well-known publican in London.

But perhaps the most interesting and striking

testimony to the courage and enterprise of English smugglers is that supplied by the ex-Emperor himself —testimony, however, which says more for the greed and recklessness of these men than for their patriotism. Observations coming from such a curious and altogether unexpected quarter are of special interest.

"During the war," said Napoleon, "all the information I received from England came through the smugglers. They are people who have courage and ability to do anything for money. They had at first a part of Dunkirk allotted to them, to which they were restricted ; but as they latterly went out of their limits, committed riots, and insulted everybody, I ordered Gravelines to be prepared for their reception, where they had a little camp for their accommodation. At one time there were upwards of 500 of them in Dunkirk. I had every information I wanted through them. They brought over newspapers and despatches from the spies that we had in London. They took over spies from France, landed and kept them in their houses for some days, then dispersed them over the country, and brought them back when wanted. They came over in boats not broader than this bath. It was really astonishing to see them passing your seventy-four-gun ships in defiance.'

In reply to the remark that they were double spies, and brought intelligence from France to the British Government, Napoleon said, "That is very likely ; they brought you newspapers, but I believe that, as spies, they did not convey much intelligence to you. They are *genti terribili*, and did great mischief to your Government. They assisted the French prisoners to escape from England. The relations of Frenchmen, prisoners in your country, were accustomed to go to Dunkirk, and to make a bargain with them to bring over a certain prisoner. All that they wanted was the name, age, and a private token, by means of which the prisoners might repose confidence in them. Generally, in a short time afterwards they effected it, as, for men like them, they had a great deal of honour in their dealings. They offered several times to bring over Louis and the rest of the Bourbons for a sum of money ; but they wanted to stipulate that if they met with an accident, or inter-ruption to their design, they might be allowed to massacre them. This I would not consent to."

These observations are not less remarkable for their agreement with evidence derived from other sources than for the proof they afford of Napoleon's profound knowledge of everything connected with his *régime.*

This character for straightforward dealing was not always, however, maintained by the smugglers, for, if report be true, there were instances in which, after receiving payment for the escape of prisoners, they overpowered them when—in a double sense— "half seas over," and handed the fugitives over to English cruisers.*

Apropos of the system of carrying on a traitorous intercourse with the enemy in war-time, we have it on record that all through the last war with France the daily newspapers and correspondence were regularly carried to Bonaparte by a family then resident at Bexhill, in Sussex. In plain English, the majority of the smugglers seem to have been ready to turn their hands to any dirty job by way of raising the wind.

* For an interesting account of an episode of this nature see "Mes Pontons," by Louis Garneray.

So far back as the beginning of last century the public records supply evidence of the calling to which smugglers betook themselves in time of war. Thus, in January, 1703, the capture of a man called William Snipp, at Lydd, is reported, together with two other men, "part of the old gang of those who were *owlers* (smugglers of wool) in the late war," all of whom were openly in communication with French sloops which came to the coast.

Some idea of the activity with which these clandestine communications with the enemy were carried on may be gathered from the following extracts from the public records of this period :—

July 25th, 1702.—Some French letters sent from a privateer and others found on the beach near Seaford ; all delivered to the Secretary Hedge's office.

October 8th.—Near Seaford two persons seized and sent to the secretary.

January 4th, 1703.—At Newhaven, five Frenchmen and a boy taken.

March 5th.—At Felpham, two French prisoners.

May 3rd.—A Frenchman, from Calais, with letters and papers, under Beachy Head in the night.

May 6th.—Three French prisoners at Pagham.

May 27th.—Five or six French prisoners near Shoreham. Captain Joosloe set on shore from Dieppe. Shoreham, three French prisoners more ; three came on shore in long-boat, and made their escape through the country.

October 2nd.—Mr. Herne seized ; brought up per messenger.

December 12th.—Major Boucher, Captain Ogilby, and five more out of France seized at Beachy Head by express ; brought up by messengers. Out of a small hoy, near Selsea, seized five Frenchmen ; committed to Chichester gaol, broke prison, and retaken by J. Field.*

It may not be out of place to remind our readers that at the consultation of smugglers at Rowland's Castle, previous to the murder of Galley and Chater, it was proposed to have them secretly conveyed to France, notwithstanding that the two countries were then at war with each other, a fact which presupposes the existence of a clandestine intercourse unknown to the authorities.

At the trial of the men concerned in the brutal murder of Hawkins on Slindon Common it was elicited that one of the murderers had crossed to Gravelines, in France, and entered himself into the corps of the Irish brigade, thus affording further proof of these clandestine communications between the two countries.

So notorious were these facts at the time that many patriotic men sought a means of preventing the mischief to the country which was wrought by the smugglers. In the course of a speech in the House of Commons, in January, 1749, advocating a substitute for impressment as a means of manning the fleet, the following observations on this subject were made :—

"The smugglers not only exhaust our national wealth, and carry it to our enemies, but at the same time—what is of infinitely worse consequence—they carry them intelligence of every step that is taken in this kingdom ; so that they at once destroy our wealth and our honour, producing at once beggary and defeats. Nor can they bring back intelligence from our enemies, for as soon as they land at the French ports, they are carried before the Intendant,

* Egerton MS. 929, quoted in " Smuggling in Sussex "—Sussex Archæological Collection, Vol. X.

and examined upon oath concerning the situation of
vessels on the English coasts, and at the same time
sworn not to discover what they see there."

In the month of April, the same year, James
Toby, an old smuggler, was convicted for carrying
wool to France. It was also proved that he held a
correspondence with the French during the late re-
bellion (1745), and furnished them with swivel guns
for their privateers.

CHAPTER VII.

Profits on Smuggling—Trade Secrets—Methods of Procedure—Collecting
a Freight—Engaging a Vessel—Cost of Tubs—Customs of the Trade—
Causes of the Decline of Smuggling—Definition of Smuggling.

HAVING followed the author thus far, the reader may
possibly be curious to know what the actual profits
amounted to on a branch of trading which offered
such irresistible attractions to our forefathers, and
tempted men of all classes to risk life, limb, and
liberty in its pursuit.

In the preceding pages it has been more than
once remarked that amongst the smuggling fraternity it was an axiom that if they could save
one cargo out of three they considered themselves
fairly well recouped for all their labour and expense. This, however, supplies no clue to the
actual money value of the goods on delivery, their
first cost, or the various expenses necessarily incurred in transit from one port to another.

The information that follows, and which must
be regarded in the light of "trade secrets"—communicated to the writer from time to time by a very

celebrated, and, in his day, successful smuggler, will help to throw a light on certain points, regarding which information has so far been withheld, and may be accepted as perfectly reliable. The writer's informant, moreover, is a remarkable exception to the rule which governed the career of most contraband traders, in so far that instead of ending his days in pinching poverty or the poorhouse, he succeeded in carving out for himself during the later half of his life an honourable career, which brought a competency for old age in the shape of a pension from his former employers, which he is still enjoying.

It must be premised that the information applies to the trade in spirits alone, and refers to the busiest days of the "scientific period" of smuggling, viz., from about 1825 to 1840 :—

"If I intended bringing over a cargo, I would arrange for all the likely parties I knew of to meet me on a certain day for the purpose of deciding on the number of tubs. Each person would 'venture' so many, paying down to me, on the spot, £1 for each tub ventured. Another £1 per tub would be lodged in the bank to pay expenses. Supposing we arranged for a hundred and fifty tubs, I would take the £150 advanced, look out for a likely boat, and make a bargain with the owner for the trip across. If the captain preferred it he would be paid a lump sum, say £100, out of which he paid the crew, arranging with them as best he could—there were always plenty of chaps ready to chance a run across in those days, and then, you see, they could always venture a few tubs themselves, if they liked.

"Sometimes the freighter would pay down half the amount agreed on before starting, say £50, besides which he would agree for £25 per man of the crew, of which £20 would be paid down. If times were bad, of course men could be got for less, £15 or £10 may-be. The captain would then engage a crew on his own terms, paying, perhaps, £3 or £5 per man down.

"In buying the tubs over in France, £1 would fetch twenty-one shillings, while the tubs would cost generally 18s. each, according to the bargain you made with the merchant, who, in addition, always allowed one tub in a score, and two in a hundred, which was called 'scorage' tubs, and always went to the owner of the boat, who, before sharing profits, would deduct so much for 'freight and average.'

"Sometimes the tubs could be bought for as low as 16s. each, the difference going into the pocket of the purchaser, to cover small expenses, such as 'sinking-stones,' food, etc., for the crew.

"A tub—or half-anker, as it used to be called before my time, weighed about fifty-six pounds when full, and contained four gallons of brandy, costing from four to five shillings per gallon in France; the same costing in England thirty-six shillings, duty paid. So, by getting the stuff 'run' clear of duty—thirty-two shillings a gallon it was in those days—a pretty good profit could be made on a cargo of a hundred tubs.

"Each tub cost the venturers £2, the same, if charged duty, costing about £6.

"Of course, if the cargo was lost, the venturers just lost the £1 paid down, the other pound being only paid to the freighter after the tubs had been delivered, and if they were lost the money was drawn out of the bank again and paid back to the venturers.

"The tubs were always supplied by the merchant

ready 'slung.' I generally bought my cargoes at Roscoff, though I have been to Cherbourg and other ports for goods. The spirit you got in those days was beautiful stuff—mild, and fine-flavoured ; indeed, you can't get anything like it now.

"The spirit was almost always supplied un-coloured—white brandy it was called—a tub of colouring mixture being supplied with the tubs by the merchant for the purpose of colouring the spirit after it had been run. I sometimes made my own colouring mixture with burnt sugar, and it was just as good as that supplied by the merchant.

"The average strength of the liquor supplied was 70° above proof, but I have known cargoes brought over as much as 180° above proof. You see, it could be brought over at less expense like that, a hundred tubs making three hundred when mixed to the right strength ; besides, brandy of this strength was sold cheaper in proportion, or at about thirty shillings the four-gallon tub. Of course it required fewer tubs and caused less trouble to the merchant. But if cheaper to buy—costing to the venturer, when reduced to its proper strength, about 2s. 6d. a gallon— the mixing gave a lot of trouble. It had to be done after landing, and oftentimes there was a difficulty in getting enough tubs to put the liquor into after it was mixed, so that, on the whole, it gave more trouble than it was worth, in my mind."

So far, the successful smuggler. No doubt "trade customs" varied somewhat in the different counties, but the above particulars will quite sufficiently enable the reader to understand why the temptation to smuggle proved in so many instances stronger than frail humanity of sixty years ago was able to withstand.

What, it will naturally be asked, chiefly contributed to put down the contraband trade ? Opinions
differ somewhat widely on this point. The truth is
that various causes, all tending in the same direction,
worked to this end. Old smugglers, who are naturally a little disinclined to see any virtue in a preventive
man, will tell you that the informer did more than
anything else to destroy the trade ; and there can be
no doubt that the treachery of men, who were nothing
loth, sometimes, to sacrifice their own kith and kin for
the sake of lucre, very greatly increased the risks.
Others, again, who, though possibly interested in the
trade, were never brought into contact with the preventive men, and therefore, less prejudiced, declare
that after the establishment of the coastguard the
beach was too well watched to admit of a landing
without almost certain detection. Then, again, there
are those who attribute the decadence of smuggling
to the " limit laws," under which boats were liable to
seizure and detention—if not forfeiture—when discovered outside of their limits. But what certainly
put the final touch to all the contributory causes was
the large reduction in the duties—especially on
spirits ; and when the possible profits bore no proportion to the risks, smuggling, on the scale, and
according to the methods of old, died a natural death.
That smuggling is extinct no one will venture to
assert, in view of the frequent prosecutions that occur;*

* The following extract from a " Statement concerning Smuggling "
in the Customs Report for the year ended 31st March, 1891, is worthy
of notice :—

Year.	Quantities Seized.		Number of Convictions.	Penalties Recovered.
	Tobacco.	Spirits.		
1882	25,653 lbs.	432 gallons.	1,516	£3,529
1891	16,756 ,,	239 ,,	4,704	£8,126

The larger seizures occurred for the most part on the shores of the river
Humber.

but that it will ever again be conducted in the manner and with the audacity described in these pages, seems in the highest degree improbable.

Finally, after a full and impartial consideration of the matter, and with a complete knowledge of the facts, we may appropriately conclude our survey of smuggling days in the words of an Italian writer of the last century, whose "Treatise on Crimes and Punishments," published in 1764, earned for him a European reputation:—"Smuggling, though a real offence, is owing to the laws themselves: for the higher the duties, the greater is the advantage and, consequently, the temptation, which temptation is increased by the facility of perpetration, when the circumference that is guarded is of great extent, and the merchandise prohibited small in bulk" (Beccaria).

THE END.

Printed by Cassell & Company, Limited, La Belle Sauvage, London, E.C.